CW00730228

THE CAMBRIDGE COMPANION TO IAN MCEWAN

This *Companion* showcases the best scholarship on Ian McEwan's work and offers a comprehensive demonstration of his importance in the canon of international contemporary fiction. His whole career is covered, and the connections as well as the developments across the oeuvre are considered. The essays offer both an assessment of McEwan's technical accomplishments and a sense of the contextual factors that have provided him with inspiration. This volume has been structured to highlight the points of intersection between literary questions and evaluations, and the treatment of contemporary sociocultural issues and topics. For the more complex novels – such as *Atonement* – this book offers complementary perspectives. In this respect, *The Cambridge Companion to Ian McEwan* serves as a prism of interpretation, revealing the various interpretive emphases each of McEwan's more complex works invite, and shows how his various recurring preoccupations run through his career.

DOMINIC HEAD is Professor of Modern English Literature at the University of Nottingham, where he served as Head of School, 2007–10. His previous books are *The Modernist Short Story* (Cambridge, 1992), *Nadine Gordimer* (Cambridge, 1994), *J. M. Coetzee* (Cambridge, 1997), *The Cambridge Introduction to Modern British Fiction, 1950–2000* (Cambridge, 2002), *Ian McEwan* (2007), *The State of the Novel* (2008), *The Cambridge Introduction to J. M. Coetzee* (Cambridge, 2009) and *Modernity and the English Rural Novel* (Cambridge, 2017). Also, as editor: *The Cambridge Guide to Literature in English*, third edition (Cambridge, 2006), and *The Cambridge History of the English Short Story* (Cambridge, 2016).

A complete list of books in the series is at the back of this book.

THE CAMBRIDGE
COMPANION TO
IAN MCEWAN

EDITED BY
DOMINIC HEAD
University of Nottingham

CAMBRIDGE
UNIVERSITY PRESS

CAMBRIDGE
UNIVERSITY PRESS

University Printing House, Cambridge CB2 8BS, United Kingdom

One Liberty Plaza, 20th Floor, New York, NY 10006, USA

477 Williamstown Road, Port Melbourne, VIC 3207, Australia

314–321, 3rd Floor, Plot 3, Splendor Forum, Jasola District Centre, New Delhi – 110025, India

79 Anson Road, #06–04/06, Singapore 079906

Cambridge University Press is part of the University of Cambridge.

It furthers the University's mission by disseminating knowledge in the pursuit of education, learning, and research at the highest international levels of excellence.

www.cambridge.org
Information on this title: www.cambridge.org/9781108480338
DOI: 10.1017/9781108648516

© Cambridge University Press 2019

This publication is in copyright. Subject to statutory exception and to the provisions of relevant collective licensing agreements, no reproduction of any part may take place without the written permission of Cambridge University Press.

First published 2019

Printed and bound in Great Britain by Clays Ltd, Elcograf S.p.A.

A catalogue record for this publication is available from the British Library.

Library of Congress Cataloging-in-Publication Data
NAMES: Head, Dominic, editor.
TITLE: The Cambridge companion to Ian McEwan / edited by Dominic Head, University of Nottingham.
DESCRIPTION: Cambridge ; New York, NY : Cambridge University Press, 2019. | Includes bibliographical references and index.
IDENTIFIERS: LCCN 2018057999 | ISBN 9781108480338 (hardback : alk. paper) | ISBN 9781108727297 (pbk. : alk. paper)
SUBJECTS: LCSH: McEwan, Ian–Criticism and interpretation.
CLASSIFICATION: LCC PR6063.C4 Z625 2019 | DDC 823/.914–dc23
LC record available at https://lccn.loc.gov/2018057999

ISBN 978-1-108-48033-8 Hardback
ISBN 978-1-108-72729-7 Paperback

Cambridge University Press has no responsibility for the persistence or accuracy of URLs for external or third-party internet websites referred to in this publication and does not guarantee that any content on such websites is, or will remain, accurate or appropriate.

CONTENTS

CONTRIBUTORS

ASTRID BRACKE writes on twenty-first-century British fiction and nonfiction, ecocriticism and narratology, climate crisis and floods. Her monograph, *Climate Crisis and the Twenty-First-Century British Novel*, was published in 2018. She is Lecturer of British Literature at HAN University of Applied Sciences, Nijmegen (the Netherlands).

RICHARD BROWN is Reader in Modern Literature at the University of Leeds, where he is Programme Leader for the English Literature BA and the Modern and Contemporary MA Pathway. He has published widely on the work of James Joyce as well as on many other modern and contemporary writers from Shakespeare to J. G. Ballard and Bob Dylan. Previous work on Ian McEwan includes essays on *The Innocent* and *Saturday*.

PETER CHILDS is Professor of Modern and Contemporary English Literature at Newman University, Birmingham, UK. He has published widely on post-1900 literature and on such writers as E. M. Forster, Ian McEwan, Julian Barnes, and Paul Scott in particular. His books include *Contemporary Novelists: British Fiction Since 1970* (2005) and *Aesthetics and Ethics in Twenty-First Century British Novels* (2013).

THOM DANCER has written on Ian McEwan's *Saturday* in the journal *Novel*. His work on contemporary fiction more generally has appeared in *the minnesota review* and *Contemporary Literature*. He is Assistant Professor of English at the University of Toronto.

DOMINIC HEAD is Professor of Modern English Literature at the University of Nottingham, where he served as Head of School, 2007–2010. His books include *The Modernist Short Story* (1992), *The Cambridge Introduction to Modern British Fiction, 1950–2000* (2002), *Ian McEwan* (2007) and *Modernity and the English Rural Novel* (2017). Also, as editor: *The Cambridge Guide to Literature in English*, third edition (2006), and *The Cambridge History of the English Short Story* (2016).

DAVID JAMES is a Professorial Research Fellow at the University of Birmingham. Among his books are *Modernist Futures* (2012) and *Discrepant Solace* (2019), and edited volumes such as *The Legacies of Modernism* (2012) and *The Cambridge Companion to British Fiction since 1945* (2015). He co-edits the series *Literature Now*.

BEN KNIGHTS is Emeritus Professor of English and Cultural Studies at Teesside University, UK. A former director of the UK English Subject Centre, his research interests include the history and pedagogies of English, and masculinities in narrative. His most recent book is *Pedagogic Criticism: Reconfiguring University English Studies* (2017).

MICHAEL LEMAHIEU is Associate Professor of English at Clemson University and co-editor of the journal *Contemporary Literature*. He is the author of *Fictions of Fact and Value: The Erasure of Logical Positivism in American Fiction, 1945–1975* (2013) and co-editor of *Wittgenstein and Modernism* (2017). He is the recipient of a 2018–2019 American Council of Learned Societies (ACLS) Fellowship.

DAVID MALCOLM teaches at SWPS University of Social Sciences and Humanities in Warsaw. He has written on the work of Jean Rhys, Graham Swift, John McGahern, and John Berger. His books include *Understanding Ian McEwan* (2002). He has also published on short fiction and modern poetry.

JUDITH SEABOYER teaches nineteenth-century and contemporary fiction at the University of Queensland. She has published three essays on Ian McEwan's work: one on realism, one on *The Comfort of Strangers* as a reading of the underlying power of sadomasochism in patriarchal society, and the third on *Black Dogs* as Virgilian pastoral. Her present literary research looks at why classical pastoral is being reworked in contemporary literature.

ELUNED SUMMERS-BREMNER is Senior Lecturer in English at the University of Auckland, New Zealand. The author of *Insomnia: A Cultural History* (2008), *Ian McEwan: Sex, Death and History* (2014), and *A History of Wandering* (forthcoming), she is currently working on a history of the sea and human emotions, and on the literature of the Second World War.

LYNN WELLS is the author of *Allegories of Telling: Self-Referential Narrative in Contemporary British Fiction* (2003) and *Ian McEwan* (2010), as well as a number of other publications on contemporary British fiction. Dr Wells' scholarship focuses on literary ethics and urban fiction. She has held a number of leadership positions in Canadian universities, and is currently Associate Vice-President Students at MacEwan University in Alberta, Canada.

1945   Second World War ends; atomic bombs are dropped on Hiroshima and Nagasaki. Clement Attlee wins election and forms a Labour government. George Orwell, *Animal Farm*.

1947   Truman Doctrine and the beginning of the Cold War. Malcolm Lowry, *Under the Volcano*.

1948   Ian Russell McEwan born on June 21 in Aldershot.

1949   North American Treaty Organization founded. George Orwell, *Nineteen Eighty-Four*.

1950   William Cooper, *Scenes from Provincial Life*; Rose Macaulay, *The World My Wilderness*; Angus Wilson, *Such Darling Dodos*.

1951   Winston Churchill elected as Conservative Prime Minister.

1954   Kingsley Amis, *Lucky Jim*; Iris Murdoch, *Under the Net*.

1956   Suez crisis. Eight-year-old McEwan living at an army camp in Libya. Angus Wilson, *Anglo-Saxon Attitudes*.

1959   Sent to school at Woolverstone Hall, a state boarding school in Suffolk.

1961   Construction of the Berlin Wall begins.

1962   Anthony Burgess, *A Clockwork Orange*; Doris Lessing, *The Golden Notebook*.

1963   John le Carré, *The Spy Who Came in from the Cold*.

1964   Labour Party wins general election, Harold Wilson becomes Prime Minister. Angus Wilson, *Late Call*.

1965   Malcolm Bradbury, *Stepping Westward*.

1967   McEwan attends the University of Sussex to read English and French, graduating in 1970. UK Sexual Offences Act decriminalizes homosexuality. Angela Carter, *The Magic Toyshop*.

1969   John Fowles, *The French Lieutenant's Woman*.

1970   Germaine Greer, *The Female Eunuch*. Read by McEwan in 1971. Conservative Party wins general election, Edward Heath Prime Minister.

1970–1 MA in creative writing (with modern fiction) University of East Anglia. Taught by Angus Wilson and Malcolm Bradbury.

1972 Trip to Afghanistan. Angela Carter, *The Infernal Desire Machines of Doctor Hoffman.*

1973 Britain joins the European Economic Community. Martin Amis, *The Rachel Papers*; Iris Murdoch, *The Black Prince.*

1974 Moves from Norwich to take a room in Stockwell. Makes contact with Ian Hamilton's *New Review.* Labour Party wins second general election of the year, after a hung parliament, Harold Wilson becomes Prime Minister. Martin Amis, *Dead Babies.*

1975 First book published, the collection of stories *First Love, Last Rites.* Malcolm Bradbury, *The History Man.*

1976 Somerset Maugham Award for *First Love, Last Rites.*

1977 Angela Carter, *The Passion of New Eve.*

1978 *In Between the Sheets* and *The Cement Garden.* Iris Murdoch, *The Sea, the Sea.*

1979 Conservative Party wins general election, Margaret Thatcher becomes Prime Minister. Angela Carter, *The Bloody Chamber and Other Stories.*

1980 *The Imitation Game* transmitted as a BBC 'Play for Today'. Screenplay published 1981.

1981 *The Comfort of Strangers.* Salman Rushdie, *Midnight's Children.*

1982 Marries Penny Allen. The Falklands War, April to June.

1983 Named by *Granta* magazine as one of top twenty young British novelists. First performance of *Or Shall We Die?* wins *The Evening Standard* award for best screenplay for *The Ploughman's Lunch.* Conservative Party wins general election, Margaret Thatcher begins second term as Prime Minister. Graham Swift, *Waterland.*

1984 Miners' strike. Martin Amis, *Money*; Angela Carter, *Nights at the Circus.*

1985 *Rose Blanche.*

1987 Publication of *The Child in Time*, which wins the Whitbread Novel Award. Conservative Party wins general election, Margaret Thatcher begins third term as Prime Minister. The Great Storm in England kills eighteen people and destroys 15 million trees in southern England.

1988 Salman Rushdie, *The Satanic Verses*; David Lodge, *Nice Work.*

1989 Publication of *A Move Abroad*, containing the oratorio for *Or Shall We Die?* and the screenplay for 'The Ploughman's Lunch'.

The Berlin Wall is taken down, signalling the beginning of the end of the Cold War. Martin Amis, *London Fields*; Kazuo Ishiguro, *The Remains of the Day*; Jeanette Winterson, *Sexing the Cherry*; Julian Barnes, *A History of the World in 10½ Chapters*.

1990   *The Innocent*. Unification of East and West Germany. Hanif Kureishi, *The Buddha of Suburbia*.

1991   Gulf War begins. Dissolution of the Soviet Union and definitive end of the Cold War.

1992   *Black Dogs*. Conservative Party wins general election, John Major becomes Prime Minister. Adam Thorpe, *Ulverton*.

1993   Awarded the French Prix Fémina Étranger. Irvine Welsh, *Trainspotting*.

1994   *The Daydreamer*. Jonathan Coe, *What a Carve Up!*

1995   Divorced from Penny Allen. Martin Amis, *The Information*.

1997   *Enduring Love*. Marries literary journalist Annalena McAfee. Labour Party wins general election, Tony Blair becomes Prime Minister.

1998   Publication of *Amsterdam*, which wins the Booker Prize. Good Friday Agreement reached in Northern Ireland. Julian Barnes, *England, England*.

1999   Awarded the Shakespeare Prize.

2000   Awarded the Commander of the Order of the British Empire (CBE). Zadie Smith, *White Teeth*.

2001   *Atonement*. Labour Party wins general election, second term for Tony Blair as Prime Minister. Terrorist attacks on the World Trade Center in New York and other targets.

2002   Wins the W. H. Smith Literary Award, the National Book Critics Circle Award for fiction, and the *Los Angeles Times* Book Award, all for *Atonement*.

2003   The Iraq War, or Second Gulf War begins.

2005   Publication of *Saturday*, which wins the James Tait Black prize for fiction. Labour Party wins a third term under Tony Blair. 7/7 London suicide bombings. Zadie Smith, *On Beauty*.

2007   *On Chesil Beach*. Discovers he has a long-lost brother, Dave Sharp.

2008   Book of the Year award for *On Chesil Beach* at the British Book Awards. *For You* published, libretto for Michael Berkeley's opera.

2010   Publication of *Solar*, which is awarded the Bollinger Everyman Wodehouse Prize. Hung parliament after the general election.

Coalition government between the Conservatives and the Liberal Democrats, with David Cameron as Prime Minister.

2012 *Sweet Tooth.*

2014 *The Children Act.* 'No' vote in national referendum on Scottish independence.

2015 Conservative Party wins general election with a majority, David Cameron Prime Minister.

2016 *Nutshell.* 'Leave' vote in United Kingdom European Union membership referendum.

2017 Conservative Party forms minority government after snap election, with Theresa May as Prime Minister.

ABBREVIATIONS

The following abbreviations and editions are used for references to McEwan's work:

Am   *Amsterdam* (London: Jonathan Cape, 1998)
At   *Atonement* (London: Jonathan Cape, 2001)
BD   *Black Dogs* (1992; London: Picador, 1993)
CA   *The Children Act* (London: Jonathan Cape, 2014)
CG   *The Cement Garden* (1978; London: Picador, 1980)
CS   *The Comfort of Strangers* (1981; London: Vintage, 1997)
CT   *The Child in Time* (London: Jonathan Cape, 1987)
D   *The Daydreamer* (1994; London: Red Fox, 1995)
EL   *Enduring Love* (London: Jonathan Cape, 1997)
FL   *First Love, Last Rites* (1975; London: Picador, 1976)
FY   *For You* (London: Vintage, 2008)
I   *The Innocent* (1990; London: Picador, 1990)
IBS   *In Between the Sheets* (1978; London: Vintage, 1997)
IG   *The Imitation Game* (1981; London: Picador, 1982)
MA   *A Move Abroad: 'Or Shall We Die?' and 'The Ploughman's Lunch'* (London: Picador, 1989)
MP   *My Purple Scented Novel* (London: Vintage, 2018)
N   *Nutshell* (London: Jonathan Cape, 2016)
OCB   *On Chesil Beach* (London: Jonathan Cape, 2007)
RB   *Rose Blanche* (1985; London: Red Fox, 2004)
S   *Saturday* (London: Jonathan Cape, 2005)
So   *Solar* (London: Jonathan Cape, 2010)
ST   *Sweet Tooth* (London: Jonathan Cape, 2014)

DOMINIC HEAD

Introduction

Ian Russell McEwan (1948–) holds a pre-eminent place in late twentieth-century and contemporary British fiction. His standing as one of the most significant British writers since the 1970s is well established, and the interest in his work extends beyond Britain, especially to the United States and Europe, where he is widely read (and studied): his works have received both popular and critical acclaim, and he is, apart from Salman Rushdie (1947–), perhaps the most truly *international* author among his peers, the novelists of his generation, born in the 1940s: Martin Amis (1949–), Julian Barnes (1946–), Graham Swift (1949–). The larger underlying claim, which this *Companion* explores in its different facets, is that McEwan is at the forefront of a group of novelists who reinvigorated the ethical function of the novel, in ways that embody a deep response to the historical pressures of the time. Indeed, from the perspective of literary history, McEwan occupies a central role in a new wave of British novelists whose mature writing began to emerge in the Thatcher era, all of whom found different ways to address the moral problems that presented themselves in Britain from the late 1970s through to the 1990s, a period characterized broadly by the growth of self-interest, the expansion of corporate power and the collapse of the Welfare State. At the same time, McEwan has expanded our understanding of the novel's capacity – and especially the various ways in which the discourse of the novel can intersect with the discourses of science – so that the attempt to place him historically must address the history of ideas as much as his social and political context.

McEwan engages fully with the ideas as well as the social preoccupations of his time, so that his novels sometimes seem to treat these questions head-on, or at least less obliquely than is customary in a novelist's work. The following topics have all figured prominently in his writing: politics; male violence and the problem of gender relations; science and the limits of rationality; nature and ecology; love and innocence; and the basis of morality. Yet, if his work has sometimes been seen as over-dependent on ideas, he has also pre-empted his critics by treating the problem of ideas self-consciously, and by making it subordinate to questions of narrative technique; and he is also a great stylist, so his readers can always take pleasure in his carefully-wrought spare prose. This *Companion* has been structured to highlight the points of intersection between literary questions and evaluations, and the treatment of contemporary sociocultural issues and topics.

McEwan's work has received much praise and public recognition. His first book, the collection of stories *First Love, Last Rites* (1975), won the Somerset Maugham Award (1976). In 1983, he was named by *Granta* magazine as one of the 20 Best Young British Novelists and was awarded *The Evening Standard* award for best screenplay for *The Ploughman's Lunch*. He has won the Whitbread Novel Award for *The Child in Time* (1987) and the Booker Prize in 1998, for *Amsterdam*. He has also been short listed for the Booker on four other occasions: for *The Comfort of Strangers* (1981), *Black Dogs* (1992), *Atonement* (2001) and *On Chesil Beach* (2007). He won the French Prix Fémina Étranger in 1993, and the Shakespeare Prize in 1999. He was awarded the W. H. Smith Literary Award, the National Book Critics Circle Award for fiction and the *Los Angeles Times* Book Award for *Atonement*, all in 2002. *Saturday* won the James Tait Black prize for fiction in 2005, and McEwan has also won the Book of the Year award for *On Chesil Beach* at the British Book Awards in 2008, and the Bollinger Everyman Wodehouse Prize for *Solar* in 2010. He was awarded the CBE in 2000.

There are several ways in which McEwan's life can be seen to inspire his social preoccupations. For example, his background seems to relate strongly to his frequent portrayal of new kinds of family dynamic, and especially how a changing class structure impacts on domestic space. McEwan was born on 21 June 1948 in Aldershot. His Scottish father David McEwan was a soldier in the British army (later an officer), and his mother was Rose Lilian McEwan, whose previous husband had died in the Second World War, and by whom she had already had two children. In 2007, McEwan discovered that he had an elder brother, Dave Sharp, given up for adoption during the war.[1] In the early years of his childhood, McEwan lived at British military bases, both in Britain and abroad in Singapore and Libya, so he was not rooted in any specific place or region. A different sense of displacement ensued when McEwan's family found themselves in a form of class limbo, when his father was 'commissioned from the ranks'.[2] Because both parents were working class, the family experienced 'a curious kind of dislocated existence'.[3]

His childhood also produced a nascent political consciousness, stemming from his existence as (in his words), an 'army brat'[4]: the Suez crisis of 1956, which emphatically demonstrated the waning of Britain as a world power, occurred when McEwan was eight, and living in Libya, where anti-British sentiment was running high. When he saw the 'service revolver' strapped to his father's waist, McEwan claims to have 'understood for the first time that political events were real and affected people's lives' (*MA*, p. 27). Here, in McEwan's introduction to the screenplay for *The Ploughman's Lunch* (1983), in which parallels are drawn between Suez and the Falklands campaign, the writer retrospectively locates the birth of his political consciousness with the waning of Britain as a colonial power.[5]

McEwan's education was also unusual, but in ways that put him in the vanguard of class transition. Aged eleven, he was sent to a state boarding school in Suffolk, Woolverstone Hall, which he has characterized as having 'the trappings of a public school', yet with an intake of 'grammar-school level working-class lads from central London'.[6] McEwan's later education was also illustrative of a changing world. He attended two new universities: he was an undergraduate at the University of Sussex (1967–70), and he was the first student to study creative writing (with modern fiction, 1970–1) at the University of East Anglia. The new universities of the 1960s and 1970s, and the expansion of Higher Education they embodied, signalled a key step in the democratization of learning, and the University of Sussex was a particular focus for new (and often radical) social and political thought. In 1972 McEwan experienced the counter-culture first hand, following the 'hippy trail' to Afghanistan.

In 1974, he moved from his flat in Norwich to take an attic room in Stockwell. At this time, he made contact with Ian Hamilton's *New Review*. Through this key literary journal, he was introduced to, as he puts it, 'my generation' of writers, including Martin Amis, Julian Barnes and Craig Raine. If, with hindsight, this looks like a new literary establishment in the making, it was also 'remarkably open', in a meritocratic spirit.[7] The idea of a meritocratic society was another key marker – or aspiration – that can be associated with McEwan's generation, experiencing the upheavals of class change in post-war Britain.

McEwan's later family life also has a bearing on his perception of social change. He has been married twice; first in 1982, to Penny Allen, with whom he had two sons. They were divorced in 1995, but the first marriage ended in acrimony, and a dispute over custody of the children. McEwan's second marriage, in 1997, was to literary journalist Annalena McAfee. Interviewed in 1998, and whilst avoiding any direct comment on his personal life, he remarked that 'no one ... has an ordinary family life', given the 'incredible cross-alliances and third wives, second husbands, children by previous marriages, lovers who live in – mayhem, at street level'.[8] To some extent

McEwan's domestic life corresponds with this social trend, which has continued during his lifetime, with the traditional stable nuclear family becoming increasingly less commonplace, a point reinforced by the discovery, mentioned above, of a long-lost brother in 2007.

The key social and political changes of McEwan's lifetime, then, have also affected him personally, influencing his creativity. That influence, however, has not resulted in extravagant technical innovations in the manner of novelists such as Angela Carter or Salman Rushdie, writers who fashioned new fictional forms in direct response to a rapidly changing society, and who rendered in new imaginative forms the consequences of feminism and migrancy. In McEwan's work, there is continuity with a longer-term examination of the function of the novel, a process that has extended through modernity and into postmodernity. Placing McEwan in the canon of post-Second World War British writers, therefore, is not straightforward. He may not be overtly experimental, in the manner of Carter or Rushdie, but this does not mean his work is devoid of innovation, a quality that is held in balance with his interrogation of tradition. One source for the traditional element in this balance of influences is suggested by his early mentors. During his MA year, McEwan was taught by both Angus Wilson and Malcolm Bradbury, two writers whose work addresses the liberal identity in crisis.[9] The disturbing themes of McEwan's early work seem to take him in an entirely new direction; but his later preoccupation with the self and moral responsibility is apparent, even here, a facet of McEwan's ongoing intent to reconnect narrative fiction with moral sense, and, in some measure, to develop the sense of liberal identity crisis that one associates with Wilson and Bradbury, but for a new generation. The literature of shock (especially evident in early works by Martin Amis as well as McEwan) can be seen as one strategy for awakening the collective conscience in an era of bewildering social transition. So, although McEwan's later works are more obviously engaged with political questions, with interpersonal relationships, and with literary influence, we should not overlook the continuity as well as the sense of development through the oeuvre: his ongoing interrogations of the relationship between ethics, fiction and the act of writing are evident even in the disturbing early fiction.

The *Companion* begins with a detailed look at the emergence of McEwan as a writer, through a series of works with thematic coherence. His career began in startling fashion, with three books that achieved a degree of notoriety, and which earned him a reputation for writing unpleasant shorter fictions preoccupied with violence and deviant sexuality. As I have intimated, it is obvious now that McEwan's early work embodied a challenge to a staid literary establishment. His two short story collections, *First Love, Last*

Rites (1975) and *In Between the Sheets* (1978), and the novella *The Cement Garden* (1978), had a significant impact on the literary scene, making an important contribution to the 'post-consensus' renaissance in British fiction. McEwan's second longer work, *The Comfort of Strangers* (1981), is the culmination of this early phase, a work offering a hint at one direction his subsequent fiction would take: at its heart there is a considered evaluation of one effect of ideas and belief systems, an interest that sees him breaking out of his early stylistic straitjacket. At the same time, the early shock lit reveals its own concern with broader social questions. As Eluned Summers-Bremner shows in Chapter 1, McEwan's early work is distinctive, a voice emerging from a mood of national despondency, and reflecting on concerns arising from the erosion of the British welfare state, in a longer trajectory of historical reflection on the slow dismantling of the post-Second World War political consensus.

Discovering the connections between the early and later fiction requires us to see beyond the surface differences – which, superficially, suggest a maturation away from the early shock lit and towards a denser form of prose with greater social amplitude. Yet this can be problematic in two ways: if this simple account overlooks the early burgeoning moral sense, it also downplays the ways in which McEwan continues to disturb and unsettle us: his is an 'art of unease', in Kiernan Ryan's phrase.[10] If McEwan's early writing, especially the claustrophobic interiorized short stories, signals a turning away from the kind of social embodiment current in the English novel, at the same time he catches a generational mood, the sense of dislocation chiming with a broader public feeling. This is the germ of his interest in morality, which progressively became more central to his compositional processes, and the dilemmas presented in his fictions. His conviction that 'we are innately moral beings, at the most basic, wired-in neurological level' leads to a significant advance in the novel's concern with morality, as McEwan comes increasingly to link moral questions to his interest in scientific advancements, especially in evolutionary psychology, but also in neuroscience. He is inspired by the understanding that evolution produces instinctive social behaviour, made possible by the imagination and the ability to empathize, though in the writing of a novel these connections become rich and indeterminate. It is this 'wired-in' capacity for morality that fiction both feeds and responds to: 'fiction is a deeply moral form in that it is the perfect medium for entering the mind of another. I think it is at the level of empathy that moral questions begin in fiction', he has said.[11]

McEwan makes moral questions central to his work by presenting us with ways in which his characters are tested by a contingent world, and the moral dilemmas that result from the unforeseen event. McEwan's readers know that he is renowned for his vivid rendering of such scenes, which build to suggest a world view troubled by randomness, chaos. Indeed, the failure to cope with the random nature of experience is a recurring aspect of McEwan's treatment of character, leading, for example, to: Briony Tallis's crime (*Atonement*, 2001); the initial failure of Stephen Lewis to cope with grief (*The Child in Time*, 1987) and Joe Rose's problematic response to his stalker, Jed Parry – but especially to the delusional and destructive behaviour of Parry himself (*Enduring Love*, 1997).

Readers of McEwan have come to expect his novels to make use of an engrossing set piece – the abduction of a child in a supermarket (*The Child in Time*), a ballooning accident (*Enduring Love*), an encounter with ravenous wild dogs on a remote mountain road (*Black Dogs*, 1992), a car accident (*Saturday*, 2005), a moment of catastrophic misinterpretation (*Atonement*) – to frame the moral dilemma of his novels. And such treatments are often more complex than they first appear. In Chapter 2, Lynn Wells shows how McEwan's ethical reflections are highly self-conscious, sometimes involving ironic interrelationships between the narrator, the characters and the implied reader: we have to look beyond the plotlines, the presentation of actions, and resist the simple interpretation of those scenes with a seemingly incontestable moral purport. At the same time, as Wells makes clear, these complications of the moral treatment do not prevent us from getting a purchase on the ethical questions emerging from McEwan's contexts. In several of his novels the conflicts between altruism and self-interest are clearly linked to historical and political questions, especially where political power, and the role of the state, impinges on interpersonal relationships.

Where consolation comes, in such a vulnerable and disturbing world, it is always compromised. Even in the 'positive' resolutions of novels like *The Child in Time*, *Enduring Love* and *Saturday*, we are still unsettled. If Joe Rose is ultimately proved 'correct' about Jed Parry, his responses to the stalking have exposed his inadequacies; and Parry's destructive delusion persists. In *The Child in Time*, the reconciliation of Stephen and Julie, and the birth of the new child, cannot compensate for the loss of their daughter Kate, which remains unresolved. The thwarting of the intruders at the end of *Saturday* leaves us troubled about new perceptions of inequality, opened up by neuroscience, but also by the world 'outside' privileged spaces. The ultimate refusal of consolation for McEwan's readers comes at the end of *Atonement*, when we realize that the reuniting of the lovers is Briony's invention.

If McEwan denies consolation in an unpredictable and unreliable world, there is a counter-dynamic formed by McEwan's preoccupation with models of knowing: his works betray an ongoing search for systematic ways of

understanding the world, as a defence against contingency. Where explana-
tory systems are absent (as they are, for example, for the children in *The
Cement Garden*, and for the protagonists in *The Innocent* and *Amsterdam*),
or are inappropriate or inadequate (as for Colin and Mary in *The Comfort
of Strangers*, Jeremy in *Black Dogs*, Joe Rose in *Enduring Love* or Briony
Tallis in *Atonement*), an inner lack is exposed, often with catastrophic
consequences.

An interest in science figures prominently in the oeuvre, embracing a range
of topics, including: quantum physics (*The Child in Time*); evolutionary
psychology (*Enduring Love*); neurosurgery (*Saturday*) and climate crisis
science (especially in *Solar* but also in *The Child in Time*). In his nonfiction –
in articles and essays about science – McEwan often seems to celebrate and
revere the achievements of science in a straightforward fashion. In his
fiction, however, the engagement of science is invariably more metaphorical, and also more ambiguous. McEwan engages with a cultural moment
in which popular science has become more advanced, with eminent scientists writing bestsellers in which complex ideas are mediated for an increasingly sophisticated general readership. As Astrid Bracke demonstrates in
Chapter 3, McEwan sees science and literature as complementary parallel
traditions, although they are often explored through the tensions and
oppositions they reveal, as well as the potential resolution of these oppositions. For Bracke, this complementarity is exemplified in climate change
novels like *Solar*. Despite the ecocritical disappointment with this novel, it
belongs to a category of climate change fiction that does not simply reflect
contemporary perceptions, but which may also have a role in shaping
public discourse.

Prominent ideas – social and philosophical, as well as scientific – abound
in the oeuvre. There is, for example, the overtly political screenplay 'The
Ploughman's Lunch' (broadcast 1983); and the self-conscious debate about
the relative merits of rationality and spirituality in *Black Dogs*, in which the
starkness of the opposition is subtly undermined and deconstructed. In this
novel, as in others, ideas and the achievement of fictional suspense are not
mutually exclusive. McEwan's great skill has been to use ideas (especially
ideas drawn from popular science) to enrich his evocation of contemporary
life. The prominence of ideas in successive novels has sometimes been taken
as an invitation to question his accomplishment as a novelist: the ideas, it is
suggested, are not always assimilated into convincing fictional worlds. This
is the focus of Chapter 4 by Michael LeMahieu, which develops the account
of McEwan's reliance on science for creative inspiration, and then extends
that seminal concern as an aesthetic consideration. LeMahieu shows how
McEwan's novels of ideas are always something more than this implies, with

an aesthetic dimension beyond their ideational bases: they are animated by ideas, but never overwhelmed by them.

McEwan's portrayal of character and the quest for identity that underpins it sits in an interesting tension with ideas and with systemic explanations. The emphasis is often on the *quest*, not on the resolution of it. Yet McEwan's interest in science, and especially in scientific explanations for consciousness and emotional response, suggests a resource that is less equivocal, reducing consciousness to neurological function. For McEwan, however, science does not supply bald factual confirmation about consciousness; rather, scientific models provide explanations for consciousness, and the basis of selfhood, that the novelist subjects to scrutiny. The neurologist Antonio Damasio, a direct influence on McEwan, has expressed scepticism about 'science's presumption of objectivity and definitiveness', intimating that 'scientific results, especially in neurobiology' should be seen as 'provisional approximations, to be enjoyed for a while and discarded as soon as better accounts become available'.[12] This is in tune with McEwan's use of science, which suggests a form of complementarity where neither literature nor science can lay claim to be a definitive authority about consciousness, or to have exclusive access to it.

McEwan's concern with locating the self has much affinity with realist models of the past, but in a new guise. As he summarizes his persuasive dismantling of the realism/experimentalism dichotomy that has influenced much thinking about fiction in post-war Britain, Andrzej Gasiorek cites McEwan's view that experimentation 'should have less to do with formal factors . . . and more to do with content – the representation of states of mind and the society that forms them'.[13] This view has a lasting relevance to McEwan's work, and his steady focus on states of mind and cultural shaping forces.

One way in which that preoccupation with inner and outer worlds is manifested is through McEwan's long-term interest in Cold War themes, another career-spanning concern, reaffirmed with the publication of *Sweet Tooth* (2012), an artful and self-conscious deliberation on fictional representation. *Sweet Tooth* occasions a re-evaluation of *The Innocent*, the most neglected of McEwan's novels, perhaps because of the stylistic departure it embodies, with its mood and plot directly influenced by the Cold War spy novel. Like *Sweet Tooth*, *The Innocent* uses the Cold War as a way of framing its deliberation on the moral state of Britain (in this case the setting is 1955–6, in the former, it is 1972). As in *The Innocent*, in *Black Dogs* the treatment of individual motivation and choice becomes a central focus, and – as Richard Brown demonstrates in Chapter 5 – a way of articulating a wider anxiety about ethics and responsibility in post-war Europe, anchored in the generation-defining experience of the fall of the Berlin Wall in 1989. In Brown's account, the densely allusive *Sweet Tooth* makes intelligence (in the sense of espionage) interact with cultural intelligence in a sophisticated exploration of civilized values, from which intellectual freedom emerges as its own best defence.

The conventional wisdom that the novel is the medium in which public themes and concerns receive their most powerful expression in the private realm requires significant re-articulation to account for the treatment of interpersonal relationships in McEwan. David Malcolm, in Chapter 7, shows how McEwan is interested in both public institutions, on the one hand, and the minutiae of the personal, on the other, revealing powerful extremities of treatment: his observations can be microscopically physical, but can also engage with public themes on a grand scale. The interaction of public and private is crucial to McEwan's fictional worlds. Malcolm illustrates the ways in which the personal and the public interpenetrate each other, and how institutions can constrain, but also enable the personal: either way, the trajectory of public life is intimately related to the private realm. In addition to tracing this recurring fascination with the public-private nexus, Malcolm's chapter also presents a typology of interpersonal relationships, discovering six categories of relationship in a range of relative positivity and negativity.

Perhaps the most important social change that had an impact on McEwan in his formative years was second-wave feminism. He recalls that he read Germaine Greer's *The Female Eunuch* in 1971 and found it 'a revelation' because it 'spoke directly' to his family's life, and the problem of his father's dominance.[14] Some readers may find this surprising. Feminism is certainly engaged, in important preliminary ways, in both the screenplay for *The Imitation Game* (1980) and *The Comfort of Strangers* (1981); but it is only in his work of the mid-1980s – in the oratorio for *Or Shall We Die?* (1983) and in *The Child in Time* (1987) – that McEwan produces a more overt response to the implications of feminism. Yet the more subtle influences discernible in his treatment of sexuality and gender abound. Several of the chapters discover common ground between early and later fictions in this connection, and also between stories, novels screenplays, and other publications: the oratorio for 'Or Shall We Die?' (text published 1989), for example, marks a significant moment in McEwan's transition towards a greater comprehension of feminist principles, foreshadowed in the screenplays collected in *The Imitation Game* (1981). McEwan's ongoing interest in male-female relationships is another route in to his investigations into the state of society, and the ways in which it impinges on individual identity and behaviour.

Still more prominent in McEwan's oeuvre is his concern with male experience. Adam Mars-Jones's famous critique of *The Child in Time*, as an exemplary instance of the dubious new man in British fiction, identifies a turning point in McEwan's career, and the beginning of a fresh investigation of masculinity, which can be construed more positively. In this novel, McEwan is not interested merely in the psychological nature of gender identity (important though that is): he is equally concerned with the connection between mainstream masculinity and patriarchal power. The question of masculinity is revisited in different ways throughout the oeuvre, from the dysfunctional narrators of the short stories, through the rape fantasy of *The Innocent*, the personal feud in *Amsterdam*, to the unsettling of Joe Rose's worldview in *Enduring Love*. The professionalism of Henry Perowne in *Saturday* is a fascinating case study in masculinity, which is subverted in the figure of *Solar*'s Michael Beard. All of these instances illustrate the ways in which the relational and provisional matter of gender is a textual matter. In Chapter 8, Ben Knights offers a thorough investigation of masculinity, evaluating the scope of McEwan's contribution to a model of thinking about gender that now seems like a generational concern, a model that has less purchase on twenty-first century society. If debates about gender have now gravitated towards identity wars, Knights reminds us that the wider debate about masculinity in the 1980s and 1990s was focused on the formation or questioning of patriarchy, and on the related dynamics of power. Underpinning this preoccupation with masculinity and patriarchal authority there is, as Knight shows, a continuing search for alternative models.

In Chapter 6 Peter Childs investigates a topic intimately related to questions of masculinity in the oeuvre: the construction of childhood. *The Child in Time*, McEwan's first major novel, is at the heart of his interest in childhood, and how the child is central to the self-definition of British society. Against the manipulations of the child – the *Authorized Child-Care Handbook*, which reveals the political construction of childhood; and the question of children's imagination, as a publishing construction – this novel seeks to connect childhood and adulthood in a thoughtful account of self-realization, in a world where disconnection is the root of both personal tragedy and social decay. As Childs shows, the fascination with childhood, which has endured throughout McEwan's career, from the early stories of the 1970s through to recent works including *The Children Act* (2014) and *Nutshell* (2016), is also a barometer for social care in a broad sense. From his early concern with child neglect and abuse, McEwan progresses to ponder the loss of children and the childlessness of adults in novels of the 1980s and 1990s, and has latterly dwelt on vulnerable children, as a way of investigating the role of the state in the twenty-first century. In *The Children*

Act, the legal construction of the child becomes the focus of self-enquiry and moral agency, in a typically self-conscious treatment. McEwan's own publications for children, *Rose Blanche* (1985), and *The Daydreamer* (1994), are also interesting in this connection. *The Daydreamer*, in particular, emerges as another attempt to re-think the categorization of childhood, with (as Childs shows) its recurring theme of transformation.

The *Companion* ends with four chapters that are more explicitly concerned with formal questions, although they also register the profound interrelationship of McEwan's recurring themes and concerns. One aspect of McEwan's celebrated status as a stylist is his distinctive contribution to the novella, a genre that arguably reached its pinnacle in the late nineteenth and early twentieth centuries. Novellas like *Amsterdam*, with its focused critique of the left-leaning elite who did well in the Thatcher era, and *On Chesil Beach* (2007), with its apparently precise anatomy of sexual mores, reveal how McEwan uses the novella as an incisive instrument of cultural analysis. Chapter 9 examines these works, as well as *The Cement Garden* and *The Comfort of Strangers*, demonstrating McEwan's fascination with the novella, and the ways in which he uses the distinctive features of this form, usually associated with earlier writers, such as James, Conrad, and Lawrence: he has revived the fortunes of a form once thought to be the most sophisticated mode of shorter fiction.

The social and political focus of McEwan's fictions signals a deep reliance on an extended tradition of realist writing, reaching back to the great exponents of nineteenth-century socio-political realisms. Using the varied capacities of the realist tradition – the ability to register the dilemmas surrounding vertiginous social change, as well as the capacity to record a contingent reality – McEwan reworks realist codes in a variety of ways to engage social and political questions. Returning to the Cold War as a case study in McEwan's treatment of social and political reality, Judith Seaboyer, in Chapter 10, discovers a sophisticated form of post-realism at work in *Black Dogs* and *The Innocent*, and also in Part Two of *Atonement*, in its powerful blend of metafiction with verisimilitude and historical accuracy.

Critics have often been drawn to observe the connections between McEwan and canonical modernist writing, for example, in the treatment of time in *The Child in Time*, or the echoes of Woolf's *Mrs Dalloway* in *Saturday*. In Chapter 11, Thom Dancer concentrates on McEwan's later works, *Atonement, Saturday, Solar* and *The Children Act*, to consider the influence of modernism, and especially how McEwan extends some of the stylistic features of literary impressionism. Working in the spirit of 'meta-modernism' – an approach that traces twenty-first century engagements with the innovations of the early twentieth-century – Dancer reveals how

McEwan 'reaches back' to earlier technical influences, given the intellectual cul-de-sac he sensed in postmodernist experimentation. The emphasis here is on how McEwan makes aspects of modernist style relevant for the new conditions of living, writing and thinking in the twenty-first-century, conditions in which the strategy of 'making new' is no longer available. In particular, McEwan revitalizes modernist impressionist aesthetics, but without the transgressive politics, or the grand claims of literary innovation they once carried. Dancer shows how the legacies of modernism issue in a more limited function for literary effects, no longer transcendent, but rather a reminder of our human failings.

McEwan's particular brand of literary self-consciousness embraces different strategies, from the counter-intuitive ethical implications of the early shock lit, through to the extended treatments of narratorial unreliability in *Black Dogs* and *Atonement*, where the point of the fictions hinges on an engagement with narrative technique. In Chapter 12, David James examines McEwan's narrative artifice, revealing its several sources: he shows how *Atonement* (for example) combines influences from modernism, metafiction and nineteenth-century realist characterization. James shows how McEwan's work draws attention to its own procedures, but without disrupting the affective experience of reading. Indeed, James shows how McEwan's various methods for commenting on his creativity oblige us to reflect on our own critical habits, in a venerable tradition of reflexive fictional prose.

This overview of McEwan's preoccupations and the coverage of the *Companion* signals many points of intersection between McEwan's artistic, social, political and ethical emphases. In an attempt to capture this pervasive ideational interaction, the chapters herein are written on thematic topics, rather than on individual works in a chronological sequence. The intention is to provide several intersecting perspectives on his work, and a more complex understanding about his richest works, rather than treating them in individual chapters. Readers of this book will thus be able to gain a multi-faceted perspective on the most discussed fictions, which are read through more than one lens. For example, in the case of *The Child in Time*, emphasis can be placed on its concerns with gender and climate change (Chapter 3), or the prominence of ideas (Chapter 4), or the construction of childhood (Chapter 6). Similarly, *Atonement* can be read through separate, but complementary lenses: morality (Chapter 2), the modernist legacy (Chapter 11) or formal hybridity (Chapter 12). And these layers of reading reveal the kind of complementarity not easily attained in a single reading: if we consider McEwan to be 'dressing up' as Briony (Chapter 8), does this staging of masculinity in relation to narrative unreliability suggest a complementary or parallel reading to the emphasis placed on Briony's guilt as a response to modernist style in Chapter 11? Or, as Chapter 12 suggests, does McEwan's assembled literary heritage in *Atonement* sit self-consciously at odds with Briony's practice as a novelist? As Chapter 10 suggests, this extraordinarily complex work can also be read as a metafictional mapping of the literary history of novelistic realism and its influence. This book has been designed, then, to serve as a prism of interpretation, revealing the various interpretive emphases each of McEwan's more complex works invite, and to show how his various recurring preoccupations run through his career. This intention to open up our understanding of McEwan, in the various readings the fiction inspires, is presented in a spirit of invitation: to encourage and stimulate further variety in the future criticism of this leading contemporary novelist.

NOTES

1 See Dave Sharp and John Parker, *Complete Surrender* (London: John Blake, 2008).
2 'Mother Tongue: A Memoir', in *On Modern British Fiction*, ed. Zachary Leader (Oxford: Oxford University Press, 2002), pp. 34–44 (p. 35). The piece was first published in *The Guardian*, 13 October 2001.
3 Liliane Louvel, Gilles Ménégaldo, and Anne-Laure Fortin, 'An Interview with Ian McEwan', *Études Britanniques Contemporaines*, 8 (1995), pp. 1–12 (pp. 1, 3).
4 'Mother Tongue', p. 36.
5 In *The Child in Time* (pp. 69–74), Stephen Lewis's childhood recollections seem to be McEwan's.
6 'Mother Tongue', p. 36.
7 'Wild Man of Literature (c1976): A Memoir', *The Observer*, 'Review', 7 June 1998, p. 16.
8 William Leith, 'Form and Dysfunction' (author profile), *The Observer*, 'Life', 20 September 1998, pp. 4–5, 7–8 (p. 8).
9 Malcolm Bradbury, *The Modern British Novel*, revised edition (London: Penguin, 2001), p. 437.
10 Kiernan Ryan, *Ian McEwan* (Plymouth: Northcote House/British Council, 1994), pp. 2, 4, 5.
11 Louvel, Ménégaldo, and Fortin, 'An Interview with Ian McEwan', p. 4.
12 Antonio Damasio, *Descartes' Error: Emotion, Reason, and the Human Brain* (1994; New York: Quill, 2000), p. xviii.
13 Andrzej Gasiorek, *Post-War British Fiction: Realism and After* (London: Edward Arnold, 1995), p. 180; Ian McEwan, 'The State of Fiction: A Symposium', *New Review*, 5 (Summer 1978), 1, pp. 14–76 (p. 51).
14 'Mother Tongue: A Memoir', pp. 41–2.

I

ELUNED SUMMERS-BREMNER

'Shock Lit'

The Early Fiction

The stories in Ian McEwan's 1975 collection, *First Love, Last Rites*, shocked many readers with their subject matter (murder, paedophilia, incest, infantile regression) and the nonjudgemental manner of their telling. A second collection, *In Between the Sheets* (1978), and first short novel/novella, *The Cement Garden* (1978), employ a similarly dispassionate tone – *The Cement Garden*'s details are 'blank, precise, passive', in Hermione Lee's description – and the subjects are no less disturbing.[1] Castration, bestiality and sadomasochism feature in the stories, while incest recurs in *The Cement Garden*, an account, told by fifteen-year-old Jack, of the summer he, his sisters and younger brother spend alone in the family house after both parents die, the children having buried their mother's body in a trunk in the basement. A further short novel (or novella), *The Comfort of Strangers* (1981), featuring murder and sadomasochistic sex, exhibits a strangely detemporalized, dreamlike kind of narration. In all of his work to this point, McEwan places readers within the largely enclosed, bleak worlds of his characters in such a way that it is difficult to see any escape from them.[2]

While reviewers and critics of *First Love* were by turns disturbed and impressed by McEwan's stylistic control of gruesome subject matter McEwan himself expressed surprise at the perturbed reactions.[3] 'Lurid physical detail' rendered with 'cold dissociation' feature in 'Burroughs, Celine, Genet and Kafka', as he told John Haffenden in 1985.[4] And McEwan is not the only English fiction writer of the time to present bleak, unsettling subject matter in clean-lined prose. The work of Angela Carter in the late 1960s and early 1970s and J. G. Ballard in the early to mid-1970s comes to mind. Jeannette Baxter has suggested surrealism as a context for McEwan's early work and Dominic Head notes that its 'iconoclasm' might represent 'the intellectual wing of the punk movement, catching a mood in which raw cultural forms are generated to disturb the status quo'.[5]

There is clearly something in this, for all that both surrealism and punk were more formally experimental than are most of McEwan's carefully constructed stories. But the early work can also be seen to be historical in a less immediately obvious sense. In a 1994 interview, McEwan described the stories as originating in a search for 'de-socialised, distorted versions' of his own existence, and as functioning 'like dreams about [his] own situation', something he often only understood long after a particular story's writing.[6] The same can often be said of the time and places of a work of fiction's making, which leave traces in a work that can be seen more readily afterwards. While many situations in early McEwan exhibit the kind of bizarre certainty we associate with dream and perhaps especially nightmare scenarios, the dreamlike is also a way to describe the context of the early work: 1970s Britain.

As elsewhere in Europe and America, the 1970s in Britain were experienced as less clearly purposeful than the flamboyantly delineated 1960s, with their youthful idealism and breaking of taboos. And, although most ordinary families in Britain were better off at this time than previously, for much of the decade the nation was in the kind of stasis that approached the nightmarish in its inability to move forward politically.[7] In the early to mid-1970s, Britain faced an oil and electricity crisis resulting in a three-day working week, acute industrial unrest, high inflation, a stagnant economy and a mood of 'declinism' that Andy Beckett describes as having shifted, in 1974–5, 'from the anxious to the apocalyptic'.[8] Given that politicians were unable to propose clear ways ahead, it should not surprise us if we encounter fiction in the decade that portrays sealed up or self-referential worlds. And the early McEwan's concern with adolescence and adolescent interests, as well as with how older adults remember this time of problematic, if temporary, stasis, is paralleled by a decade in which little that was strikingly definitive seemed to occur.

Additionally, there is sometimes in McEwan's early work a conflation of historical periods in which the merging is not entirely seamless, where 1950s or 1960s features appear in the setting of the 1970s and are accompanied by its mood of despair. Although we need not expect fiction to create a fully recognizable world, it is possible to read this contiguity as a part of the distortion involved in inhabiting the 1970s themselves, a decade unavoidably engaged in looking back, if only because the postwar consensus, if it ever existed, comes to a perceptible end in the period.[9] In 'Homemade', for instance, a story about a young man's first sexual experience that is an exercise in part-homage to postwar American novelists, a mismatch between the story's two narrative voices – the fifteen-year-old narrator is uncommonly articulate and wise, indicating an older self in a later moment of recollection – accentuates the fact that two distinct historical periods seem to be involved.[10] Although the story evokes the 1950s – in the allusion to the

Elvis Presley song 'Teddy Bear' and in the exploration of a bombed out cellar – the extended bleakness of the story's descriptions of the narrator's relatives' working conditions might equally belong to the 1970s, which gives us to understand that it is in the 1970s that early postwar ways of doing things come to an end (*FL*, pp. 9, 11, 14–15).

The teenage narrator and his cousin Raymond are represented as older than their peers (*FL*, p. 13), and yet their older relatives are regarded by the narrator as hopelessly innocent and earnest, like the young. 'Priz[ing] themselves' for never missing a day at work despite their exhaustion and on making to the narrator small monetary gifts they can ill afford (*FL*, p. 15), these older men in working class occupations represent the wartime and early postwar mindset in which going without some kinds of pleasure was a way to contribute to the overall well-being of the nation. Personal sacrifices were made in these earlier periods to ensure that Britain won the war, built and maintained the welfare state despite financial indebtedness, and kept up morale in the bleak, early years of the Cold War.[11]

The historical slippage of a decade or more symbolizes or accompanies the temporal slippage the narrator desires insofar as he wants to 'have fucked' (*FL*, p. 23) rather than to experience fucking, and to bypass childish things. By contrast, older working relatives bound to the ennui more often associated with adolescence, or in the historical sense to time understood according to the postwar logic of sacrifice for invisible outcomes, represent 'the childhood of the nation'. They are oriented towards a benign future with which it is not their task to contend. Yet, neither the story's adults nor its children know why they are pursuing certain courses of action, while the means, so vigorously pursued, compensate for this absence of reason by producing secondary satisfactions which themselves produce a nonsensical momentum. The male relatives work excessively, cousin Raymond staggers 'determinedly' but 'pointless[ly]' to the finish line of the school cross-country race (*FL*, p. 17), and the narrator's sister Connie, in a parody of 1950s domestic servitude, 'ecstatic[ally]' fetches all manner of miniature household objects upon learning that her brother wants to play 'Mummies and Daddies' with her, quickly reaching a state of beatific wonder (*FL*, p. 20).

While other stories in *First Love, Last Rites* are striking for their absence of expressed emotion – 'Butterflies', for instance, the confession of a child molester and murderer, and 'Conversations with a Cupboard Man', in which a man who has suffered significant hardships is apparently blasé about them – the theme of play-acting runs through several other stories, from 'Solid Geometry' to 'Cocker at the Theatre' and 'Disguises'. 'Last Day of Summer', a haunting tale of a preadolescent boy's first encounter with adult relationships and longings, in a household in which several adults variously care for two children, is also a story about the social experiments of the 1960s and 1970s. The sadness yet to be felt by the twelve-year-old narrator at the story's close is signalled earlier, as Jenny's care for another woman's daughter indicates the care for each other and their environment that is not quite shown by the other characters. These people are living a relatively free-form existence, but it does not seem to enliven them.

If play-acting is a way to describe a decade in which a 'muddled, backward-looking social consensus' comes to an end without there being a recognizable replacement, 'Disguises', which features, as do 'Butterflies' and 'Conversations', damaged humans who regress and in doing so harm themselves and others, reveals the danger of attachment to this way of being.[12] Working the territory of disguises that reveal themselves to be disguises and, thus, do not function as intended, the story, set in the early 1960s, also portrays adults who act in childlike ways. This was in fact a feature of the 1960s in the West, as hippies in flamboyant dress consciously worked at living more authentically in the present, distinguishing themselves from the 'anonymity' of 'the straight world' in which 'people prey on each other mercilessly' while imagining they are merely conforming to social conventions.[13] Here, however, adults prey on children, not only directly by means of sexual abuse, but also by fudging age markers, so that it becomes increasingly unclear to ten-year-old Henry what kinds of behaviour can reasonably be expected of adults and how children should act in response to them.

The story is a rendition of a de-romanticized 1960s from the viewpoint of the 1970s, in which little but dressing up and partying remains of the previous decade's hopeful innocence and in which time is strangely undifferentiated, as signalled by the self-referentiality of the story's opening line: 'Mina that Mina' (FL, p. 100). A sense of sealed-up adult conspiracy is conveyed by Mina's theatrical public's 'kn[owing] about Mina' and understanding the 'melodrama of desperation' that disrupts her last stage performances, although this understanding is more difficult to affirm when applied outside the theatre as Mina, a clearly unsuitable guardian, takes charge of orphaned Henry. Here again, adult Mina is the child and Henry cannot himself reliably take this role, as he learns when he tries to join in with his aunt's manic capers (FL, p. 100). Like an adult, he is worried by Mina (FL, p. 105), and when she makes him dress in girls' clothes and calls him to sit on her knee, he panics, noting that there is 'something dark' in her that he does not understand (FL, p. 107). This is proven when, later, she forces him to drink alcohol and molests him.

It is worth noting that this story is also about the effects of homophobia, which may in certain times and places confine queer people to a kind of childhood or adolescence. Lives that are not readily furnished with clear trajectories and desired endpoints can fall in upon themselves or become a series of default experiments. And while Mina is clearly mentally unstable, as a person who is probably queer she also belongs to a social group that, at the time of the story's setting, and arguably its writing, was regarded by many heterosexuals as intrinsically transgressive, with no evident relation to heterosexual familial arrangements. Mina's own transgressions against young Henry's innocence may thus appear to her less insupportable and less damaging than they are.

Sex between men was decriminalized in Britain in 1967, but public sexual contact was still prohibited and suspected breaches vigorously pursued, while sex between women continued to be publicly unaddressed by hetero-sexual lawmakers.[14] In 1972–3 in Notting Hill, London, a commune known as 'Colvillia' served as an experimental living space for those of queer persuasion and/or those who wished to witness the expressive possibilities of those who were. The environment was, as one Gay Liberation Front activist put it, 'unstructured to a degree that was terrifying if you had led any kind of structured life', although experiments in self-expression were not limited, at the time, to communal living situations in which queer people predominated.[15]

While this kind of environment may have formed part of the conscious or unconscious cultural currency of 'Disguises', the world depicted in the story is much harsher and bleaker. McEwan astutely summons a moment of disillusion – that of late middle age, that of being unhappily gay, and that of being in a decade, the 1960s (or the 1970s), in which injunctions to transgress can be very much less than liberating – that perfectly suits his trademark dispassionate rendition of base behaviours. The story is about the end or abolishment of childhood, a theme McEwan explores in greater depth in *The Child in Time*, and which here consists in a young boy's seeing the pitiful and bitter condition of certain adult lives without his having a way to parse the phenomenon, and, crucially, without seeing in time the danger it poses to him and to his young female friend, Linda. When the language of Henry's thoughts breaks down at the end of the story, reflecting in part his growing drunkenness, he registers that dressing 'like somebody else' (*FL*, p. 125) is to enter a zone of contortion, like crooked syntax, in which adults can do things to children without experiencing blame, but he still needs to know who Mina thinks she is when she abuses him. As Henry watches Linda, terrified, being pulled onto an older man's lap as the man undresses, he realizes that there are no disguises in this context. None of the guests is 'baffled by each other' (*FL*, p. 124), and a disguise is simply a means to condone destructive intent. Mina does not need to think anything when

Henry is there to represent her unhappiness. McEwan has again honed in on one of our worst tendencies: to call our worst depravities by other names.

The theme of stasis, associated with adolescence, recurs in *In Between the Sheets* (1978), McEwan's second short story collection. Bookended by stories featuring characters who gain sexual pleasure from being made physically powerless, other stories in the book ('Reflections of a Kept Ape', 'Two Fragments: March 199–', 'Dead as They Come') display worlds in which sexual or other expressive possibilities are curtailed by internal or external conditions. The relation of the surreal to the everyday is a strong theme in the collection, indicating the conflicts that can result when realities outrun the terms available for defining them. 'Two Fragments: March 199–' is set in a dystopian future in which social order has broken down. Henry and his young daughter inhabit a cityscape littered by '[h]uman refuse', rotting vegetation and the burned remains of once-domestic animals (*IBS*, p. 39). This is an extended version of the 'strange, declining social world' Tom Nairn associated with Britain in the 1970s, some features of which, such as sewage and other rubbish, proliferated in urban areas during the 1978–9 'Winter of Discontent'.[16] In common with other stories in the collection, an absence of creativity produces a problematic excess. Henry's friend Diane remarks that the inhabitants of the story's world 'make nothing' (*IBS*, p. 49). Such purposelessness is evidenced by the many manufactured, now largely useless objects with which people are surrounded as well as by the meal Henry is forced to share with a Chinese family, a meal described by the couple's daughter as 'muck' and '*piss*' (*IBS*, p. 57), after he helps the girl's father move a cupboard into their dwelling.

'Reflections of a Kept Ape' and 'Dead as They Come' also deal with absences, that of literary productivity in the former story and that of human intimacy in the latter. In 'Reflections of a Kept Ape', an ape who is the lover of a young novelist, Sally Klee, discovers that instead of producing a second work of fiction she has been daily typing out, with dutiful regularity, the text of her first successful novel. Both the ape and his human lover, it emerges, are living in the aftermath of a once desiring partnership. And while the ape could be said to inhabit a dreamlike world with adolescent qualities – his self-consciousness and the subjecting of mundane actions to acute reflective scrutiny are reminiscent of this state – he is in fact engaged in complex thought about the relation of past to future, a concern that, like Sally's writing, was both pressing and difficult to articulate in the Britain of the story's era.

If we tend to associate our simian predecessors with mimicry and an absence of artistic creativity, here it is the ape, not the human, who tells the story and who exhibits a capacity for self-reflection and complex self-representation his lover seems to lack, indicating human regression. He arranges himself on the chaise longue 'in an attitude of simian preoccupation' in case his lover should look in on him and reflects on the human tendency to repeat behaviour to no clear end (*IBS*, pp. 24, 27). He runs and reruns 'fantasy footage' of himself reading Sally's writing and enabling her to improve it (*IBS*, pp. 28–9), which act of covert reading he then performs. He waits before going into Sally's study lest he appear, 'even to [him]self, precipitate', and is prepared for 'the universal law which preordains a discrepancy between the imagined and the real', even for 'disappointment' (*IBS*, pp. 30–1). On discovering that his lover has not, after all, been producing new work, he wonders if he could 'convince [him]self of alternative descriptions of the situation' in which he finds himself (*IBS*, p. 34), thus evincing precisely the kind of creativity involved in writing fiction.

The ape, then, has a sophisticated sense of temporality, but it is oriented towards Sally's paralysed situation. As well as preparing for possible disappointment he engages in 'speculation' and 'nostalgia' (*IBS*, p. 27), looking forward and back, which reminds us of humanity's biological legacy from the ape and questions the idea that we have moved beyond it. (A more complex understanding of different evolutionary paths for apes and humans has emerged since McEwan's story was written.) The story ends with the repetition of an earlier moment in the zoo in which the ape first noticed humans looking in at him. As he squats behind Sally Klee at her writing desk, as he squatted behind his mother then, he philosophically confirms Sally's static situation as, earlier, the watching humans confirmed his. The 'impossible idea' that Sally will ever turn and notice him also implies the impossibility of her having new readers because, this time, there are no 'spectral figures' looking in (*IBS*, p. 35).

'Dead as They Come', which features an inhuman lover in the form of a mannequin with which a successful businessman falls in love and with which he experiences a fantasized relationship, similarly charts a kind of regression, as, imagining his beloved unfaithful, the protagonist then murders her. But it is 'In Between the Sheets' that continues the interest of 'Reflections of a Kept Ape' in the relation of literary creativity to sexuality and human intimacy, while demonstrating the uncertain masculinity that it became possible to acknowledge in the 1970s, if not always express effectively. The story, which concerns the relationship Stephen Cooke, a writer, has with his teenage daughter Miranda, begins with Stephen awakening from a wet dream, itself often regarded as an adolescent phenomenon. Stephen's estrangement from his wife, we learn, was largely the result of his fear of her orgasms and consequent inability to satisfy her sexually, which sense of inferiority is almost perversely reiterated by Stephen when he chooses scruffy cafés as their meeting places and visits his former home to ask Miranda to stay with him, but has no words ready to say to his former partner.

Although the story begins with the wet dream, the dream's content is not immediately given and we only learn later that the scene which follows has in fact been the material that gives rise to it. Here, Stephen and his ex-wife meet in a café. We then see Stephen at his daily writing work before buying presents in Oxford Street for Miranda's birthday. On finding, at home, that the presents cause a sense of 'loathing' and seem condescending, Stephen lies down on the unmade bed, fingers the stain from the preceding night's dream and falls asleep (*IBS*, pp. 83–4). Because what follows is a scene in which Stephen's daughter Miranda lies naked from the waist up on her bed while another girl, Charmian, sits astride her buttocks and rakes her fingernails back and forth across Miranda's back 'for her birthday', and because the more mundane material of the wet dream is not yet given, it is quite easy to assume that this scene is part of Stephen's nocturnal, sexual dream life. Incestuous desire is thus suggested. Stephen's ringing the doorbell of Miranda's mother's house, however, disrupts the bedroom activity and shows the scenario to have been real. Stephen invites Miranda and her friend to stay with him in the school holidays. While Stephen works at his writing with 'customary numbness' in the days that follow, he also begins writing down the content of the dream, in which his wife is in the café of their meeting and he is the coffee machine that fills a coffee cup, resulting in the sexual emission (*IBS*, p. 89).

The dream thus seems to be inseparable from writing, perhaps from the making of a story. On the day after the dream, Stephen has reviewed a pamphlet on Victorian attitudes to menstruation (*IBS*, p. 83), and when Miranda and Charmian come to stay the bed they share has sheets of deep red that had been a wedding present for Miranda's parents 'from a time when all sheets were white' (*IBS*, p. 93). The juxtaposition of red and white and the earlier reference to menstruation reminds us of female adolescence, and a sense of the illicit is intensified when Stephen, 'horrified' but 'elated', hurries into his study because he has an erection. Later he awakens from fractious sleep thinking he has heard a sound, goes, naked, to the bathroom to urinate and again hears it. It is the sound of a woman approaching orgasm. Stephen is halted in anxiety outside his daughter's bedroom door; Miranda opens the door and tells her father that she cannot sleep. Miranda climbs back into bed and Stephen sits on the edge of the bed while Miranda tells him of sometimes feeling frightened when she wakes in the middle of the night. Father and daughter agree that there is really nothing to be frightened of on such occasions.

The story's ending in a moment of shared fear, in which the sexual element seems only to have existed in Stephen's imagination, turns the earlier, actual fears experienced 'between the sheets' with his wife into something more innocent and childlike, like the snowy, 'dazzling white' of Miranda's upturned throat when she sleeps, finally (*IBS*, p. 96). And yet, until the ending, Stephen's writerly profession of imagining and reimagining actual situations 'in between . . . sheets' of paper makes it difficult for the reader to discern exactly where reality begins and ends. The possibility of re-encountering 'the frame of all anxieties' (*IBS*, p. 94) in the form of female sexual pleasure, a possibility for which the earlier bedroom scene has pre-pared us, seems to take Stephen back in time to the life he shared with Miranda's mother, a time which, given Stephen's fear, was not unlike adolescence. When Miranda asks to be told something to help her go to sleep – in childhood, this would probably have been a story – Stephen mentions the bag of presents in the hall cupboard, which reaffirms him as an adult. And yet the presents are also now no longer condescending, a word emphasizing the gap in understanding between adult and adolescent, because Miranda's appearance in the hall, her white nightdress hiding her body, had made her 'any age', and her statement of fear enabled a similar, truthful statement from her father.

If in this period of encounter groups and interests in popular psychology the recognition and expression of childlike fears was more routinely allowed to adults than previously, McEwan's first short novel, *The Cement Garden* (1978), tested readers' tolerance for regressive behaviours further. Detailing the lives of four children after their parents die and before social services are informed of their circumstances, the novel turns on its head the situation in which the nuclear family serves as the social form for the restriction of sexual impulses. The death of the children's father is presented as less significant than fifteen-year-old narrator Jack's first orgasm, which occurs at the same time. Jack (then fourteen) and his older sister Julie play sexual games with their younger sister, Sue, and at the end of the novel Jack and Julie have sex immediately after being discovered together by Julie's boyfriend Derek, expressing no shame at the activity. The children's father's death is only included in the story, we are told, to explain how the children came to have a large quantity of cement available (*CG*, p. 9), under which, when their mother dies, they hide her putrefying corpse in a chest in the house's basement.

Although the children seem to inhabit a moral vacuum, it is clear that the family itself, before the parents' deaths, was similarly lacking. No friends or other relatives visit, so there are no points of comparison. The children's father torments their mother and takes the decision to concrete over the garden unilaterally. But the self-referential situation of the family is also present in their surroundings which, like those of 'Butterflies' and 'Two Fragments: March 199–', form a 'Winter of Discontent' kind of environment. The partly cement-covered garden is echoed by the half-formed state of the neighbourhood, in which other houses have been destroyed to make space for a motorway that was never built (CG, p. 21). The landscape is one of weeds and torn metal, tower blocks with rain-wrought stains cascading down them, and 'cracked asphalt' aprons (CG, p. 22). The only external environments referred to are school, some unvisited shops, and the snooker hall in which Julie's boyfriend Derek plays, itself containing a debased form of family, because the couple who own it treat Derek as though he were a child (CG, pp. 93–4).

As David Malcolm notes, while the novel seems 'strangely suspended' in its own time or timelessness, because most of the temporal references are to Jack's experience, there are features which place the story somewhat earlier than its time of writing. The detail of Julie's 'starched white petticoats' (CG, p. 19) belongs to a 1950s or early 1960s era, the house contains no television, and Tom and his school friend play up the road 'in and out of ruined prefabs' (CG, p. 65), a recognizable postwar reality.[17] The clothing Julie's boyfriend Derek wears, however, and the clothing Julie later buys belongs to the 1960s or 1970s. The sense these references help to create of a postwar dream-world of indeterminate time is supported by Jack's inability to mark the passing of time in a house which seems to have 'fallen asleep' (CG, p. 65). And Julie's reference, once social services are called at the story's end, to the entire summer as a 'sleep' (CG, p. 127) helps to confirm the suspension of moral judgement that pervades the story, although it does not explain it.

The children do not report their mother's death because they are afraid of being separated, but while she is not properly gone, they feel compelled to perform a mimicry of family, as though trapped in a timeless moment. The loss of Jack's and Julie's parents means that there is no family to move away from, so their own emergent sexual identities are deprived of reference.[18] The paradox of the children's shared isolation as a result of the unmourned corpse leads the pair to perform the incestuous acts that attract the attention of Julie's boyfriend Derek, who is interested in the house's financial value as well as resentful because he has not himself been allowed to have sex with Julie (CG, p. 124). On the national level, Malcolm observes that the 'restoration of order by the police' at the novel's end 'eerily prefigures the attempted recovery and reimposition of traditional values that marked British political life in the 1980s', the turning in toward the nation and the focus on financial gain that characterized the Thatcher era.[19] If the corpse in the basement is an allegorical figure for the nation's self-image in the 1970s that is decaying but not yet properly buried, so that there is nothing to mourn or to rally around either, it is hard not to see the Thatcherite 1980s as inevitable.

The containment that is stylistically and thematically central to *The Cement Garden* is also a theme of McEwan's next work, *The Comfort of Strangers* (1981). But the setting of Venice, or an unnamed city very like it, and a style which is slightly more impressionistic than that of much of McEwan's work to this point are new developments. In the book, two English people, Colin and Mary, who are lovers but do not live together, are on holiday in Venice. On getting lost one evening they are invited by a man named Robert to his bar, and, meeting him again next day, visit his apartment where they meet Caroline, his wife. It turns out that Robert and Caroline have been interested in the couple, in particular Colin, for considerably longer than Colin and Mary have been aware. On a final visit Mary is drugged and Colin is murdered while Robert and Caroline have sex with him.

The city that is indistinguishable from Venice provides a background in which it is relatively easy for Colin and Mary to fail to notice the threat that Robert and Caroline pose to them. The layout of the streets is disorientating to the visitor, the sound of the canals gently soothing and the English couple seem to exist in a dream world in which, because they are 'on holiday' as they frequently remind each other, their actions do not need to be subjected to much scrutiny (*CS*, p. 13). Yet the novel suggests that both characters are at some distance from themselves as well as from each other, which distance they regard as a form of closeness, and that this tendency not to subject their views of themselves and their relationship to critical thought, which paradoxically sustains the relationship, is what enables the sinister Robert to gain power over them. The fact that Colin's and Mary's intimacy is 'a matter of perpetual concern' like 'too many suitcases', shows that their interest is in another object, a closeness that needs attention, rather than in each other as such, as is the case with new or more obviously impassioned lovers (*CS*, p. 13). When either partner would become annoyed by the 'cloying susceptibilities' of the other, their exploration of the city's streets would be the way in which they reunited (*CS*, p. 13). Thus, when they encounter evidence of the damaging intimacy shared by Robert and Caroline, in which Robert subjects Caroline to physical harm to the extent (eventually revealed) that her back has been broken, their earlier failure to address the matter, beyond a cursory mention, seems to derive from a sense of their own urbanity and relative disinterest in romantic passion.

Colin and Mary are both portrayed as childlike, and references to childhood increase in the novel once they meet Robert and Caroline, who met in childhood and whose sadomasochistic relationship is seemingly rooted in Robert's childhood experiences of humiliation by his sisters (CS, pp. 33–40). On the day after their first encounter with Robert, Colin and Mary are unable to get a waiter to serve them and when Robert takes them to his apartment the pair awaken in a bed deprived of their clothes, an unusual treatment of guests. When Robert takes Colin on a tour of the apartment and Colin makes fun of Robert's misogynistic views of relations between the sexes, Robert casually punches Colin in the stomach, causing him to collapse (CS, p. 77) but Colin does not relay this experience to Mary.

In fact, after their visit to the other couple, Colin and Mary seem to act out a version of Caroline and Robert's codependency, minus the sadistic element, as they stay in their hotel for four days making love, talking about childhood and memory, and congratulating themselves on how successfully in love they are (CS, p. 83), a view that their earlier careful behaviour with each other makes less than believable. But they do not talk about the cause of this behaviour (CS, p. 85). Even when Mary remembers that a photograph in Robert's and Caroline's apartment is of Colin, and this unsettling fact is returned to, its implications are not discussed (CS, pp. 91–2). At the beach, Colin tells Mary that Caroline is a prisoner to Robert before the couple swim far out to sea, as if to demonstrate their freedom. The importance of the sadomasochistic relationship is suggested by each of them privately thinking that their recent closeness has been a kind of 'parasitism', a 'conspiracy of silence disguised by ... talk' (CS, p. 97), but, again, these insights are not discussed with each other.

The prose of *Comfort of Strangers* sometimes has a sensuousness that onomatopoeically conveys the lulling effect of the city's watery canals and mirage-like reflections, while alliteration and assonance, especially at the openings of chapters, create the effect of days blurring into each other without the need for thought. For instance, when Colin and Mary have been lured to Robert's bar, the chapter in which Robert tells the story of his treatment at the hands of his father and sisters begins with a series of 's' sounds that transmit the way the water's gentle lapping, the couple's fatigue and growing drunkenness, and the sinuosity of Robert's story will lead them to relinquish any doubts they might have about him when, yet more fatigued and thirsty, they encounter him the following morning. Thus, they allow him effectively to imprison them in his and Caroline's apartment (CS, p. 19). Although the English couple discuss such matters as 'the politics of sex' and 'patriarchy' (CS, pp. 17, 84), they do not relate these concerns to their own situation, and their 'collusion' in this oversight makes them 'vulnerable' to each other, 'easily hurt' by discovering that they have distinct 'needs and interests' (CS, p. 17). It is as though their relationship is artificially sustained by an absence of address, which means that time can be spent unravelling misperceptions, the question of shared feelings and shared thoughts being displaced. Yet this makes their relationship into something of a mirage itself, and this is confirmed by the fact that, while Colin and Mary are the story's central characters, the narrative provides no instances of a shared point of view. And, as Malcolm notes, the strategy of 'recounting speech indirectly' and providing external views of characters' actions, such as after Colin's murder when Mary's 'lack of affect' is said to augment the suspicion of the police that derives from the couple's having been unmarried, increases the sense of detachment in the narration.[20]

McEwan has said in interview that his move to writing screenplays after finishing *The Comfort of Strangers* was in part because he 'had been tied to a restricted aesthetic of the novel' that he later found 'quite puzzling', and that the 'depressing, dark quality' of his early writing may have indicated his sense, at that time, of the limits of fiction itself.[21] Most of the characters in McEwan's early work have a limited ability to access and enact their own desires and, for them, the nuclear family structure and the couple relationship often fail to serve as enablers of growth and change. McEwan's later novels, by contrast, avoid this impasse by introducing events that threaten conventional familial structures rather than obscurely confirming them. At the same time, his early work's attention to reprehensible behaviour, stultifying environments and departures from the most fundamental human laws demonstrate an interest in ethical questions that the 1960s opened up for consideration in the west, but did not resolve.

There are sociohistorical ironies in the taboo-breaking of McEwan's early fiction. Given that the 1960s was a decade he described, in terms of London life at least, as having 'passed [him] by', his development as a writer runs in something of the opposite direction to the movement from 1960s idealism and expressiveness to 1970s despair and torpor I have remarked as having taken an incapacitating political form in Britain.[22] McEwan's early work may have stood out with shocking clarity amid the prevailing mood of national despondency because it coincided with an event that was almost impossible to pinpoint to one definitive moment: the fading of the British welfare state and the climate of wartime agreement that had produced it. British citizens were inclined to believe in the unlikely longevity of this political arrangement, because there was nothing obvious with which to replace it; McEwan's seemingly unnerving ideas and postures of resistance to a stultifying status quo would soon take a very different and unexpected political form in the policies of the Thatcher government (with which policies he would be in disagreement). Growth and change would be re-equated with the nuclear family, and the public spaces McEwan lamented not being able to envisage in narrative form in the late 1970s and early 1980s would be repackaged as opportunities for growth in private hands. If the early work shows McEwan to have rendered, in striking form, a version of the crises of the early postwar decades that preceded the loss of a previously assumed consensus, it had also mapped out ground to move beyond, as his later work would show.

NOTES

1 Hermione Lee, 'First Rites', Review of *The Cement Garden*, *New Statesman*, 29 September 1978, p. 416.

2 Jeannette Baxter, 'Surrealist Encounters in McEwan's Early Work', in *Ian McEwan: Contemporary Critical Perspectives*, ed. Sebastian Groes (London: Continuum, 2009), pp. 13–25 (p. 13); Dominic Head, *Ian McEwan* (Manchester: Manchester University Press, 2007), p. 35.

3 See, for instance, negatively, John D. O'Hara, *Library Journal*, 1 June 1975, p. 1241; equivocally, Rosaline Wade, 'Quarterly Fiction Review', *Contemporary Review*, 227 (1975), 1314, pp. 45–9; and more positively, Michael Mewshaw, 'Sounds Lurid, Reads Poignant', *The New York Times Book Review*, 28 (September 1975), pp. 32, 34; Neil Schmitz, *Partisan Review*, 43 (1976), 4, p. 646 and William Abrahams, *Sewanee Review*, 85 (1977), 1, pp. 111–15.

4 John Haffenden, *Novelists in Interview* (London: Methuen, 1985), pp. 168–90 (p. 169). See also Christopher Ricks, 'Adolescence and After: An Interview with Ian McEwan', *The Listener*, 12 April 1979, pp. 526–7 (p. 527), and 'Points of Departure', interview with Ian Hamilton, *The New Review*, 5 (1978), 2, pp. 9–21 (p. 19).

5 Baxter, 'Surrealist Encounters'; Head, *Ian McEwan*, p. 33.

6 Liliane Louvel, Gilles Ménégaldo and Anne-Laure Fortin, 'An Interview with Ian McEwan', reprinted in *Conversations with Ian McEwan*, ed. Ryan Roberts (Jackson: University Press of Mississippi, 2010), pp. 67–78 (p. 67).

7 Nick Hubble, John McLeod and Philip Tew, 'Introduction: Britain in the 1970s – Controversies and Cultures', in *The 1970s: A Decade of Contemporary British Fiction*, eds. Hubble, McLeod and Tew (London: Bloomsbury, 2014), pp. 1–13 (p. 1).

8 Andy Beckett, *When the Lights Went Out: Britain in the Seventies* (London: Faber and Faber, 2009), pp. 126, 129, 132, 172, 177.

9 Richard Toye, 'From "Consensus" to "Common Ground": The Rhetoric of the Postwar Settlement and Its Collapse', *Journal of Contemporary History*, 48 (2013), 1, pp. 3–23. For a sense of McEwan's feelings about the 1970s, see 'Points of Departure', interview with Ian Hamilton, reprinted in *Conversations with Ian McEwan*, ed. Ryan Roberts, pp. 3–18.

10 Louvel, Ménégaldo and Fortin, 'An Interview with Ian McEwan', p. 68.

11 See Tom Nairn, *The Break-Up of Britain: Crisis and Neo-Nationalism* (London: NLB, 1977), pp. 68–9; Sam Goodman, 'History in 1970s Fiction', in *The 1970s*, eds. Hubble, McLeod and Tew, pp. 117–44 (p. 121); David Kynaston, *Austerity Britain: 1945–51* (London: Bloomsbury, 2007), pp. 19–59 and Todd McGowan,

The End of Dissatisfaction? Jacques Lacan and the Emerging Society of Enjoyment (Albany: State University of New York Press, 2004), pp. 31–40.

12 Nairn, *The Break-Up of Britain*, p. 68.

13 Guy Strait, 'What Is a Hippie?' (1967), reprinted in *'Takin' It to the Streets': A Sixties Reader*, eds. Alexander Bloom and Wini Breines (New York: Oxford University Press, 1995), pp. 280–1 (p. 281).

14 Beckett, *When the Lights Went Out*, p. 211.

15 The remark was Andrew Lumsden's, quoted in Beckett, *When the Lights Went Out*, pp. 216–17.

16 Nairn, *The Break-Up of Britain*, p. 67; Malcolm Bradbury, *The Modern British Novel* (London: Penguin, 1993), p. 418.

17 David Malcolm, *Understanding Ian McEwan* (Columbia: University of South Carolina Press, 2002), p. 54.

18 See Head, *Ian McEwan*, p. 48.

19 Malcolm, *Understanding Ian McEwan*, p. 65.

20 David Malcolm, 'Narrational Strategy, Intertextuality and Their Functions in Ian McEwan's Early Fiction', in *Approaches to Fiction*, ed. Leszek S. Kolek (Lublin, Poland: Folium, 1996), pp. 161–77 (pp. 171–2).

21 Jon Cook, Sebastian Groes and Victor Sage, 'Journeys without Maps: An Interview with Ian McEwan', in *Ian McEwan*, ed. Sebastian Groes, pp. 123–34 (p. 131).

22 'Points of Departure', p. 14.

2

LYNN WELLS

Moral Dilemmas

The moral intensity of Ian McEwan's later fiction is captured in one iconic moment: in *Enduring Love* (1997), a helium balloon bearing a boy is out of control, jostled by gusting wind. The narrator, Joe Rose, who is having a picnic with this wife Clarissa Mellon on the hillside, runs to the rescue, as do five other men, and they attempt to hold on to the balloon's trailing ropes and pull the boy to safety. While Joe and four others let go, one of the men, a doctor named John Logan, hangs on and falls to his death, unnecessarily so, because the balloon would have landed safely had all the men persevered. In recalling the event, Joe reduces the situation to a stark ethical choice, with altruism at one extreme and self-interest at the other, concluding that 'treading that line, keeping the others in check, and being kept in check by them, is what we call morality' (*EL*, p. 14). This famous scene of acute moral crisis is just one of a number that McEwan has written over the past thirty years, which include an encounter between a distraught father and a beggar (*The Child in Time*, 1987); a confrontation with an abusive man in a restaurant (*Black Dogs*, 1992); a moment of catastrophic misinterpretation around a sexual assault (*Atonement*, 2001); and an altercation following a car accident (*Saturday*, 2005). McEwan has explained his predilection for writing such dramatic scenarios, noting that they gave him 'a means of exerting a hold over the reader' while allowing him to 'have action *and* ideas'.[1] Focusing on five of his most celebrated later texts, this chapter explores McEwan's efficacy as a contemporary moral writer, with an emphasis on how these distinctive scenes of ethical representation are rendered more complex by his evolving narrative aesthetic.

Although McEwan's credentials as a moral writer came under scrutiny early in his career, today he is seen as the heir apparent of a lineage of British moral novelists reaching back to Daniel Defoe and Samuel Richardson, extending through the great realist writers of the nineteenth century to twentieth-century luminaries such as Joseph Conrad, Henry James and Iris Murdoch. Dominic Head suggests that McEwan 'is possibly the most significant of a number of writers ... who have resuscitated the link between morality and the novel for a whole generation, in ways that befit the historical pressures of their time'.[2] Since the late 1980s, when McEwan returned to writing fiction in earnest, those pressures have included 'the growth of self-interest, the expansion of corporate power and the collapse of the Welfare State'.[3] With *The Child in Time*, he tackles the greed and self-interest rife in Britain under Prime Minister Margaret Thatcher. In *Black Dogs*, McEwan turns his attention to the aftermath of the Second World War, as experienced both in the recent fall of the Berlin Wall and through the traumatic memories of his characters. The Second World War also provides a backdrop for *Atonement*, though with an emphasis on the belated reconstruction of events, from the perspective of a character wrestling with a crisis of conscience. In *Saturday*, McEwan moves squarely to confront the problems of the new millennium, such as the effects of globalization and international terrorism. With its focus on individual psychology, *Enduring Love* might be seen as an outlier; however, Joe's self-absorbed behaviour reflects the social mores of 1990s London, where self-interest flourished in the wake of Thatcherism. In these novels, McEwan draws parallels between the iniquities of the social worlds in which the characters find themselves and their own actions. By making explicit the connection between individual and collective morality and, by using discrete scenes such as the balloon episode as concentrated dramatizations of his broader moral vision, McEwan has positioned himself as 'the latter-day humanist, concerned with the need for the human spirit to confront its own dangerous impulses'.[4]

While McEwan tries to avoid prescriptive moralism in his novels, he has definite attitudes toward the relation between ethics and fiction. In an early interview, he stated his intention to avoid 'any programmatic moral manipulation', keeping that impulse 'in some kind of abeyance', while hoping to 'generate a degree of compassion for the right people, even if the right people are in some other sense the wrong people'.[5] By 2001, McEwan had modified his stance to make room for some careful positioning of the reader by the text: 'you're not necessarily taking sides, it's not necessary always to produce a moral attitude, but in the greater scheme of things you are bound to place the reader in some form of critical attitude towards the circumstances'.[6] Key to McEwan's perspective on the moral role of fiction is his belief in its ability to stimulate a range of responses, from the judgmental to the sympathetic. In 1995, he articulated what would become his frequently expressed viewpoint on the power of fiction to generate moral understanding: 'fiction is a deeply moral form in that it is the perfect medium for entering the mind of another. I think that it is at the level of empathy that moral questions begin in fiction'.[7] In keeping with this perspective, McEwan wrote the opening scene of *Enduring Love* to allow readers to imagine the moral dilemma created by the balloon incident from both sides; he declared, 'what better enactment of morality?'[8]

Despite the undeniable emotive power of such dramatic set pieces, they do not tell the whole story of McEwan's impact as a moral writer, especially in his later fiction. In these highly self-conscious texts, scenes of intense ethical interaction are embedded in fictional structures that involve elaborate and deeply ironic interrelationships between the author, the narrator, the characters and the implied reader. His deft manipulation of these sorts of narrative relationships, in combination with his sophisticated use of generic forms and styles, adds complexity to the overall presentation of actions and ideas, confounding the simple interpretation of scenes with seemingly obvious moral valence.

Enduring Love is a striking model of McEwan's mature aesthetic, especially in light of the specific narrative context that surrounds that opening episode. Despite the event's immediacy, Joe's narration of it occurs later, as part of an overall retrospective address to an implied reader. Joe recalls how he placed value on recounting the balloon incident as precisely as possible, admitting other perspectives, especially Clarissa's; hours afterwards, they retell what happened, collaboratively shaping details, 'hammering the unspeakable into forms of words, threading single perceptions into narrative' (*EL*, p. 30). By repeating their story, they aim to master the horror of Logan's death and to assuage the 'sickness of guilt' that Joe cannot shake, despite his insistence that he was not the first to let go of the ropes (*EL*, p. 29). His remorse is exacerbated by his and Clarissa's childlessness and the contrast between his letting go of the rope and the determined courage of Logan, a father and a 'good man' who gave his life to save the boy, who eventually landed unharmed (*EL*, p. 31). Joe's lingering sense of guilt coupled with Clarissa's praise of Logan's self-sacrifice would seem to suggest a preferred answer to the ethical quandary posed by Joe in his narration of the event: of the two alternatives, altruism is morally superior to selfishness.

Despite the text's apparent valorization of selfless behaviour, however, it is Joe's choice of self-preservation that prevails as the dominant moral viewpoint since his purview as first-person narrator allows him to subsume any competing perspectives. Joe repeatedly defends his choice of survival over heroism, deeming it an act of justifiable 'self-love' (*EL*, p. 19), even in retrospect: 'the child was not my child, and I was not going to die for it' (*EL*, p. 15). The subtext of Joe's focalized narrative is his desire to persuade the reader of the rightness of his actions, both in the moment and in the weeks that follow, when he is stalked by one of the would-be rescuers, Jed Parry, who suffers from a form of religious erotomania. While Jed's obsessive pursuit of Joe may seem to be a random occurrence, it quickly becomes apparent that Jed serves as Joe's 'inverted mirror image',[9] the negative reflection of the 'easeful life' (EL, p. 18) that Joe's privileged class status affords him. Their conflict reflects the widening class disparity in post-consensus England: Joe, a popular science writer, is dissatisfied with his career, but his marriage to Clarissa, an English lecturer, has led to a 'free and intimate existence' with 'a below average share of worries' (EL, p. 8), whereas Jed lives troubled and alone on a family pension. Although Jed's deranged religiosity seems to be the opposite of Joe's insistently declared sanity, each character is an extreme manifestation of the same unbalanced narcissism that underlies the first-person narration.

A self-proclaimed rationalist, Joe makes a point of his disdain for narrative, contending it leads to 'clouded judgment' (EL, p. 41) and 'beguiles us with happy endings' (EL, p. 213). Despite his rejection of storytelling as irrational, however, he is meticulous in crafting his own narrative address, particularly those elements related to Jed. As with the accident, Joe is concerned with identifying the precise starting point for his story, changing it from the moment just before the tragic events on the hillside to the instant that he realizes he is in a covert 'relationship' with Jed (EL, p. 73). While Joe is willing to share the reconstruction of the balloon incident with Clarissa, he becomes secretive once Jed contacts him later that night, telling her that the call is a wrong number and, although he shares some information with Clarissa about Jed's threatening actions, Joe also conceals some things (he erases phone messages, for example), as he attempts to assert the masculinity he feels to be under threat. Every aspect of the story about Jed's stalking is filtered through Joe, including portions being written from others' points of view: in the ninth chapter, for instance, Joe details how he 'later construed' Clarissa's reaction to his own manic behaviour (EL, p. 79). The story's finale similarly evinces Joe's tendency to craft the narrative to his own ends, as he is able to re-establish his masculinity by rescuing Clarissa from Jed's attempt to murder her; thereafter, he stage-manages a reunion with the widow Jean Logan, during which he dramatically absolves her husband of suspected infidelity and, in the process, relieves his own guilt over John's death. As constructed by Joe, the last scene indulges in the 'narrative compression of storytelling' that he claims to abhor (EL, p. 213), with Jean's children symbolically positioned to substitute for the family denied by Clarissa's infertility and Joe poised to begin to tell them a new tale. Yet Joe's tidiness as narrator is part of an overall pattern of manipulation that prompts the reader to question both his mental stability and his moral standing.

In Enduring Love, McEwan makes clear the critical role played by the reader in contemporary moral fiction. As Martha Nussbaum argues, truly ethical reading requires a 'richly qualitative kind of seeing' that includes (as Jane Adamson puts it) 'patience, receptiveness, wise passiveness, as well as constant activity of mind'.[10] Through attentive engagement, Martha Nussbaum asserts, the reader can have 'a relation characterized by genuine altruism, and by genuine acknowledgement of the otherness of the other', along the lines of McEwan's own sense of the moral imagination.[11] This sort of engaged reading is openly thematized in *Enduring Love*; for instance, in Joe's discussion with the policeman Linley about Jed's transcribed messages, he warns him that the threats are 'not right out front,' telling him that he will need to 'read carefully' (*EL*, p. 156). Our skills as diligent readers are similarly tested by McEwan's techniques to disrupt the text's pretensions to verisimilitude. These include not only the numerous instances of narratorial unreliability, but also the 'scientific' appendix from the *British Review of Psychiatry*, purporting to substantiate Jed's mental illness, which was quickly revealed to be a fabrication, with the authors' last names forming an anagram of 'Ian McEwan'.[12] Such frame-breaking alerts readers to think beyond the persuasive intimacy of Joe's first-person narrative.

In *Enduring Love*, as we have seen, McEwan embeds a scene of moral intensity within a complex narrative framework that generates radical ambiguity, but also stimulates ethically engaged reading. McEwan's aesthetic practice in this novel provides a starting point for understanding the ethical subtexts of other later novels. What remains common is the thematization of the power of fiction (often in contradistinction to science and 'objective reason') to create narratives that provide meaning, but also have the potential to 'cloud the judgment', as Joe would have it, necessitating the reader's active engagement. Just as he does in *Enduring Love*, McEwan situates moments of ethical confrontation in *The Child in Time*, *Black Dogs*, *Atonement* and *Saturday* within conspicuously self-conscious narrative structures that complicate the moral clarity of individual scenes. In these four texts, however, the central conflicts between altruism and self-interest (or narcissism, at the extreme) are more clearly linked to the various historical and political contexts of the novels, with the power of the 'state' (broadly conceived) over individuals reflected in and dramatized by the characters' interpersonal relationships.

With *The Child in Time*, for instance, McEwan creates a parallel between the values of an extreme Thatcher-style regime and the actions of the main character, Stephen Lewis, a children's book author whose three-year-old daughter Kate is abducted at a supermarket checkout in the blink of an eye. Stephen conducts his futile search for Kate in a London cityscape dominated by a right-wing government that forces beggars to carry licences and is developing an authorized handbook to control every aspect of childhood. Stephen's initial response to the abduction, which is entirely understandable, still parallels the obsessive self-interest sanctioned by the state, as he is unable to see beyond his own needs and projects his desperate wish to find Kate onto others, including a beggar girl who he imagines resembles her. While the girl is clearly too old to be Kate, she is 'emblematic of a possible future for her' under the draconian conditions portrayed in the novel.[13] Though the beggar roughly rejects Stephen, he continues to impose his desire for his daughter onto others, since 'without the fantasy of her continued existence he was lost, time would stop' (CT, p. 8). His ethical encounter with the beggar is echoed in an episode in which he follows a girl he thinks is Kate into a 'a late Victorian type' school, where he indulges his daydream of being a child again before eventually being dismissed by the headmaster (CT, pp. 141–53). In both scenes, Stephen's fetishized desire to recover his daughter leads to a narcissistic failure to recognize others' individuality, which reflects the repressive power of the state that also constrains him.

While the set pieces with the beggar and the school girl suggest that Stephen is unable to move beyond the rampant individualism of the neoliberal state in which he is caught, McEwan complicates the ethical framework of The Child in Time by shifting the novel's 'narrative register' away from stark realism towards fantasy.[14] At points, McEwan experiments with elastic conceptions of time, associated with a particular understanding of quantum physics. Unlike the tenuous binary between objective rationality and narrative imagination represented by Joe and Clarissa in Enduring Love, here science is aligned with a more flexible, holistic and 'feminine' understanding of the universe. This conception of temporal relativism, articulated by physicist Thelma Darke, Stephen's friend and wife of Charles Darke, an erstwhile government minister, looks beyond 'the linear, sequential time of common sense' to 'a higher order of reality' (CT, p. 138), which might also signal, at the level of political commentary, a deviation from the strictures of the ruling party.[15]

While Charles can only escape from the dystopian world by retreating irrationally to an artificial version of boyhood that leads to his suicide, Stephen is able to gain access to the alternative temporal reality in ways that allow him to transcend individualism and enter a new ethical space. The second of these encounters with differential time involves a lorry he is driving behind that overturns, requiring instant evasive action from Stephen, which he experiences as an instance of Bergsonian durée, marvelling at 'how duration shaped itself round the intensity of the event' (CT, p. 95). In the first such encounter, Stephen leaves behind the constraints of the city to enter a 'noumenal' zone where both temporal and spatial laws are suspended.[16]

On his way to visit his estranged wife Julie in the country, Stephen walks through a wheat field to enter an 'obsessive landscape' (CT, p. 52) that takes him back to the moment when his young parents were at a pub, discussing their pregnancy with him and deciding whether or not to abort. This unsettling occurrence sends Stephen into a state of regression, returning him to an embryonic form, then, in a momentary loss of selfhood, apparently back to the beginning of evolution (CT, p. 60). When Stephen later describes the episode to his mother, Claire, she recounts how the sight of a boy's face in the pub window prompted her recognition of her own child as 'a separate individual' (CT, p. 175) whose life she had to protect. Through these unusual temporal experiences, Stephen develops a new sense of others' distinct being, moving him past his own traumatized self-absorption. His ethical transformation, as captured in these scenes, reaches fulfilment in his realization that the beggar girl, whom he finds dead on the street near the novel's end (CT, p. 193), never resembled his daughter and, in his acceptance of their new child, delivered by Julie, as the sign that his fixation on Kate's loss must end.

As Emily Horton argues, the novel's 'fantastic temporality' makes possible 'an alternative socio-political framework based on wholeness rather than (neoliberal) individualism'.[17] Beyond Stephen's personal metamorphosis, however, it is unclear how the moral deficiencies of the autocratic world in the text will be remedied. The ending seems to promise a better future, symbolized by the baby, whose gender, like that of the shadowy Prime Minister, is left unstated; yet the artificial sense of closure and sentimentality of the final scene highlight the text's reliance on fantasy solutions for intractable social problems. Except for the finding of the dead beggar girl, all of the scenes that signal an ethical awakening occur away from the harsh 'real' world of London: the lorry accident, the incident at the pub and the birth of the child all take place in idyllic rural settings, while in the city the restrictions continue unabated. The novel's overall ethical messaging needs to be seen in the light of this fantasy framework: the potential for ethical transformation rests with the reader's ability to understand the importance of genuine responsibility for others within the context of post-consensus Britain.

In Black Dogs and Atonement, McEwan turns to a still more oppressive political system, Nazism, as the backdrop for his depiction of moral issues. With both historical (1940s) and contemporary (late 1980s) settings, Black Dogs deals with the aftermath of the war's brutality, symbolized by the titular dogs, reportedly trained by the Gestapo to rape women, and the Majdanek concentration camp in Poland, visited by the narrator, Jeremy. Further, the persistence of repression into the late twentieth century, through extreme political systems, is embodied in Bernard's 'Big Mistake' of support-ing Communism in his youth (*BD*, p. 70). The fall of the Berlin Wall in 1989, a central event in the novel, holds out the promise of reconciliation and moral progress, yet McEwan uses it to demonstrate the enduring threat of violence in the present. Though narrated surreptitiously from a late twentieth-century perspective, *Atonement* is mostly set in the pre-war period of the 1930s and during the conflict itself, with sections devoted to the Dunkirk retreat and a military hospital in London. In both novels, the historical context of Nazi Germany serves as a metonym for personal domination, for the forceful denial of others' humanity. While both *Black Dogs* and *Atonement* involve scenes of ethical encounter that dramatize the power of oppression, each text's narrative construction has a critical bearing on its moral inflection.

With Jeremy, the first-person narrator of *Black Dogs*, McEwan presents a moral perspective antithetical to that of Joe in *Enduring Love*, one founded (apparently) on selflessness rather than narcissism. Like both Joe and Stephen, Jeremy is a writer, though not a professional; he chooses to write the history of his estranged in-laws, June and Bernard Tremaine, partly in an effort to assuage the loss of his own parents and the experience of domestic violence in his youth, which produced 'a sense of childish unbelonging' (*BD*, p. 17) persisting into adulthood. Jeremy continues to long for parental acceptance, which he finds by listening to the stories of Bernard and June. Similar to Joe and Clarissa in *Enduring Love*, this couple represents the polarities of scientism and emotionalism: Bernard, a government official and amateur entomologist, was a fervent supporter of Communism until con-fronted with irrefutable evidence of its destructiveness, whereas June, who is more of a 'mystic' and 'intuitionist' (*BD*, p. 19), lost faith in the ideology once she became aware of its ruthless indifference to individual human life. June associates the cruelty of Communism with Bernard's scientific curiosity, which leads him to kill a dragonfly against her wishes when she is in the early stage of pregnancy; in a scene comparable with Claire's realization in the pub scene in *The Child in Time*, June feels 'responsible not only for the life that was growing inside her, but for all life' (*BD*, p. 78). Jeremy's ostensible purpose in writing June and Bernard's history is to reconcile their world-views, thereby 'marrying' two incompatible 'systems' (*BD*, p. 73), in a parallel with the union of East and West Germany. What becomes clear, however, is that Jeremy's narrative, by virtue of being focused on others, provides him with the vicarious experience of some key ethical encounters that propel him gradually towards altruism.

By being willing to listen carefully to both Bernard and June, Jeremy demonstrates his openness to respect others' points of view, recording each voice faithfully, despite their vagaries of memory. He acknowledges that 'a morality must be distilled from a sequence of actions' (*BD*, p. 50) when lives are translated into stories, yet he mostly refrains from passing judgement. He does, however, admit to rejecting initially June's belief in 'the healing power of love' (*BD*, p. 60), which overwhelmed her after her traumatic attack by the black dogs in the French countryside after the war. June regards this event as a metaphysical turning point, an encounter with 'evil' through which she 'discovered God', and she devotes the remainder of her life to contemplating its meaning, so that it becomes 'mythologized' for her, despite her protestation to the contrary (*BD*, p. 59). This closed-off perspective leads to the breach with Bernard, who struggles to see beyond the certainty of his own worldview. After June's death, however, Jeremy tries to make Bernard relent to her kind of 'magical thinking' that sees a moral value in life, with 'rewards and punishments' and 'a deeper pattern of meaning' (*BD*, p. 80). This broadening of Bernard's attitude is evident in his private game of believing that June is transmitting ghostly messages to him through the faces of other women. In a scene reminiscent of Stephen's misrecognition of the beggar girl, Bernard imagines he detects June's presence in the face of a young woman in the crowd at the Wall, who later intervenes to prevent him from being beaten by neo-Nazis. In this encounter, Bernard is willing to sacrifice his safety to save a Communist protester from danger, another lesson in altruism that informs not only Jeremy's narrative, but also his own personal development. In the novel's climactic ethical engagement, Jeremy confronts an abusive father who strikes his young son in a restaurant, reacting with rage, and challenging him to fight. When the fight is stopped by a woman saying '*ça suffit*', the same phrase that June used to subdue the black dogs, Jeremy withdraws, 'horrified' by his own brutality (*BD*, p. 131). Jeremy's realization of his need to replace violence with compassion, achieved through his recording of June and Bernard's moral dilemmas, generates an appeal to the reader to reject systems of personal and political domination in favour of self-sacrifice and compassion.

The title of McEwan's most famous work, *Atonement*, suggests a similar impulse to elevate altruism over self-interest, particularly through the expiation of wrongdoing against others. McEwan has a different understanding of the word's meaning, which one day 'came apart' for him into 'at-one-ment', which he interprets as 'reconciliation with self'.[18] This telling remark, with its emphasis on self-absolution, reveals much about *Atonement*, a prime example of McEwan's mature aesthetic in which narrative layering complicates the reader's engagement with the text's moral implications. The ostensible purpose behind the novel's multisectioned narrative is an act of penitence by Briony Tallis, the central character, for her youthful crime of falsely claiming that Robbie Turner, the son of the charwoman on her family's estate, raped her cousin, Lola Quincey, an accusation that leads to his incarceration and, eventually, his death. Yet McEwan's text does not convey selfless contrition; rather, it betrays an investigation of authorial manipulation apparent through the intricate imbrication of the different levels of the narrative.

Although Part One is ostensibly told from a third-person point of view, there are hints of Briony's role as retrospective author and covert narrator; her sister Cecilia complains of 'seeing strangely, as though everything was already long in the past, made more vivid by posthumous ironies she could not quite grasp' (*At*, p. 48). This section describes the incidents leading up to Robbie's arrest, which take place on one summer's day in 1935 on the Tallis estate, when the adolescent Briony inadvertently becomes aware of Robbie's love for Cecilia, provoking confusion and misunderstanding. The childish melodrama 'The Trials of Arabella', about a princess who marries a peasant, which Briony has written and plans to have performed by her visiting cousins, is intended to impress her older brother Leon, for whom she harbours a secret desire, as she also does for Robbie. This sentimental production, with its stock characters, is displaced by a series of misinterpreted occurrences: Briony's witnessing of Cecilia's plunge into a fountain to retrieve pieces of a broken heirloom vase; her reading of an explicit letter sent accidentally to Cecilia by Robbie; and her interrupting in the library of Robbie and Cecilia's first sexual encounter. The fountain scene leads Briony to believe that she has been conceiving of things in the 'wrong genre' (*At*, p. 45), that she needs to move beyond the simplicity of fairy tales to the serious realities of adult life. From Briony's perspective six decades later, the narrator reflects on her evolution as an author, from imitating 'folk tales' and 'drama with simple moral intent' to achieving 'an impartial psychological realism' that came to characterize her mature fiction, 'known for its amorality' (*At*, p. 41). Nonetheless, through the perspective of the older narrator, Briony admits that she is conscious of 'self-mythologising' and crafting the story based on her 'subsequent accounts' (*At*, p. 41) rather than on what actually happened, or on her development on that particular day.

Part One culminates in the novel's primary ethical encounter in which Briony accuses Robbie of rape, despite being initially unsure of his guilt, because of her inflated sense of her powers as a writer and her projection of her own desires onto others. Persuaded that Robbie is a 'maniac' (*At*, p. 119) and 'the incarnation of evil', Briony is also convinced that 'there had to be a story' (*At*, p. 115) and that it 'was writing itself around her' (*At*, p. 166). When confronted with Lola's sexual assault, Briony does not maintain 'god-like' neutrality (*At*, p. 115), but rather positions herself as the heroine of her own tale, while asserting her need for order through a child's world view. Although she does not clearly see her cousin's assailant (later revealed to be Leon's friend Paul Marshall) and Lola provides no corroboration of her attacker's identity, Briony assumes that Robbie is the rapist, continuing the pattern of wilful misinterpretation begun with the fountain and library scenes: 'everything fitted; the terrible present fulfilled the recent past' (*At*, p. 168). While her accusation satisfies her 'passion for tidiness' (*At*, p. 7) in narrative, with 'all fates resolved' (*At*, p. 6) in clear moral terms, she finds the procedure of confirming Robbie's guilt unsettling – she does not like to confirm that she 'saw' him ('less like seeing, more like knowing' *At*, p. 170) – and her later narrative consciousness imbues the recollection with the germ of the idea that her histrionic imagination may have engendered a fatal falsehood. Yet, in the moment, she neutralizes her doubts and persists in her indictment of Robbie, supported by the authorities, who are inclined to suspect him owing to his lower-class status. From her retrospective position as narrator, Briony seems to accept responsibility at the end of Part One for ruining Robbie's life, saying that she 'trapped herself' (*At*, p. 170). Yet Parts Two and Three expose Briony's ongoing tendency to create fantasy narratives that might exonerate her, although the reader understands (if only retrospectively) the subtext of self-accusation involved in the construction of the narrative.

Parts Two and Three are set against the backdrop of global tyranny, an analogy for individual domination as in *Black Dogs*, but the war also serves as a stage on which Briony invents her own fantasized story of personal redemption. Once Robbie is released from prison, he becomes one of the thousands of soldiers escaping the Nazis by retreating to the beach at Dunkirk. While Part Two, with its appalling violence, conveys historical accuracy (supported by McEwan's real-life research), it also evinces a fictiveness that reveals Briony's authorial influence. For instance, in a folk tale scene, partly conditioned by Robbie's feverish state, he aids an old woman in the seaside resort of Bray in capturing her escaped pig, believing that the act will have magical consequences. The name of Robbie's sidekick in this venture, Corporal Nettle, connects to a scene in Part One in which Briony plays a juvenile game of flaying nettles, imagining herself an Olympic champion. Echoes such as this reinforce the novel's recursive structure, destabilizing the verisimilitude. In Part Three, which details Briony's service as a nurse, the realist elements are similarly disrupted. A character created by her own hand, Briony models herself on the heroine Florence Nightingale, abasing herself to menial work, having her identity stripped and becoming 'N. [for Nurse] Tallis' (*At*, p. 275) while spending her evenings writing early drafts of her story, a 'clever fiction' to 'satisfy her vanity' (*At*, p. 320). When her manuscript is rejected for lacking 'the backbone of a story' (*At*, p. 320), she resolves to take moral action by confronting Paul and Lola at their wedding, which takes place in the countryside, away from the horrors in the city. When she loses courage, she moves to another fantasy ending, tracking down Cecilia in her south London home where she also finds Robbie alive, promises to set the record straight through a formal statement and 'a new draft, an atonement' (*At*, p. 349).

While Briony's decision to write Robbie and Cecilia's story seems to indicate a genuine desire to make amends, her authority over all aspects of the text, established by her initials at the end of Part Three, reveals a consistently self-absorbed portrayal of others. In the epilogue 'London, 1999', the elderly Briony, in the early stages of dementia, returns to the Tallis estate for a birthday celebration. Narrating now in the first-person, she is candid about her research with the real Corporal Nettle to lend accuracy to her account of the war, suggesting that she is finally being forthright about the construction of her tale, which she continued in various drafts over fifty-nine years. She claims that the latest version is factual, but cannot be published for legal reasons until after Lola and Paul's deaths. Though she admits the truth about Robbie and Cecilia's having died during the war, she refuses to assign them that fate, which she deems 'the bleakest realism'; instead, she leaves the ending of her final draft such that the lovers 'survive and flourish' (*At*, p. 371), a kind of wilful 'amnesia' that matches her own failing memory. Claudia Schemberg's argument is representative of the view that Briony's choice to deny herself Robbie's forgiveness, despite the happy ending, proves that she 'has learned how to imaginatively put herself into the position of other people';[19] however, it is also possible to argue that Briony's preference for fantasy resolution, underscored by the final ingratiating production of *The Trials of Arabella* at her party, is consistent with her narcissistic control of others throughout the text, belying the sincerity of her atonement. Through his careful construction of interconnected narrative layers, McEwan challenges his readers to assess the implications of Briony's stark assertion that there is no 'entity or higher form' to which the novelist can appeal for forgiveness (*At*, p. 371). We are left to reflect on novelistic processes of manipulation and the difficulty of true engagement with others.

Like *Atonement*, *Saturday* involves sophisticated narrative techniques that raise questions about the novel's overall moral stance, which seems initially to reinforce values consistent with British imperialistic hegemony. Set on February 15, 2003, the day of a mass protest in London against Prime Minister Tony Blair's plan to take Britain into the Iraq War, *Saturday* is centred on one day in the life of a neurosurgeon, Henry Perowne, as he travels around the city. With its obvious echoes of *Mrs Dalloway* and *Ulysses*, the novel is imbued with literariness, including a sense of inevitability that Perowne's day will end as it begins, safely in bed with his successful wife, Rosalind. Yet Perowne himself dislikes literature, especially fiction of the 'magical realist' variety, which he views as 'the recourse of an insufficient imagination, a dereliction of duty' (*S*, p. 67), preferring the irrefragable clarity of science and mathematics. While the text is largely focalized through Perowne's point of view, McEwan deftly shifts the perspective of the third-person narration at key moments, employing a 'cool, stylistic neutrality' that creates a subtle distance between the narrator and the character, breaking the reader's identification with Perowne.[20] When the narrator intervenes to describe Perowne on the balcony of his opulent London townhouse, watching the protesters assemble below, 'imagin[ing] himself as Saddam, surveying the crowd with satisfaction' (*S*, p. 62), the depiction contains an implicit critique of the doctor's imperious worldview. Ostensibly, he is critical of the crowd's naivety, as he sees it, playing into Saddam Hussein's hands; but it is a curious act of empathy, which taints him with its suggestion of power. Through such pointed use of irony, McEwan engages his readers to consider the ethical ramifications of continuing British cultural supremacy in the contemporary world.

The conflict in Britain between the dominant English culture and the forces of global change are captured in the novel's central ethical set piece, the altercation between Henry and a violent thug, Baxter, who represents the perils posed by international terrorism and domestic unrest in the new millennium. The cityscape through which Henry moves shows signs of poverty and increased multiculturalism. In one observation, he reflects how three women in burqas on the street look 'like kids larking about at Halloween'. His 'visceral' distaste for their appearance is rooted in a conviction about gender inequality, yet he is quick to dismiss the more nuanced perception of 'relativists' like his daughter (*S*, p. 124). This scene is a local instance of the novel's broader tendency to evoke 'an all-encompassing cosmopolitanism that it then paradoxically marginalizes'.[21] From Henry's viewpoint, London is 'a success, a brilliant invention', with its citizens 'harmonious for the most part' (*S*, p. 5); he is not oblivious to inequality, but his professional disposition inclines him to see human difference as a consequence of the genetic lottery, rather than a consequence of race or class. Henry's complacency is disrupted by his sighting of a burning plane streaking past the British Telecom Tower in the early hours, an eerie reminder of the 9/11 attacks. Though this terrorist menace does not materialize, his drive through the protester-thronged streets in his luxury car later in the day brings him into direct contact with another danger, the 'simian' Baxter (*S*, p. 88), whose vehicle the doctor hits after being granted privileged access by the police to a blocked thoroughfare. Faced with the possibility of a prolonged violent assault, Henry chooses to save himself by calling on his scientific knowledge, diagnosing Baxter's incurable Huntingdon's disease and holding out the hope of treatment to him. While Henry assures himself that he 'was obliged, or forced, to abuse his own power' (S, p. 111), he has 'humiliated' Baxter (S, p. 152), setting the stage for eventual retribution. This initial encounter between Henry and Baxter allegorizes a global situation in which powerful nations suppress the disadvantaged, especially migrants from impoverished nations, generating resentment and resistance.

The final confrontation plays out a scenario of domestic terrorism that ends with the invader subdued, implying that the text sanctions the right of the dominant culture to defend itself aggressively. When Baxter and his henchmen penetrate the formidable security at the Perowne townhouse, assaulting Rosalind and menacing her pregnant daughter Daisy with rape, it is justifiable in the world of the text that Henry takes action to protect them. Yet the reasonableness of this episode is subverted by its symbolic valence, which extends beyond the characters to the novel's political allegory. This ironic distance is signalled by the critical role that literature plays in resolving the conflict, in direct contradiction to Henry's dismissal of fiction's real-world effects. Baxter is 'transfixed' by Daisy's recitation of Matthew Arnold's poem 'Dover Beach' (S, p. 278), having an emotional response that leaves him vulnerable. While Baxter reacts to the reading as nostalgic, saying the poem 'makes [him] think about where [he] grew up' (S, p. 222), Henry interprets what he hears as connected with the looming battle in Iraq, mishearing the line 'when desert armies stand ready to fight' (S, p. 221). This double misinterpretation highlights the importance of readerly engagement in assessing a text's ethical import, a point reinforced by McEwan's self-conscious invocation of Arnold, whose conception of culture (highly influential into the twentieth century) includes art's potential to overcome the divisiveness of class conflict. Baxter's final subjugation by Henry, who once again wields his medical knowledge to gain the upper hand, represents Britain's triumph over perceived threats to its culture, both from within and without. Although *Saturday* seems to reinforce Henry's world view, the narrator's comment that London is 'waiting for its bomb' (S, p. 276) undermines the character's sense of his own impregnability. Through carefully crafted irony, McEwan urges a more nuanced reading of the novel's ethical encounters that warns about the consequences of unchecked power.

Since the late 1980s, McEwan has been producing fiction that comments on the major dilemmas of our time, reflecting the injustice of historical and contemporary political systems and highlighting the tendency of individuals to choose self-interest over care for others. McEwan's own conception of the moral imagination is closely tied to the power of fiction to allow us to better understand one another. As these five novels demonstrate, however, ethical engagement with his work requires scrupulous attention to the narrative contexts in which his moral investigations appear. McEwan's mature aesthetic involves sophisticated use of narrative layering, generic manipulation, ironic focalization and overt self-consciousness, all designed to challenge readers to look beyond surface representations. When approaching a McEwan novel with these textual aspects in mind, the reader experiences 'the radicality and uniqueness of the moral situation itself', thereby achieving a deeper insight into the mindset of the text and the author who wrote it.[22]

NOTES

1 Adam Begley, 'The Art of Fiction CLXXIII: Ian McEwan' (2002), in *Conversations with Ian McEwan*, ed. Ryan Roberts (Jackson: University Press of Mississippi, 2010), pp. 89–107 (p. 97).

2 Dominic Head, *Ian McEwan* (Manchester: Manchester University Press, 2007), p. 1.

3 Ibid., p. 2.

4 Malcolm Bradbury, *The Modern British Novel*, revised edition (London: Penguin, 2001), p. 536.

5 Christopher Ricks, 'Adolescence and After' (1979), in *Conversations with Ian McEwan*, ed. Roberts, pp. 19–25 (p. 25).

6 Jonathan Noakes, 'Interview with Ian McEwan' (2001), in Ibid., pp. 79–88 (p. 87).

7 Liliane Louvel, Gilles Ménégaldo and Anne-Laure Fortin, 'An Interview with Ian McEwan' (1995), in Ibid., pp. 67–78 (p. 70).

8 David Lynn, 'A Conversation with Ian McEwan' (2006), in Ibid., pp. 143–55 (p. 149).

9 Kiernan Ryan, 'After the Fall', in *Ian McEwan's Enduring Love*, ed. Peter Childs (London and New York: Routledge, 2007), pp. 44–54 (p. 52).

10 Martha C. Nussbaum, *Love's Knowledge: Essays on Philosophy and Literature* (Oxford: Oxford University Press, 1990), p. 36; Jane Adamson, 'Against Tidiness: Literature and/versus Moral Philosophy', in *Renegotiating Ethics in Literature, Philosophy, and Theory*, eds. Jane Adamson, Richard Freadman and David Parker (Cambridge: Cambridge University Press, 1998), pp. 84–110 (p. 98).

11 Nussbaum, *Love's Knowledge*, p. 48.

12 Laura Miller, 'Ian McEwan Fools British Shrinks', *Salon Books*, 21 September 1999. Retrieved from: www.salon.com/1999/09/21/mcewan_2/ (accessed 25 January 2018).

13 Paul Edwards, 'Time, Romanticism, Modernism and Moderation in Ian McEwan's *The Child in Time*', *English*, 44 (Spring 1995), 178, pp. 41–55 (p. 41).

14 Ben Knights, *Writing Masculinities: Male Narratives in Twentieth-Century Fiction* (London: Macmillan, 1999), p. 213.

15 McEwan was inspired by his reading in popular science, especially David Bohm's *Wholeness and the Implicate Order* (London: Routledge, 1980). In the novel, Bohm is referred to as a 'colleague' of Thelma's (*CT*, p. 118).

16 Edwards, 'Time, Romanticism, Modernism and Moderation', p. 53.

17 Emily Horton, *Contemporary Crisis Fictions: Affect and Ethics in the Modern British Novel* (London: Palgrave Macmillan, 2014), p. 121.

18 Kate Kellaway, 'At Home with His Worries', *The Observer*, 16 September 2001. Retrieved from: www.theguardian.com/books/2001/sep/16/fiction.ianmcewan (accessed 26 January 2018).

19 Claudia Schemberg, *Achieving 'At-one-ment': Storytelling and the Concept of the Self in Ian McEwan's 'The Child in Time', 'Black Dogs', 'Enduring Love', and 'Atonement'* (Frankfurt: Peter Lang, 2004), p. 85.

20 Elizabeth Kowaleski Wallace, 'Postcolonial Melancholia in Ian McEwan's *Saturday*', *Studies in the Novel*, 39 (2007), 4 (Winter), pp. 465–80 (p. 470).

21 Ibid., p. 467.

22 Adam Zachary Newton, *Narrative Ethics* (Cambridge, MA: Harvard University Press, 1995), p. 12.

3

ASTRID BRACKE

Science and Climate Crisis

While critics have paid most attention to the depiction of science in *Enduring Love* (1997), McEwan's concern with science runs through much of his oeuvre, from the physics of *The Child in Time* (1987) via evolutionary psychology in *Enduring Love* and brain surgery in *Saturday* (2005) to climate crisis science in *Solar* (2010). As Emily Horton notes, McEwan's fiction presents 'science, *in dialogue with* literature'.[1] *Enduring Love*'s protagonist Joe is a writer of popular science works, whose relationship with his wife Clarissa frequently reads like a thinly veiled allegory of the clash of science and literature: he is apparently the rational one, trying to understand the world through science; she is a literary scholar, an expert on Keats, and more likely to approach the world through storytelling. Through such means, *Enduring Love* illustrates the way in which McEwan conceives of science and literature as parallel traditions, best understood as two spheres of knowledge production that are not antithetical. Similarly, Joe can be said to need Clarissa precisely for the 'necessary critical check' that literature provides to his rationalism.[2] As Jonathan Greenberg puts it, the novel 'hold[s] out hope for a rapprochement between the sciences and the humanities'.[3] *Enduring Love* may even depict a 'third culture' in which the common ground between science and art is explored and celebrated. The third culture, a term associated with especially John Brockman, responds to the growing popularity of science writing in the late twentieth century. This trend turned science into the space in which the public debate happens and made scientists 'the new public intellectuals, leaders of a new kind of public culture'.[4]

In its exploration of science and literature through Joe and Clarissa, *Enduring Love* echoes the conversations in *The Child in Time* between Stephen, a writer, and Thelma, a physicist. *Enduring Love* also anticipates *Solar* and the impatience of scientist Michael Beard with the artists and storytellers he encounters. In this essay, my focus is on how the relationship between science and art is played out in the novels themselves as well as in their critical reception, particularly after the publication of *Solar*. Central to the depiction of science and art in McEwan's novels is the setting up of an opposition between the two fields that is subsequently destabilized. As such, the novels depict art and science in conversation, resisting resolution in favour of one or the other. While *The Child in Time* uses science – in combination with gender – to offer some form of consolation in a time of climate crisis, many critics felt that *Solar*'s depiction of science and climate change is unsatisfactory. This dissatisfaction with the novel is largely tied in with its genre, as well as the character of Michael Beard, who is a much less sympathetic representation of the scientist than many of McEwan's earlier scientist protagonists. In what follows, I read *The Child in Time* and *Solar* in relation to each other and place these works in the larger framework of McEwan's writings on science, art and climate crisis.

Art and Science

While McEwan suggests that he has 'always' been interested in science, this interest comes to the fore in his oeuvre especially from *The Child in Time* onwards.[5] In interviews, he has frequently commented on the role that science plays in his life; science, he has said, is the 'only available and credible metaphysics'.[6] McEwan's novels are consequently inspired by the work of a range of scientists. The primary scientific influence on *The Child in Time*, for instance, is David Bohm, mentioned in the novel as one of Thelma's colleagues (*CT*, p. 118). In *Wholeness and the Implicate Order* (1980), referenced in the novel's acknowledgements, Bohm emphasizes the value of scientific knowledge as a source of spiritual wholeness – a sentiment echoed by Thelma's approach to physics. Patricia Waugh places *Enduring Love* in a broader novelistic response to popular science writing in the 1980s and 1990s, including works by A. S. Byatt, Graham Swift and Jim Crace. Like these works, *Enduring Love* is influenced by the rise of popular science and especially by the increasing use of novelistic techniques by writers such as Richard Dawkins and E. O. Wilson.[7] Wilson's work is important not only to Joe, but also to McEwan. His enthusiasm about the idea of consilience – popularized by Wilson in his 1998 book of the same name – shows that McEwan's interest lies not so much in favouring art over science or the other way around, but in bringing the two together. In *Consilience*, Wilson proposes an integration of 'knowledge from the natural sciences with that of the social science and humanities'.[8] Other influences on *Enduring Love* are Robert Wright's *The Moral Animal* (1994) – on evolutionary psychology – and Antonio Damasio's exploration of the false opposition of reason and emotion. Of the three novels explored in this essay, *Solar* is the only one which is not explicitly tied to a particular scientific work: the only book mentioned in the acknowledgements is Walter Isaacson's biography of Einstein. Even though McEwan mentions a number of (climate) scientists with whom he had conversations during the writing of the book, none of them seemed to have such an explicit influence as, for instance, Bohm and Wilson had on the earlier books. Nonetheless, *Solar*'s depiction of science shows traces of the work of the political scientist John Gray, especially as set out in *Straw Dogs* (2002). Katrin Berndt proposes that in the novel, 'Gray's ideas are translated into narrative through a comical exposure of the incommensurability of technological advancement and social progress'.[9]

Typical of McEwan's depiction of science – both in his fiction, as well as his non-fiction and interviews – is the comparison between science and art, including literature. For instance, though describing literature and science as being parallel traditions, he speaks about science as 'invading' the territory of novelists.[10] Through their exploration of cognitive and evolutionary psychology, he holds, biologists have entered what was previously the main remit only of literature, namely human nature.[11] He has also repeatedly remarked that science and scientists offer a more productive view of the world than the arts. In the humanities, he suggests, 'all intellectuals are required to be card-carrying pessimists. You have to go to the sciences today to find any real sense of wonder, any real joy in the intellectual life'.[12] The pessimism that McEwan notes here is illustrated by Beard's view of artists in *Solar*. When he spends a few days in the Arctic as part of an environmental initiative to bring scientists and artists together, he is struck by what he sees as the futility of their endeavours. One of them, Stella Polkinghorne, designs, for Tate Modern, a life-sized Monopoly set on a playing field, entitled *Do Not Pass Go*, a piece intended as an indictment of 'a money-obsessed culture', but which produces 'rising sales' of the board game itself (and so the makers of the game drop their legal case against her) (*So*, p. 51). Another artist creates ice sculptures and – although he is presented as someone who maintains an optimistic view about the possibility of 'profound inner change' in humanity – he is noted professionally for such things as polar bear ice carving, the ephemeral nature of the art mirroring the precarious predicament of the species depicted (*So*, p. 66). Instead of the sense of wonder that McEwan identifies in the sciences, these artists' works express the kind of 'indulgent pessimism' that he believes characterizes liberal arts culture. Beard and McEwan come to the same conclusion after their stay in the Arctic: answers should come from good rules and policy, not from art.[13] Conversely, the artists aboard the ship display a peculiar sense of self-loathing: Beard, they feel, is the only one doing something real (*So*, p. 74).

Yet McEwan's novels should not be seen as mere dismissals of art and literature in favour of science. Rather, in his fictions a dialogue takes place between art and science without leading to an ultimate resolution. The novels tend to display a kind of double move in which art is critiqued and frequently said to be lacking, yet in the end proves central and invaluable to the novels, as well as to their depiction of science. While characters might frequently be explicitly in favour of a scientific view of the world – like Joe in *Enduring Love* and Michael Beard in *Solar* – the narrative itself works against this. As Waugh proposes in relation to *Enduring Love*, 'Joe's attempts, from the beginning, to position every event in relation to some shibboleth of the grand narrative of current ultra-Darwinism, [are] undone again and again by McEwan's plot'.[14] As part of this internal debating, *Enduring Love* depicts a dialogue between art and science that is prefigured in *The Child in Time* and recurs in *Solar*. Joe is the writer of popular science works and as such increasingly struggles with his desire for doing original work, rather than merely describing that of others. He is critical of storytelling – both in terms of the works his wife Clarissa studies, as well as in the form of nineteenth-century 'anecdotal' scientists (*EL*, p. 48). Yet storytelling plays a significant role in his making sense of the events unfolding in his life. While for much of the novel the reader is perhaps likely to side with Clarissa, and her belief that Joe is misinterpreting his stalker's madness, the appendices at the end of the novel, though also fictional, affirm that Joe was right all along. The first appendix is a spoof of a scientific publication, created by McEwan – and submitted to, although not accepted by, the *Psychiatric Bulletin*.[15] As such, the appendix is proof that Joe's rationalism and scientific approach was justified: as he had believed himself, Jed Parry indeed suffers from de Clérambault syndrome. At the same time, the appendix functions as a critique of science by echoing the Sokal affair: the publication of a spoof article by the physicist Alan Sokal in the journal *Social Text*. Sokal aimed to expose the journal's lack of intellectual rigour and critique the field of postmodern cultural studies as being too political and too friendly to fashionable phrases and debates. Finally, the first appendix of *Enduring Love* is metafictional: the last names of the spoof article's authors – Wenn and Camia – are an anagram of 'Ian McEwan'. As such, the text of the novel draws attention to itself, by including a passage that is made to look real, but is fictional, and by foregrounding the existence of a narrative beyond that of Joe and Clarissa's, written by an author who plays with narrative reliability and the constructedness of narratives. Consequently, like *The Child in Time* and *Solar*, *Enduring Love* refuses closure in terms of favouring either science over art or the other way around. Through an interplay between characters and text – including the appendix – the novel achieves the kind of dialogue that characterizes all of McEwan's science novels.

A similar dynamic between literature and science is sketched in *The Child in Time*, more so than in *Solar*. In the former, the focus (and circumstance) of Stephen Lewis's career-defining book as a children's writer becomes crucial to the lives of his friends, Thelma, a physicist, and her husband Charles, a promising politician, who is inspired by it to leave his political life behind. Conversely, Stephen's conversations with Thelma about science liberate him and assist him in the gradual process of facing his trauma. As Horton suggests, science in *The Child in Time* is not detached from everyday realities, but becomes 'an accessible source of renewed inspiration, combining with literature and theory to endorse a change to the neoliberal status quo'.[16] While the characterization of *The Child in Time* and *Enduring Love* suggests a kind of balancing in their depiction of science and art, the kind of consilience advocated in the former, and the dialogue that happens in the latter, is absent from *Solar*. Its exclusive focalization through Beard and the little room afforded to other perspectives makes this novel read – at least at first sight – as only pessimistic about the value of art and literature in a time of climate crisis. Beard is suspicious of storytelling, and people who tell and study stories (*So*, p. 147). He perceives the artists in the Arctic as misguided amateurs taking part in a debate that should be left to scientists and policy makers (*So*, pp. 77, 80). Literature has a function for Beard only when he can use it for a purpose, as when he seduces his first wife Maisie by quoting a passage from Milton (*So*, p. 200). Yet a different kind of story emerges in *Solar* that illustrates the equivocation typical of McEwan's work. Because *Solar* is a satire, its depiction of science needs to be interpreted as part of this satire. As an unlikeable, unreliable and unappealing protagonist, Beard himself is probably the most obvious way in which the novel satirizes science. Yet there are other means by which this is achieved as well. Beard's work on solar energy is not his own, and the Nobel Prize that cemented his reputation loses its lustre once the reader learns of the rumour that the Nobel Committee could not decide between three front runners and selected the fourth choice – Beard – instead (*So*, p. 50). As Berndt suggests, the novel's satire of science serves to challenge 'the belief in the salvational potential of scientific progress not only because the latter is unfit to solve problems such as humankind's destructive exploitation of natural resources, but also because, or so the text suggests, such romanticization is at the root of mechanisms that allow humans to delude themselves into expecting deliverance from their own inventions'.[17] Beard is the perfect character in this respect: his belief in science's progress is really the only thing he can still hold on to, and that which he is using as a mask for essentially making a profit out of environmental crisis.

While Beard, of all of McEwan's protagonists, is the one most critical towards art, he too is shown to rely on art and literature. For Beard as much as for the characters in *The Child in Time* and *Enduring Love*, science may be fundamental, but there is no escaping the power of story. While Joe, though critical of storytelling in his own way is at least aware of his own reliance on storytelling (*EL*, p. 28), Beard is not. When trying to convince investors of the importance of solar energy, Beard tells a story. It is a story his postdoctoral researcher Aldous had told him years earlier, about a man chopping down trees. Interestingly, Beard's retelling is not just a retelling: he alters a few significant details, thereby – unwittingly? – foregrounding the centrality of storytelling to his own project. In Aldous' story, a man is cutting down trees to drink the sap, thereby creating a wasteland. The moral of the story is that the man would have been better off drinking the resource that was readily available – rain – much like Aldous believes people should use solar energy rather than fossil fuels (*So*, p. 27). In his retelling, Beard keeps the analogy between the rain and sunlight intact. Yet, whereas Aldous told the story in an attempt to inspire Beard to help save the planet, Beard is telling the story to make money. Consequently, he changes a few details to make the story more appealing to his potential investors. In Aldous' story, the man was to blame for creating a wasteland, whereas in Beard's retelling the issue of blame is left out. Instead of making it explicit that the man knows he is causing the devastation, Beard says merely that the man 'knows the forest is vanishing' (*So*, p. 153). Though this detail might seem to be minor, the way in which Beard alters the story is a strategic decision. Putting the blame on the man would have sounded as if Beard was blaming his audience – who work in the energy industry – for environmental destruction. He knows that this would make them less sympathetic to his project, so he takes the matter of blame out of the story.[18] To Adam Trexler, it is passages like these – when Beard relies on the kind of storytelling that he is usually so suspicious of – that demonstrate how in *Solar* 'science is left so ignorant of individual motives that fiction becomes essential once again'.[19]

Reading *The Child in Time*, *Enduring Love* and *Solar* against each other, then, shows that their depiction of art and science is not about privileging one over the other as a way of understanding the world, or solving big problems. Rather, the two should be seen in dialogue, hinting at the kind of consilience that McEwan finds so appealing in Wilson's ideas. A similar kind of resolution of bringing together disparate perspectives is suggested in *The Child in Time*, though not so much through consilience as through gender.

Gender in *The Child in Time* and *Solar*

The similarities between *The Child in Time* and *Solar* – both are explicitly about science and both are set against the background of climate change – invite comparisons. In *The Child in Time*, climate change is explored primarily through global warming and the novel is filled with references to unusually high temperatures and freak weather. Interestingly, climate change is not presented in the novel as an environmental or social problem, but is explicitly politicized. In the dystopian Thatcherite state in which *The Child in Time* is set, everything – including the weather – is related to the government.[20] In late spring, the temperature passes the 100 degree Fahrenheit mark, inspiring 'patriotic exultation in the popular press'. The high temperatures are interpreted as 'serving the Government well' (*CT*, p. 69) and the overt connection between weather and the government anticipates Margaret Thatcher's evolving policy on climate change. She was soon (1988) to present global warming as a massive risk to humanity and proceed to use it as justification for her politics. As Anabela Carvalho argues, Thatcher attempted to control the definition of the climate change issue: 'instead of ignoring the problem, she appropriated it and made several high-profile interventions to set the agenda in line with neo-liberal principles'.[21] Consequently, global warming began to serve the Thatcherite agenda for investment in nuclear power, privatization of the electricity industry and the termination of the coal mining industry.

A possible solution to the dystopian realities of the novel is offered by gender, particularly the feminization of science suggested by Thelma and the spiritual connection to the world offered by Stephen's estranged wife Julie. Indeed, *The Child in Time* is, as Ben Knights puts it, a 'green parable', concerned explicitly with gender, and an understanding of its treatment of science needs to be filtered through this lens.[22] Thelma is concerned with what she calls a 'feminising' of physics – and, indeed, all science – through quantum mechanics. As she tells Stephen, quantum mechanics would make science 'softer, less arrogantly detached, more receptive to participating in the world it wanted to describe' (*CT*, p. 43). When at the end of the novel Stephen finds his way back to his wife Julie, who is living in a cottage in what remains of the countryside, the need for a 'feminisation' of society is underscored. Even before the almost mystical event of the birth of their child, Julie is described as very much attuned to the nonhuman natural world, somehow less caught up in the urban and political scene that Stephen has become part of. Indeed, it is especially in passages in which Thelma speaks about her work, and in those relating to Julie, that the novel's status as 'an ecofeminist parable' comes to the fore. The novel suggests, Greg Garrard argues, that only 'womanly times' can save humanity and the earth.[23] With both male characters in *The Child in Time* depicted as either remarkably ineffectual (Stephen) or trying to escape adulthood (Charles), it is 'the female who provides the strength that sustains the alliance'.[24] Consequently, Jago Morrison has suggested that *The Child in Time* exemplifies how, following the earlier oratorio *Or Shall We Die?* (1983), gender became a distinct response to history and politics in McEwan's work.[25]

Given the centrality of gender to *The Child in Time*'s depiction of science and climate change, some critics have tried to seek out similar themes in *Solar*. In his analysis of the novel, for instance, Axel Goodbody suggests that, like *Or Shall We Die?* and *The Child in Time*, *Solar* proposes that a feminization of society might present a solution to climate change and the destructive potential of male rationalism.[26] Yet while *The Child in Time* emphasizes femininity, *Solar* leaves little space for a similarly gendered exploration. Instead, it is a novel depicting both masculinity in crisis – best illustrated by the often-referenced scene in the Arctic, when Beard fears that his penis might snap off in the sub-zero atmosphere, after he has had to relieve himself (*So*, p. 59) – as well as a kind of hypermasculine celebration of Beard's sexual conquests. Either way, describing the novel as suggesting that only 'womanly times' can save the world seems inadequate and only viable if the almost complete obliteration of the female perspective is interpreted as a means of foregrounding the importance of this same perspective. In *Solar*, women's perspectives are ridiculed, marginalized and wholly refracted through Beard's perspective. An example of this is Beard's girl-friend Melissa, one of the few characters who explicitly ponders the reality of climate change. Yet her words and emotions are only made available to the reader through Beard, who recollects a conversation they had. Melissa told him that to take climate change seriously 'would be to think about it all the time'. Consequently, like everyone she knows, she decides not to take it too seriously, because daily life, she suggests, 'would not permit it' (*So*, p. 165). Melissa paraphrases the writer John Lanchester, who has proposed that 'we're reluctant to think about [climate crisis] because we're worried that if we start we will have no choice but to think of nothing else'.[27] In many ways, this avoidance of climate change and the refusal to explore it head-on is central to *Solar*, which, as a whole, refuses to engage with feelings other than profit and greed when it comes to climate crisis. The only character willing to do something about it for the planet's sake rather than his own – Aldous – is killed off early in the novel. While his work is instrumental for Beard's later success and his nominal environmental cause, Aldous does not get to say much in the novel. By not letting Aldous and Melissa speak in the novel, the narrative largely represses the 'violently disruptive emotions of mourning and terror' inherent to climate crisis, which McEwan, Garrard suggests, 'has chosen not to address' but which nonetheless shine through in especially Melissa's perspective.[28] Richard Kerridge has similarly argued that in *Solar*, 'McEwan avoids the task of imagining for us, and showing us in artistic form, the feelings we do not yet dare to have'.[29] Focalizing the novel through Beard, then, not only results in preventing a feminine perspective of the kind that Goodbody suggests, and which was central to *The Child in Time*, but it also results in a depiction of climate change and science that many critics found inadequate, especially following the accomplishment of McEwan's earlier science novels.

Solar and the Problem of Genre

In *Solar*, as in *Enduring Love*, science and literature are frequently placed in opposition to each other. The narrative perspective in *Solar*, more than in *Enduring Love*, results at first sight in a favouring of science over literature and the arts. Yet while *Enduring Love* is frequently explored in terms of the dichotomy of science and literature – and the potential resolution thereof – a different conversation surrounds *Solar*. Criticism of this novel focuses largely on how a novel should depict science and especially climate crisis. This issue becomes prominent in *Solar*, much more than in *Enduring Love* and *Saturday*, because of Beard and the criticism that he as a character received. The focus on science in the novel is consequently overshadowed by a critique of characterization and particularly, as I discuss in the final pages of this essay, of genre. Although some reviewers, such as Nicholas Lezard, praised *Solar*, other reviewers were not as positive. James Urquhart found the novel's plot 'two-dimensional', while Jason Cowley described how the novel leaves the reader 'trapped' in Beard's company, confined by his 'cold reductiveness'.[30] Others, particularly those concerned with the depiction of climate crisis in literature, find Beard a (morally) unsuitable character for a novel about climate change. To these critics, the text's humorous elements 'did not do justice to the goal of increasing public awareness of the serious threat that global warming represents', as Berndt puts it.[31] Of course, as McEwan has argued, *Solar* was never meant to be a novel about climate change – it was merely meant to be 'the background hum' of the book; however, this justification does not fully resolve the difficulties presented by the work's presentation of character.[32]

Underlying many of these critiques of characterization and narrative perspective in *Solar* lies another issue: that of the novel's genre. Given McEwan's realist depictions of science in, for instance, *Enduring Love* and *Saturday*, readers and critics may have expected a similarly realist treatment of climate change science. *Solar*, however, is an allegory: Beard's constant yearning for more food, more sex and more success is illustrative of the kind of greed that brought humanity to the brink of extinction, symbolized by the melanoma that Beard develops (*So*, p. 238).[33] Beard's behaviour, Kerridge suggests, 'represents the collective failing of wealthy consumers to change their behaviour in response to the threat of global warming'.[34] Yet in exploring the novel as allegory, critics have also touched on – and puzzled over – whether the novel works as an allegory and whether allegory is a genre suited to the problem of climate crisis. The latter issue is of particular concern to ecocritics, many of whom have long approached literature as a possible means of inspiring political action or change. Tying these aims in with allegory, and particularly with *Solar*, has proved to be difficult.

McEwan had been thinking about writing about climate change for years but, as he said in interview, 'it just seemed so huge and so distorted by facts and figures and graphs and science and then virtue. I just couldn't quite see how a novel would work without falling flat with moral intent'.[35] Its vast temporal and spatial scale, questions of blame and cause and effect make it difficult to write about climate change. How to address climate crisis in literature and art has been a key concern for ecocritics over the past few decades, and genre is a crucial factor in these discussions. In his critique of *Solar*, Kerridge approaches it as a realist novel, albeit one that lacks 'the full emotional and moral range of which the realist novel is capable'.[36] Indeed, he has proposed that literary realism may be highly appropriate to depicting climate crisis, current responses to it – including the frequently contradictory ones – as well as the consequences of climate change as it is happening right now.[37] Timothy Clark, in contrast, writes off realistic fiction: 'the main artistic implication of trying to represent the Anthropocene must be a deep suspicion of any traditionally realist aesthetics'.[38] He offers gothic, science fiction and myth as genres more suitable to climate crisis. Others, like Ursula Heise and Timothy Morton, have pointed to experimental modes of narrative, such as collage, or digital imagining, as in Google Earth.[39]

Matters of genre also come to the fore within McEwan's oeuvre. In *The Child in Time*, he explicitly chose dystopia as his genre. The novel is clearly recognizable as a dystopia in which global warming has worsened, the countryside is destroyed in the name of efficiency and an unchecked Thatcherite government is in power. *Solar* is very much set in the present and lacks the sense of futurity characterizing *The Child in Time*. And *Solar*, unlike *The Child in Time*, is meant to be an allegory, as McEwan himself has emphasized. Writing a moralizing book, he suggests, would have ruined it for him – what he needed was a get-out clause. What he landed on was that *Solar* would be 'an investigation of human nature, with some of the latitude thrown in by comedy'.[40] For McEwan, then, it seems that in writing about climate crisis, comedy – and specifically allegory – was the only option. Few critics seem to believe that this was a good decision, an exception being Evi Zemanek, who in an early article on *Solar* proposes that the novel's quality depends on its allegory and that this allegory 'solves a great problem of representation when one decides against dramatizing hurricanes or floods'.[41] Yet, for many critics, it is precisely the fact that *Solar* is an allegory about climate crisis that is the problem. Kerridge hints that McEwan's choice for allegory was escapist: more of a cop-out than a 'get-out clause'.[42] Likewise, Garrard suggests that 'McEwan himself seems to have been stumped and resorted to comic allegory as an escape route'.[43]

Almost unanimously, though, critics agree that one part of the novel did work well as an allegory: the boot room passage. When he is invited to spend some time in the Arctic with a group of artists aboard a ship frozen in the ice, Beard is struck by the state of the ship's boot room. The idea is that each of the passengers stores their outerwear in his or her own space in the boot room. After just a few days, chaos breaks out as people start taking each other's gear. Beard reflects on this in light of climate change and wonders how humankind is ever supposed to save the earth, if a small group of people cannot even keep a boot room organized (*So*, p. 78). Experiencing just this scene on the Cape Farewell expedition to the Arctic that McEwan went on in 2005 led him to believe that this – the disorder in the boot room – would be his way into a novel about climate change.[44] Indeed, the success of the boot room passage raises the question of whether McEwan should not have just stuck to this passage, instead of writing an entire novel. In his *New Yorker* profile of McEwan, Daniel Zalewski cites one of McEwan's close friends, the philosopher Galen Strawson, who suggests that 'Ian is essentially a short-story writer' whose novels are often short stories 'pushed into a novel'.[45] This sentiment is echoed by a number of *Solar*'s reviewers, including Jason Cowley, who believes the novel to have been stretched beyond its natural length, when compared with the treatment of the human drama in *Amsterdam*.[46] The answer to the question of whether *Solar* works as an allegory might be that some parts do. Nonetheless, the question mark remains about the suitability of allegory as a genre for the treatment of climate crisis and science, especially when *Solar* is compared with McEwan's earlier dystopian (*The Child in Time*) and realist (*Enduring Love*) works.

Even though McEwan suggests that allegory was the only option for him, some of his comments – not to mention his other work – reveal other possible genres. *The Child in Time* is a dystopia, which arguably does a better job than *Solar* does of painting a haunting picture of a thoroughly unpleasant future. Yet when asked about dystopia as the genre in which to write about climate change, McEwan counters that that does not interest him at all: 'we've had so many dystopias that we're brain-dead in that direction'.[47] Since McEwan made this comment in 2007, the rise and popularity of dystopian fiction seems to have proved him wrong. The past decade has seen an explosion of novels that are called 'cli-fi' or climate fictions: Novels in which the effects of climate crisis are central to the narrative and which are often dystopian.[48] These works need not necessarily only be genre fiction: Realist climate fictions such as *The Day After Tomorrow* (Nathaniel Rich) and *Flight Behaviour* (Barbara Kingsolver) depict what McEwan himself has identified as an essentially human act, central to fiction: imagining what it is like to be someone else and, in this case, to live with the effects of climate crisis. Rather than depicting a culture that has become 'brain-dead' about dystopias, awareness of environmental crisis seems to have reinvigorated the genre.

Particularly in light of the depiction of science and art the publication and reception of *Solar* present an interesting case study. In their responses to the work, critics explicitly continue a discussion that is central to McEwan's oeuvre, concerning the tension between his interests in both fields. While the relationship between the two is often depicted as problematic – especially in *Enduring Love* – some of McEwan's comments as well as *The Child in Time* suggest that the two fields are complementary, offering Stephen the science he needs to get his life back on track, and Charles the literature he needs to escape his. *Solar* continues this discussion, presenting Beard's derision of art and literature, while implying the necessity and inescapability of storytelling. The novel, and in particular its reception, also asks the question that hovers over much of McEwan's fictional work: not only what the relationship, or hierarchy, between science and literature is, but how a novel may successfully capture science and, in the case of *The Child in Time* and *Solar*, climate change. By staging dialogues between science and art in his novels, McEwan engages with the respective value of these fields, opening up the question of the role that art and literature play in depicting science. It is this point of successful communication of climate crisis and the science that surrounds it in *Solar* that has inspired so much criticism. Literary works like those by McEwan reflect not only contemporary perceptions and discourses, but may also shape the discourse about climate change. It is this second aspect that *Solar* has been seen to neglect, especially in the ecocritical assessment of it. While the conclusion of *The Child in Time* and the birth of the unnamed (and genderless) child provide a problematically simplistic answer to the Thatcherite dystopia, the refusal to hold up any kind of emotional, moral or practical path in *Solar* may have been a missed opportunity.

NOTES

1 Emily Horton, *Contemporary Crisis Fictions* (London: Palgrave, 2014), p. 25.
2 Ibid., p. 26.
3 Jonathan Greenberg, 'Why Can't Biologists Read Poetry? Ian McEwan's *Enduring Love*', *Twentieth Century Literature*, 53 (2007), 2, pp. 93–124 (p. 95).
4 John Brockman, 'Introduction', in *The Next Fifty Years: Science in the First Half of the Twenty-First Century*, ed. John Brockman (New York: Touchstone, 1995), pp. xi–xiii (p. xiii). See also Curtis D. Carbonell, 'A Consilient Science and Humanities in Ian McEwan's Enduring Love', *CLCWeb: Comparative Literature and Culture*, 12 (2010), 3. Retrieved from: https://doi.org/10.7771/1481-4374.1425 (accessed 15 February 2018).
5 Daniel Zalewski, 'Ian McEwan's Art of Unease', *The New Yorker*, 23 February 2009. Retrieved from: www.newyorker.com/magazine/2009/02/23/the-background-hum (accessed 15 February 2018).
6 Jon Cook, Sebastian Groes and Victor Sage, 'Journeys without Maps: An Interview with Ian McEwan', in *Ian McEwan*, second edition, ed. Sebastian Groes (London: Bloomsbury, 2013), pp. 144–55 (p. 148).
7 Patricia Waugh, 'Science and Fiction in the 1990s', in *British Fiction of the 1990s*, ed. Nick Bentley (London: Routledge, 2005), pp. 57–77 (p. 63).
8 E. O. Wilson, *Consilience: The Unity of Knowledge* (1998; London: Abacus, 2003), p. 12.
9 Katrin Berndt, 'Science as Comedy and the Myth of Progress in Ian McEwan's *Solar*', *Mosaic*, 50 (2017), 4, pp. 85–101 (p. 87).
10 Ian McEwan, 'A Parallel Tradition', *The Guardian*, 1 April 2006. Retrieved from: www.theguardian.com/books/2006/apr/01/scienceandnature.richarddawkins (accessed 15 February 2018).
11 Cook, Groes and Sage, 'Journeys without Maps', p. 148.
12 Ian McEwan, 'Ian McEwan & Antony Gormley: A Conversation about Art and Nature', *The Kenyon Review*, 28 (2006), 1, pp. 104–12. Reprinted in *Conversations with Ian McEwan*, ed. Ryan Roberts (Jackson: University Press of Mississippi, 2010), pp. 134–42 (p. 141).
13 As McEwan writes in a short essay about his experiences on the *Cape Farewell* expedition: 'all boot rooms need good systems so that flawed creatures can use them well. Good science will serve us well, but only good rules will save the boot room. Leave nothing to idealism and outrage, or even good art. (We know in our hearts that the very best art is entirely and splendidly useless).' See Ian McEwan, 'A Boot Room in the Frozen North'. Retrieved from: www.capefarewell.com/explore/215-a-boot-room-in-the-frozen-north.html (accessed 15 February 2018).
14 Waugh, 'Science and Fiction in the 1990s', p. 66.
15 Dominic Head, *Ian McEwan* (Manchester: Manchester University Press), p. 138.
16 Horton, *Contemporary Crisis Fictions*, p. 123.
17 Berndt, 'Science as Comedy', p. 86.
18 Ironically, he does include an implicit reference to environmentalism's founding text, Rachel Carson's *Silent Spring* – 'no birdsong' – that Aldous had not included (*So*, p. 153).
19 Adam Trexler, *Anthropocene Fictions* (Charlottesville and London: University of Virginia Press, 2015), p. 47.

20 Based on the chronology of events in the novel, it is set in 1992: when Stephen's parents meet each other, his mother Claire has just been fired from a department store where she worked for three years after the war (*CT*, pp. 166, 169), so until 1948. Next July, Claire announces her pregnancy (*CT*, p. 171), hence in 1949. Stephen recalls that when he witnesses this scene, it is forty-three years later (*CT*, p. 210). Since the scene in the pub took place in July 1949, the date of the novel is 1992.

21 Anabela Carvalho, 'Representing the Politics of the Greenhouse Effect', *Critical Discourse Studies*, 2 (2005), 1, pp. 1–29 (pp. 4, 5).

22 Ben Knights, *Writing Masculinities: Male Narratives in Twentieth-Century Fiction* (Aldershot: Ashgate, 2002), p. 208.

23 Greg Garrard, 'Ian McEwan's Next Novel and the Future of Ecocriticism', *Contemporary Literature* 50 (2009), 4, pp. 695–720 (p. 698).

24 Jack Slay, 'Vandalizing Time: Ian McEwan's *The Child in Time*', *Critique: Studies in Contemporary Fiction*, 35 (1994), 4, pp. 205–18 (p. 215).

25 Jago Morrison, 'Narration and Unease in Ian McEwan's Later Fiction', *Critique: Studies in Contemporary Fiction*, 42 (2001), 3, pp. 253–68 (p. 253).

26 Axel Goodbody, '*Die Ringe des Saturn* und *Solar*: Sinnbilder und Schreibstrategien in Literarischen Stellungnahmen zur Ökologischen Krise von W. G. Sebald und Ian McEwan', in *Ökologische Transformationen und Literarische Repräsentationen*, eds. Maren Ermisch, Ulrike Kruse and Urte Stobbe (Göttingen: Universitätsverslag Göttingen, 2010), pp. 131–48 (p. 140).

27 John Lanchester, 'Warmer, Warmer', *London Review of Books*, 22 March 2007. Retrieved from: www.lrb.co.uk/v29/n06/john-lanchester/warmer-warmer (accessed 15 February 2018).

28 Greg Garrard, '*Solar*: Apocalypse Not', in *Ian McEwan*, second edition, ed. Sebastian Groes (London: Bloomsbury, 2013), pp. 123–36 (p. 135).

29 Richard Kerridge, 'The Single Source', *Ecozon@*, 1 (2010), 1, pp. 155–61 (pp. 159–60). Retrieved from: core.ac.uk/download/pdf/58910792.pdf (accessed 15 February 2018).

30 See Nicholas Lezard: '*Solar* by Ian McEwan – Review', *The Guardian*, 26 February 2011. Retrieved from: www.theguardian.com/books/2011/feb/26/solar-ian-mcewan-lezard-review (accessed 16 February 2018); James Urquhart, '*Solar*, by Ian McEwan', *The Independent*, 14 March 2010. Retrieved from: www.independent.co.uk/arts-entertainment/books/reviews/solar-by-ian-mcewan-5527479.html (accessed 16 February 2018); Jason Cowley, 'McEwan's War Against Warmth', *The Observer*, 'The New Review', 14 March 2010, pp. 41–2.

31 Berndt, 'Science as Comedy', p. 85.

32 Zalewski, 'Ian McEwan's Art of Unease'.

33 See Rachel Holland, 'Reality Check: Ian McEwan's Rational Fictions', *Critique: Studies in Contemporary Fiction*, 58 (2017), 4, pp. 387–400 (p. 397).

34 Kerridge, 'The Single Source', p. 155.

35 Mick Brown, 'Ian McEwan Interview: Warming to the Topic of Climate Change', *The Telegraph*, 11 March 2010. Retrieved from: www.telegraph.co.uk/culture/books/7412584/Ian-McEwan-interview-warming-to-the-topic-of-climate-change.html (accessed 23 March 2018).

36 Kerridge, 'The Single Source', p. 159.

37 Richard Kerridge, 'Ecocritical Approaches to Literary Form and Genre', in *The Oxford Handbook of Ecocriticism*, ed. Greg Garrard (Oxford and New York: Oxford University Press, 2014), pp. 361–76 (p. 374).

38 Timothy Clark, 'Nature, Post Nature', in *The Cambridge Companion to Literature and the Environment*, ed. Louise Westling (Cambridge: Cambridge University Press, 2014), pp. 75–89 (p. 81).

39 See Ursula Heise, *Sense of Place and Sense of Planet* (Oxford and New York: Oxford University Press, 2008), pp. 17–67; Timothy Morton, *Hyperobjects* (Minneapolis: University of Minnesota Press, 2013), pp. 161ff.

40 Brown, 'Ian McEwan Interview'.

41 Evi Zemanek, 'A Dirty Hero's Fight for Clean Energy: Satire, Allegory, and Risk Narrative in Ian McEwan's *Solar*', *Ecozon@* 3 (2012), 1, pp. 51–60 (p. 51). Retrieved from: ecozona.eu/article/view/450/472 (accessed 23 March 2018). Trexler questions whether *Solar* can be read as an allegory at all: '*Solar* is undergirded by a scientific account of the human mind, rather than the ideal moral order of classic allegory' (Trexler, *Anthropocene Fictions*, p. 49).

42 Kerridge, 'Ecocritical Approaches to Literary Form and Genre', p. 373.

43 Garrard, 'Apocalypse Not', p. 135.

44 Brown, 'Ian McEwan Interview' and McEwan, 'A Boot Room'.

45 Zalewski, 'Ian McEwan's Art of Unease'.

46 Cowley, 'McEwan's War Against Warmth', p. 41.

47 Zemanek, 'A Dirty Hero's Fight', p. 51.

48 See Adeline Johns-Putra, 'Climate Change in Literature and Literary Studies: From Cli-Fi, Climate Change Theater and Ecopoetry to Ecocriticism and Climate Change Criticism', *WIREs Climate Change*, 7 (2006), pp. 266–82. Retrieved from: https://doi.org/10.1002/wcc.385 (accessed 23 March 2018); Trexler, *Anthropocene Fictions*.

4

MICHAEL LEMAHIEU

The Novel of Ideas

Few novelists would admit to trying to write a novel of ideas; many might resent the implication they had. 'You have to forgive my ranting', Thelma Drake apologizes to Stephen Lewis in *The Child in Time*, 'it's what comes of living alone in the country with only ideas for company' (*CT*, p. 120).[1] To compliment a novel's ideas is to risk implying it has 'only ideas', and therefore to signal a defect with, say, plot or character. One does not typically compliment the scientist for using data or the lawyer rhetoric: all novels simply have ideas. 'So intrinsic to the novelistic medium were ideas', Mary McCarthy writes, 'that it would have been impossible in former days to speak of "the novel of ideas." It would have seemed to be a tautology'.[2] In more recent times, her argument implies, the multiplicity of genres – indeed, the very existence of genre fiction – precludes the assumption that ideas are intrinsic to the novel. As a result, the novel of ideas becomes a particular subgenre, one alternately considered intellectual and highbrow or stilted and stiff. Thus, if formerly the name 'novel of ideas' seemed to be tautologous, more recently it appears contradictory. Too keen an interest in ideas disqualifies a book as a novel, or a writer as a novelist. For example, Norman Mailer's novels are not really novels, John Gardner implies in *On Moral Fiction*, owing to 'Mailer's greater interest in his ideas than in his characters'. By the same token, Gardner continues, because Saul Bellow 'cares more about his political opinion' than about 'a coherent, self-sustained fictional world', he is 'actually not a novelist at heart but an essayist disguised as a writer of fiction'.[3] All novels are novels of ideas, it would seem then, but no novels of ideas are novels. As with Stephen's fatigue with ideas in *The Child in Time* – 'the very word made him weary' (*CT*, p. 131) – the very name novel of ideas can make wary readers weary, suggesting as it does essays, lectures, or even rantings, rather than works of art.

Ian McEwan, one of the foremost practitioners working in this suspect form, writes novels of ideas that are never simply novels of ideas. To the contrary, his works feature intrigue, suspense and even knives. Having itself become a particular genre of fiction, the novel of ideas in McEwan's hands intermingles with genre fiction.[4] That his novels of ideas display such features – are in fact of a piece with them – accounts in part for the critical and popular success of his work in a form not typically considered user-friendly. 'Though he is animated by ideas', Daniel Zalewski notes, McEwan 'would never plop two characters on a sofa and have them expound rival philosophies'.[5] Through a combination of heady concepts, realized characters and suspenseful plots, McEwan's work does not overcome so much as exploit the generic contradictions of the novel of ideas. At times, his novels of ideas enact what they denote – form follows content; at other times, their performative function diverges from their constative meaning, but, either way, they consistently explore and demonstrate unexpected capabilities of the genre. In his novels, ideas animate but never overwhelm aesthetics.

The novel of ideas often plays the negative counterpart to the novel as art, an opposition that owes much to Henry James, whom T. S. Eliot famously described as possessing a 'mind so fine that no idea could violate it'.[6] For James, art is its own idea, sufficient unto itself: 'we must grant the artist his subject, his idea, his *donnée*: our criticism is applied only to what he makes of it'.[7] The idea of a work is given, granted and beyond reproach; as a result, the aesthetic object is to be considered replete and autonomous: 'only a short time ago it might have been supposed that the English novel was not what the French call *discutable*. It had no air of having a theory, a conviction, a consciousness of itself behind it – of being the expression of an artistic faith, the result of choice and comparison. I do not say it was necessarily the worse for that.' Theories, convictions, self-consciousness – James suggests these are not necessary components of a novel; their absence in no way creates 'any taint of incompleteness'.[8] This understanding emerges as the paradigmatic conception of the novel in the twentieth century. As a result, Aldous Huxley could write in 1928 that 'the real, the congenital novelists' do not write novels of ideas, which are not artful, as opposed to the art novel, which is its own idea.[9] Huxley, who did not count himself a member of that distinguished group, but who did influence the development of the novel of ideas after 1945, embraces the denigration implied by the opposition between the novel of ideas and the novel as art.

The lasting legacy of James's aesthetic ideology, McCarthy notes, is this conception 'of the novel as a fine art and of the novelist as an intelligence superior to mere intellect'. Thus, 'the power of the novelist insofar as he was a supreme intelligence was to free himself from the work-load of commentary and simply, awesomely, to show: his creation was beyond paraphrase or reduction'.[10] James's insistence that novelists show and not tell, which quickly became an old saw, appears inimical to the novel of ideas, where the attempt 'to voice explicit ideas in a novel' typically 'requires a spokes-man'.[11] As a result of this requirement, novels of ideas struggle not to subordinate plot and character to dialogue and commentary; they struggle, that is to say, not to tell more than they show. McEwan's novels of ideas, however, manage to show more than they tell, or perhaps better, they manage to do more and to mean more than they say.

McEwan's narrative fiction elaborates a sustained polemic against an understanding of modernist aesthetic ideology as art for art's sake. 'As far as I can make out', Thelma accuses Stephen, 'you think that some local, passing fashion like modernism – modernism! – is the intellectual achieve-ment of our time. Pathetic!' (CT, p. 45). Thelma's criticisms advance McEwan's own critique, which construes modernism as art's elitist retreat into itself. As opposed to the nineteenth century, which Enduring Love's science writer Joe Rose represents as a time of harmony between science and literature – Keats's beauty leads to truth; Darwin's science to grandeur – in the twentieth century, science 'became professionalized' and 'in literature and in other arts, a newfangled modernism celebrated formal, structural qualities, inner coherence, and self-reference' (EL, pp. 48–9). Amsterdam's composer Clive Linley's manifesto Recalling Beauty continues the critique of the 'whole modernist project', which it describes as ironically old-fashioned: 'the old guard of modernism had imprisoned music in the academy' (Am, pp. 21–2). The foetus in Nutshell puts it most succinctly: 'most of the modern poems leave me cold' (N, p. 14). The proliferation of novels of ideas after 1945, including those of McEwan, can be understood in part as an effect of the loosening bonds of modernist aesthetic ideology. The novel of ideas, Timothy Bewes suggests, is 'a characteristic form of postmodernity'.[12]

In their subject matter, McEwan's novels of ideas are distinctly contem-porary. More than either politics or philosophy, two traditional concerns of the genre, science predominates. The novel of ideas was once commonly thought of as ideological fiction – akin to the French roman à thèse. In the British tradition, George Orwell's Animal Farm (1945) and Nineteen Eighty-Four (1949) exemplify this conception. While McEwan is by no means a resolutely political writer, across his career he has produced works that take their ideas directly from political topics and events. For example, two minor works – the oratorio Or Shall We Die? (1983) and the screenplay The Ploughman's Lunch (1985) – were occasioned by, and in turn explicitly address, nuclear proliferation and environmental degradation. McEwan returns to the latter topic in Solar (2010), in which physicist Michael Beard treacherously pursues new forms of wind and solar energy. A second trad-itional strand in the novel of ideas is philosophical fiction: Iris Murdoch's Under the Net (1954), for example, or Bellow's Herzog (1964), from which

McEwan takes the long epigraph to *Saturday* (2005). As with the ideological novel, McEwan has occasionally worked in this form as well. *Atonement* (2001) is in many ways an exploration of the problem of other minds – of 'the failure to grasp the simple truth that other people are as real as you' (*At*, p. 40). *The Children Act* (2014) addresses the right to die and wades into what the novel describes as 'the turbulent realm of religious and philosophical ideas' (*CA*, p. 122). But more than Marx or Nietzsche, Darwin is McEwan's muse. In this respect, his works exemplify a broader transformation: contemporary novels of ideas are often concerned less with totalitarianism than with unified field theory, less with existentialism than elementary particles and less with the human condition than the human genome. Of course, certain topics – sustainability and the environment, for instance – cut across distinctions between politics, philosophy and science, and works such as *Saturday* and *Solar* are at once political and scientific novels. But in McEwan's works, as in those of his American counterpart Richard Powers, for instance, science contributes the ideas to novels that ultimately reveal the limits of scientific inquiry.

McEwan finds in the discoveries of science the stuff of fiction, whether it be quantum mechanics (*The Child in Time*), evolutionary psychology (*Enduring Love*) or neuroscience (*Saturday*). And while it is no doubt the case that at times McEwan can represent difficult scientific theories as electrifying episodes, at other times he does indulge in extended expositions of ideas. 'Come off it, Thelma', Stephen says, not plopped on a couch but sitting at the dinner table, 'Admit you're bursting to lecture me'. She is, and she does, with references to 'quantum theory' (*CT*, p. 117), 'Big Bang theory', 'unified field theory' and 'a higher order of theory' (*CT*, p. 118). So much for James's aversion to theory: 'She spoke of eigenfunctions and Hermitian operators, Brownian motion, quantum potential, the Poisson bracket and the Schwarz inequality' (*CT*, p. 119). Moments such as these explicitly perform a didactic or pedagogical function, but they also serve to establish narrative authority. Rather than an indulgence or a shortcoming, then, these lectures form part of an aesthetic strategy. While McEwan cannot reasonably expect many of his readers to understand the theories to which he refers, his novels create the sense that *he* does, thus sustaining interest without requiring full comprehension. McEwan's novelistic strategies, that is to say, are first and foremost aesthetic rather than informational: the ideas in his novels can still serve their primary purpose, even if the reader does not fully comprehend them. That is not to say the ideas in his novels have no cognitive value, but rather that their value is primarily aesthetic; they enact more than they instruct, although they often instruct as well. 'Do not forget', Ludwig Wittgenstein remarks in one of his notebooks, 'that a poem, even though it is composed in the language of information, is not used in the language-game of giving information'.[13] McEwan composes in the language of information, and at times delights in giving information, but that information is not given in 'the language-game of giving information', but rather in the language-game of aesthetic creation.

McEwan's works pull off that trick by unfolding the drama and texture of their ideational content, from the level of plot device and set piece down to that of lexical units. At times, he invigorates abstract nouns with dynamic modifiers, as in the beginning of *Enduring Love*: 'comforting geometry' (p. 2), 'ruthless gravity' (p. 16); at others, he reverses the equation, with abstract adjectives modifying dynamic nouns: 'neuronal pulse' (p. 13), 'biochemical exchanges' (p. 23). McEwan's celebrated style often performs what his conceptual investigations denote. In the opening pages of *Saturday*, one finds similar bursts of verbal constructions: 'chemical accident', 'intracellular events', 'paradoxical consequence' (p. 5), 'biological engines', 'bipedal skills', 'warm filaments', 'invisible glow', 'planetary scale' (p. 13), 'solar dust' (p. 14), 'obliging imagination' (p. 16), 'hidden order' and 'anthropic principle' (p. 17). As that novel traces the movements of neurosurgeon Henry Perowne over the course of one London Saturday in 2003, McEwan establishes authorial credibility by eagerly, perhaps overeagerly, displaying the results of his research in a technical vocabulary, including such terms as: 'trigeminal neuralgia', 'trigeminal ganglion', 'radiofrequency thermocoagulation', 'Rhoton dissector', 'multi-level lumbar laminectomy', 'vestibular schwannoma', 'right posterior frontal glioma', 'infratentorial supracerebellar route' and 'superior cerebellar vermis' (pp. 7–9). Not the typical stuff of novelistic discourse, but one gets the sense that McEwan delights in it, in both the signs and the referents. He often indicates as much, as when he refers admiringly to the 'beauty' that Einstein found in the theory of general relativity – which Perowne includes on his 'list of sublime achievement' (*S*, p. 68) – or the 'grandeur' that Darwin found in the theory of natural selection.[14] In a similar vein, McEwan speaks excitedly of reading 'the cosmologists on the creation of time' or 'the mathematician who can describe the beauty of numbers to the numbskull'[15]; and he describes sensuously the 'special pleasure' that comes from seeing by 'the light of a powerful idea' or the pleasure of indulging at 'a feast of human ingenuity'.[16]

McEwan does occasionally recycle ideas across multiple works. Readers who first encounter *Enduring Love*'s description of 'that preverbal language of instant thought linguists call mentalese' (*EL*, p. 167) might have their memories jogged by *Saturday*'s reference to 'the pre-verbal language that linguists call mentalese' (*S*, p. 81). And those who first read *Saturday*'s mention of 'a problem, or an idea, of reference' (*S*, p. 17) might hear an echo in the description in *Nutshell* of 'what is known as a problem of reference' (*N*, p. 5). These repetitions betray a certain formulaic quality, but they are exceptions and, even then, when individual phrases do recur, they do so over a period of many years: *Saturday* was published eight years after *Enduring Love* and *Nutshell* eleven after *Saturday*. Furthermore, the ideas that recur bear directly not only on the interests of particular novels, but also on the art of novel writing generally. The idea of 'preverbal language' is key to the novel's ability to represent interiority, as McEwan does so well in capturing, for example, the syntax of young Briony Tallis's thoughts in *Atonement*. And problems of reference cut across linguistics, psychology and philosophy, pertaining to the relationship between words and meanings, but also to that between individual acts and conceptual schemes. They are ideas, in other words, well-suited to language games that involve depicting the grammar of thought and representing individual lives in narrative structures.

McEwan's own remarks on the novel of ideas at times imply an opposition between ideas and narrative. Speaking in an interview about the composition of *Enduring Love*, he recalls: 'I felt I was writing a novel of ideas, but I did want a very strong narrative shelter'.[17]

McEwan insists that ideas must emerge out of the process of composition. To begin with an idea, he claims, is to reverse 'the imaginative order from which the novel takes its life'; rather than working from the ground up, 'a moral or political scheme draws you away at the very beginning, at the moment of inception, from the specific, from the detail, from the strange combination of details that give novels their curious power' (*MA*, p. x). Here in a nutshell is McEwan's aesthetic philosophy: in the imaginative order, the creative act moves from specific detail to more general ideas; the aesthetic object is not predetermined conceptually. McEwan's remarks recall Stanley Cavell's characterization of Wittgenstein's late style: 'he *writes*: he does not report, he does not write up results'.[18] Wittgenstein composed his later philosophy as a series of crisscrossing investigations; McEwan describes the creative act of writing a novel as 'an exploration or investigation' (*MA*, p. x). When the novelist becomes captivated by a particular image – and explores the details of that image – ideational content derives from aesthetic considerations.

McEwan makes these remarks just as he enters the stage of his career that features his most fully realized novels of ideas: *The Child in Time* (1987), *Black Dogs* (1992) and *Enduring Love* (1997). Elements of these novels are prefigured in earlier works, to be sure, and there are elements in later works that hearken back to them (*Saturday*, in particular, is of the same ilk), but these three books mark McEwan's turn to the novel of ideas precisely during the time in which he emerges as a major novelist. In the six-year period that elapsed between the publication of *The Comfort of Strangers* (1981) and *The Child in Time*, McEwan thought intentionally and wrote explicitly about the relationship between novels and ideas. In the preface to *A Move Abroad* (1989), as cited, he reflects back on that interlude from the other side of *The Child in Time*, relating how grappling with ideas and ideology in the oratorio *Or Shall We Die?* and the screenplay *The Ploughman's Lunch* allowed him to ponder the difference between those forms and narrative fiction. He describes those two texts as 'flights from, or tactical evasions of, novel writing' that taught him something about 'the relationship between ideas, opinions, politics, bees-in-the-bonnet on the one hand and the imagination on the other' (*MA*, p. vii). Unlike a screenplay, McEwan suggests, the novel is not conducive to encapsulating passing cultural preoccupations or occasional political debates: 'the novel is not best suited to topical issues, or catching on the wing a changing social mood. Novels take longer to cook' (*MA*, p. xxv). McEwan articulates a productive tension in his work between the timeless and the timely, for while *The Child in Time* deals with the idea of time speculatively and in general terms, it is also very much of its moment, a conditional Condition of England novel, as it were.

It is also precisely in this pivotal period when McEwan begins to think of the ideas in the novel of ideas not as ideological, so much as scientific. In conducting research for the oratorio, he relates, he came across 'accounts of contemporary physics and its diverse and extraordinary explanations of the nature of time' that nevertheless reinforced his 'belief in the insufficiency of the intellect alone in understanding ourselves or our world' (*MA*, p. xxvi). Even as McEwan turned to other forms to represent political ideas, therefore, he discovered how scientific ideas could enhance the novel form. In conducting research for *Or Shall We Die?*, he discovers the germ of not only *The Child in Time*, which reflects on 'the nature of time', but also of *Black Dogs* and *Enduring Love*, both of which dramatize the necessity of the intellect as well as its 'insufficiency' in isolation. Such a characterization may seem counterintuitive for a novel of ideas, but that is precisely McEwan's point. 'Turning points' may be, as the narrator Jeremy suggests in *Black Dogs*, 'the inventions of storytellers and dramatists' (*BD*, p. 50); but *The Child in Time* represents an important bend in the trajectory of McEwan's career.

The Child in Time is not simply a novel of *ideas*, but also a *novel* of ideas, which is to say that in that work McEwan discovered not only how a novel can accommodate ideas, but also how ideas can augment and intensify a novel. McEwan himself marks the composition of *The Child in Time* as a turning point when his interest in science leads to the realization of his aesthetic theory. Just as he would have it, the novel materializes with the writer being captivated by an image, 'by the memory, or perhaps the memory of a dream, of a footpath that emerges onto a bend in a country road' (*MA*, p. xxv). Readers will recognize this memory as the seed of one of the novel's most memorable scenes: the protagonist emerges from a footpath onto that country road, approaches a pub and through the window sees his parents' younger selves discussing whether or not to keep the baby that would become the protagonist. It is also the scene that McEwan wryly refers back to in *Saturday* as Perowne derisively describes the magical realist novels his daughter has assigned him (*S*, p. 67). The timeslip functions both as a plot device and as a means to further the novel's interests in the intersecting ideas of temporality and childhood.

Children are often the source of ideas in McEwan's work, whether they are living alone in a house (*The Cement Garden*), floating away in a balloon (*Enduring Love*), telling devastating lies (*Atonement*), or refusing the medicine that would save their lives (*The Children Act*) – or, as is the case with *The Child in Time*, being abducted in a supermarket. *The Child in Time* also features a narrator who is a successful author of children's books, a prominent politician who attempts to revert to a state of childhood and a government committee devoted to the best methods of childrearing. In many respects, the figure of the child embodies what McEwan describes as the imaginative order: as the ideas in a novel emerge from an attention to specific details, so too the child, though often absorbed by the immediacy of the moment and by the particulars of the environment, also represents temporality and potentiality – the promise of implicit ideas yet to come. At the same time, there is something vaguely threatening about the figure of a child, both in the precariousness of a presumed innocence and also in the threat of action without understanding. In a McEwan novel, any promise can double as a threat.

McEwan gravitates toward ideas that have complex aesthetic dimensions, and the figure of the child allows him to reflect on competing models of temporality that ensue from 'a shift from a Newtonian to an Einsteinian world view', which he understands as a paradigm shift from mastery of the environment to implication in it (*MA*, p. xx). *The Child in Time* begins not with the abduction of the narrator's three-year-old daughter, but rather with the narrator attending a meeting of the Official Commission on Child Care. While in the meeting, his mind returns to the traumatic event, which is narrated as it was experienced. This instance introduces a sustained exploration of the aesthetic dimensions of time, a concept which accrues numerous attributes over the course of the novel: 'lost time' (p. 12), 'uninterrupted time' (p. 14), 'absolute time' (p. 14), 'empty time' (p. 34), 'backward flowing time' (p. 43), 'contracting time' (p. 47), 'the vandalizing erasures of time' (p. 48), 'a time apart' (p. 53), 'this delicate reconstruction of another time' (p. 57), 'this slowing of time' (p. 94), 'different kinds of time' (p. 119), 'inert time' (p. 131) and 'escape from time' (p. 201). Time not only provides content, but also determines form, and all of these examples work in the service of what the novel self-referentially describes as 'the elaborate time schemes of novelists' (CT, p. 120). Not only does the narrator witness his parents discussing his conception, not only does the narrative shift almost imperceptibly between time frames, but also McEwan explicitly explores the relativity of time and space – 'a sense of relative motion, of drifting slowly backwards' (CT, p. 7). Stephen's constant search for his missing daughter Kate draws his attention to 'the slow changes, the accruing competencies' of childhood, and he cannot 'fail to feel the untapped potency of weeks and months, the time that should have been hers. Kate's growing up had become the essence of time itself' (CT, p. 8). The reader encounters these descriptions before learning exactly who Kate is and what happened to her; the child is in time, but the time is out of joint. From the outset, the movement of McEwan's narrative encapsulates his theme of temporality, which combines ideas drawn from theoretical physics and child psychology, including from three of McEwan's acknowledged sources: David Bohm's *Wholeness and the Implicate Order* (1980), Christina Hardyment's *Dream Babies* (1983) and Joseph Chilton Pearce's *Magical Child* (1977).[19]

McEwan further exploits these ideas of time to develop signature aesthetic tactics pertaining to narrative pace, perspective and temporality. Early in the novel, a new section begins in a mode that would become typical of McEwan's narratives: 'in retrospect, the events of Stephen's year, the committee year, were to seem organized round a single outcome' (CT, p. 34). This technique, of previewing an outcome that neither reader nor character can know and then looking back to a time beyond the narrative present from the perspective of that future outcome – a type of retrospective future perfect or future anterior narration – becomes key to building suspense and sustaining momentum. For example, later in *The Child in Time*, the narrator relates that, 'for years afterwards he would be baffled by his insistence on not returning to see her' (CT, p. 67); and in one of the most acute moments in *Atonement*, the seemingly impersonal third-person narrator – who readers learn later is Briony retrospectively narrating the events of a novel she has written – looks back to a moment of Robbie Turner's anticipated pleasure from the other side of an impending action's calamitous effects: 'in the years to come he would often think back to this time, when he walked along the footpath that made a shortcut through a corner of the oak woods' (*At*, p. 90).

McEwan also develops another, complementary technique in *The Child in Time*, narrating the most rapid and forceful events with deliberate and painstaking precision – the slowing down of the narrative voice inversely proportional to the speeding up of the plot's unfolding: 'in what followed, the rapidity of events was accommodated by the slowing of time ... duration shaped itself round the intensity of the event' (*CT*, pp. 93, 95). This exploration of the relativity of the phenomenal experience of time continues throughout the novel and in those that follow, as in *Enduring Love*, where the opening set piece enacts what the text denotes: 'the best description of a reality does not need to mimic its velocity' (*EL*, p. 17). While McEwan's character Thelma might instruct readers regarding the nature of time, McEwan himself exhibits the elaborate time schemes of novelists. The work tells and shows, but also does.

One thing that McEwan's novels of ideas consistently do is represent and ultimately destabilize what C. P. Snow first called in 1956 the 'two cultures' of science and literature. *The Child in Time* initiates a pattern in which McEwan develops a character who represents expertise in some realm of science that the author then mines for ideational content and thematic continuity. A physicist investigating 'the nature of time' (*CT*, p. 32), Thelma prefigures *Black Dogs*'s entomologist, *Enduring Love*'s science writer, who holds 'a doctorate on quantum electrodynamics' (*EL*, p. 75), *Saturday*'s neurosurgeon, and *Solar*'s own physicist. These scientists find counterparts in McEwan's writers: *The Child in Time*'s children's book author, *Black Dogs*'s memoirist, *Enduring Love*'s literary critic, *Amsterdam*'s composer, *Atonement*'s novelist, *Saturday*'s poet and *Nutshell*'s own poet.

Rather than conceiving of the two cultures in terms of science and literature, however, McEwan's works set up an opposition between science and religion. *The Child in Time* introduces a governing opposition in nearly all of McEwan's works, that between reason and logic, on the one hand, and 'a tendency to magical thought' (*CT*, p. 126), on the other. Nearly thirty years later, McEwan writes in *Nutshell* of the triumph of 'realism over magic, of *is* over *seems*' (*N*, p. 3). And in just about every work in between, this opposition often plays a formative one, as in *Black Dogs*, where Bernard, the insistent rationalist, refers derisively to his wife June's 'magical thinking' (*BD*, p. 80), or in *Saturday*, where the philosophical materialist Perowne insists 'the actual, not the magical, should be the challenge' (*S*, p. 67). McEwan's works often encode this dichotomy between the material world and magical thinking as reason and faith, or the opposition between the certitude of science and the succour of religion. More generally, the two sides of this dichotomy serve as points of departure from which characters are drawn and limits are encountered so that ultimately the dichotomy itself is displaced.

McEwan counteracts his respect for science with criticisms of religion. Referred to as 'the New Atheist novelist *par excellence*' and described by his late friend Christopher Hitchens as an atheist with 'the zeal of a convert', McEwan often juxtaposes magical thinking and pathological behaviour.[20] For example, the fictional case study appended to *Enduring Love* posits 'a close relationship ... between some pathological aspects of love and the tenets of the church for religious believers' (*EL*, p. 240). In *Saturday*, a similar thought occurs to Perowne, who situates the 'primitive thinking of the supernaturally inclined ... on a spectrum at whose far end, rearing like an abandoned temple, lies psychosis' (*S*, p. 17). In *Enduring Love*, Jed Parry's pathological obsession with Joe Rose often manifests as religious utterance: 'God has brought us together' (*EL*, p. 25); 'you'll come to Him too' (*EL*, p. 91); 'He has sent me to you' (*EL*, p 93) and 'I know that you'll come to God, just as I know that it's my purpose to bring you there, through love' (*EL*, p. 97). McEwan highlights the illogical nature of these professions: 'the purpose is to bring you to the Christ that is in you and that *is* you' (*EL*, p. 66). Logical positivist philosophers described such utterances as nonsense; neither verifiable nor falsifiable, they do not state a proposition but rather (obliquely) express a (veiled) emotion, to bring someone to something that resides within that someone and that in fact is that someone. McEwan criticizes, in particular, utterances that attribute a purposeful, divine trajectory to individual human lives. 'He was inviolable in his solipsism', Rose says of Parry, 'God was a term interchangeable with self' (*EL*, pp. 144, 152). *Saturday* is also unsparingly critical of 'religious feeling' and 'supernatural explanations' (*S*, p. 17), particularly of the 'restful' belief that one's prosperity, for example, forms part of a divine plan of 'an all-knowing supernatural force' (*S*, p. 74). Perowne considers pathological the failure to recognize the self-serving nature of such belief, 'a form of anosognosia, a useful psychiatric term for a lack of awareness of one's own condition' (*S*, p. 74). What for the positivists was simply nonsense is for McEwan possibly madness.

Unlike the positivists, however, McEwan's sharp criticisms of religion are not tantamount to an unequivocal elevation of science. On various levels in *Enduring Love*, for example, McEwan gives indications that Joe's rationalism and scientism leads him to overlook other, complicating factors. His vindication – he is proved correct about Parry – comes without satisfaction, because he privileges knowledge over acknowledgment, cognition over recognition. As a result of focusing myopically on the subjectivity of ethical and interpersonal factors, Joe becomes incapable of recognizing their reality.

Black Dogs embodies and enacts McEwan's inclusive modes of critique. As newlyweds, Bernard and June Tremaine hike in southern France and the characters diverge at the climactic moment. For June, the terrifying dogs she encounters represent 'emblems of the menace she had felt' (*BD*, pp. 144–5) and provoke a 'revelation' of 'extraordinary light' (*BD*, p. 151). They confirm the reality of evil and the existence of God in ways that permanently shape her worldview. Bernard does not witness the encounter, having fallen behind because he is engrossed by 'a caravan of two dozen brown furry caterpillars' (*BD*, p. 146). While June experiences terror and epiphany, Bernard's cheek is on the ground – the entomologist's equivalent of the philosopher's head in the clouds – 'to stare up close at the head of the leading caterpillar' (*BD*, p. 149). This juxtaposition distils the lifelong divide the two would feel ever after: 'rationalist and mystic, commissar and yogi, joiner and abstainer, scientist and intuitionist, Bernard and June are the extremities' between which the narrator Jeremy, their son-in-law, positions himself (*BD*, p. 19).

McEwan's novels of ideas often gender this opposition between faith and reason, characterizing their male protagonists as excessively rational and their female counterparts as insufficiently rational. In *The Child in Time*, Julie criticizes Stephen for 'a typically masculine evasion, an attempt to mask feelings behind displays of competence and organization and physical effort' (*CT*, p. 24), while she retreats to a country cottage, where she reads 'mystical or sacred texts' (*CT*, p. 52). In *Black Dogs*, June describes Bernard blinded by 'facts and figures' (*BD*, p. 43) and Bernard in turn denigrates June, who 'didn't give a damn for *truth*, for the facts' (*BD*, p. 86). In *Enduring Love*, Clarissa feels that Joe's mind 'takes no account of its own emotional field' (*EL*, p. 83), while Joe describes Clarissa as thinking that 'her emotions were the appropriate guide, that she could feel her way to the truth' (*EL*, p. 150). Even Thelma in *The Child in Time*, who as a physicist would seem to break with this pattern, is associated with a revolution in which 'quantum mechanics would feminise physics' (*CT*, p. 43). At their most effective, these characterizations augment the narrative conflict and gesture toward a critique of instrumental reason; at their least effective, and perhaps more typically, they recapitulate the premise of *Men Are from Mars, Women Are from Venus*.[21]

Black Dogs refuses any easy accounting for these standard binary oppositions, gendered or otherwise: 'it will not do to argue that rational thought and spiritual insight are separate domains', Jeremy stipulates, 'and that opposition between them is falsely conceived' (*BD*, p. 20). The novel insists on the simultaneous necessity of what June refers to 'a revolution of the inner life' (*BD*, p. 172) and of what Jeremy imagines to be Bernard's alternative, 'a set of ideas, and bloody good ones too!' (*BD*, p. 148). If McEwan's novels of *ideas* criticize appeals to supernatural forces and the claims of revealed religion, his *novels* of ideas demonstrate the limits of scientific rationalism and logical positivism in explaining human affairs. Many of those novels reach a point similar to the one Wittgenstein articulates near the conclusion of the *Tractatus*: 'we feel that even when all *possible* scientific questions have been answered, the problems of life remain completely untouched'.[22] The task of the novel of ideas, as McEwan practices it, is to represent scientific questions in such a way that does not lose sight of, and ultimately touches on, the problems of life.

McEwan's novels of ideas seek to conceive of the problems of life in a way that remains irreducible to science without resorting to mystical, magical or supernatural explanations. They seek to articulate and enact, in other words, what John Barth refers to as 'non-mystical value-thinking'.[23] Because McEwan's novels do not conflate ethics and aesthetics with religion and mysticism – as the logical positivists did – they can explore the constitution of value systems and different forms of knowing the world and of acknowledging others. And of course, one primary mode of 'value-thinking', one that can draw on science and aesthetics, is literature, which functions as a third term that troubles the binary opposition between faith and reason. McEwan does not, however, attribute any magical power to literature; he ascribes it no capacity to subsume or to transcend. Indeed, contemporary novels of ideas, including McEwan's, often reflect a cultural anxiety that science has become the sole source of ideas, that literature, once the site of invention, is now capable only of reporting discoveries from other realms. Joe Rose articulates this concern in *Enduring Love*: 'all the ideas I deal in are other people's' (*EL*, p. 75). McEwan's novels attempt, therefore, what they may not be able to accomplish: their promise of illumination is accompanied by a threat of obsolescence.

McEwan's philosophy of literature remains steadfastly secular: novels possess no inherent value. In this regard, *Saturday*'s Perowne seems to collapse the distance between author and character when he concludes that 'fiction is too humanly flawed, too sprawling and hit-and-miss to inspire uncomplicated wonder at the magnificence of human ingenuity, of the impossible dazzlingly achieved' (*S*, p. 68). McEwan's novels instead seek to inspire what one might think of as complicated wonder – the grandeur of the empirical, the beauty of the theoretical. The value of the novel is precisely in possessing no inherent value. McEwan's novels of ideas are always also about the limitations and capacities of those sprawling, hit-and-miss monuments to human flaws and human ingenuity whose implication in the messiness of human affairs precludes conceptions of aesthetic autonomy.

McEwan's novels do not aspire to being their own idea, therefore, but they remain ever preoccupied with the idea of the novel.

NOTES

1 Some of the ideas in this chapter expand on points I initially developed in the chapter on 'The Novel of Ideas' in *The Cambridge Companion to British Fiction since 1945*, ed. David James (Cambridge: Cambridge University Press, 2015), pp. 177–91.

2 Mary McCarthy, *Ideas and the Novel* (New York: Harcourt Brace Jovanovich, 1980), p. 18.

3 John Gardner, *On Moral Fiction* (New York: Basic Books, 1978), pp. 86, 92, 91.

4 Judith Seaboyer discusses how McEwan's novels of ideas manifest additional generic properties in 'Ian McEwan: Contemporary Realism and the Novel of Ideas', *The Contemporary British Novel Since 1980*, eds. James Acheson and Sarah C. E. Ross (New York: Palgrave Macmillan, 2005), pp. 23–34.

5 Daniel Zalewski, 'Ian McEwan's Art of Unease', *The New Yorker*, 23 February 2009. Retrieved from: www.newyorker.com/magazine/2009/02/23/the-background-hum (accessed 6 June 2018).

6 T. S. Eliot, 'In Memory of Henry James', in *The Complete Prose of T. S. Eliot: The Critical Edition*, Vol. 1, eds. Jewel Spears Brooker and Ronald Schurchard (Baltimore, MD: Johns Hopkins University Press, 2014), p. 650.

7 Henry James, *The Art of Fiction and Other Essays* (New York: Oxford University Press, 1948), p. 14.

8 Ibid., p. 3.

9 Aldous Huxley, *Point Counter Point* (New York: Grosset & Dunlap, 1928), p. 295.

10 McCarthy, *Ideas and the Novel*, pp. 3–4. On the novel as art form, see Mark McGurl, *The Novel Art: Elevations of American Fiction after Henry James* (Princeton, NJ: Princeton University Press, 2001).

11 McCarthy, *Ideas and the Novel*, p. 29.

12 Timothy Bewes, 'What Is "Philosophical Honesty" in Postmodern Literature?', *New Literary History*, 31 (2000), 3 (Summer), pp. 421–34 (p. 432).

13 Ludwig Wittgenstein, *Zettel*, eds. G. E. M. Anscombe and G. H. von Wright, trans. G. E. M. Anscombe (Berkeley: University of California Press, 1967), p. 28.

14 Ian McEwan, 'The Originality of the Species', *The Guardian*, 23 March 2012. Retrieved from: www.theguardian.com/books/2012/mar/23/originality-of-species-ian-mcewan (accessed 6 June 2018).

15 Ian McEwan, 'The God That Fails', *New Republic*, 244 (25 February 2013), 2, pp. 7–8. Published online as 'When I Stop Believing in Fiction', 15 February 2013. Retrieved from: https://newrepublic.com/article/112374/ian-mcewan-my-uneasy-relationship-fiction (accessed 6 June 2018).

16 Ian McEwan, 'A Parallel Tradition', *The Guardian*, 1 April 2006. Retrieved from: www.theguardian.com/books/2006/apr/01/scienceandnature.richarddawkins (accessed 6 June 2018).

17 Dwight Garner, 'The Salon Interview – Ian McEwan', 31 March 1998. Retrieved from: www.salon.com/1998/03/31/cov_si_31int/ (accessed 6 June 2018).

18 Stanley Cavell, *Must We Mean What We Say?* (Cambridge: Cambridge University Press, 1969), p. 70.

19 See Dominic Head, *Ian McEwan* (Manchester: Manchester University Press, 2007), pp. 78–84.

20 Arthur Bradley and Andrew Tate, *The New Atheist Novel: Fiction, Philosophy, and Polemic after 9/11* (London: Continuum, 2010), p. 17. Hitchens quoted in Zalewski, 'The Background Hum'.

21 John Gray, *Men Are from Mars, Women Are from Venus: A Practical Guide for Improving Communication and Getting What You Want in Your Relationship* (New York: HarperCollins, 1992).

22 Ludwig Wittgenstein, *Tractatus Logico-Philosophicus*, trans. D. F. Pears and B. F. McGuinness (1921; London: Routledge, 1961), p. 73.

23 Quoted in George Bluestone, 'John Wain and John Barth: The Angry and the Accurate', *Massachusetts Review*, 1.3 (1960), p. 586.

5

RICHARD BROWN

Cold War Fictions

The publication of *Sweet Tooth* in 2012 confirmed McEwan's interest in the Cold War themes of global politics and the individual experience, extending them into the 1970s politics of the cultural sphere and forward into the second decade of the new millennium. Its story of woman MI5 agent Serena Frome, assigned to the secret literary project of supporting a writer, Tom Haley, who is not entirely unlike the early McEwan himself, allowed him to perform a self-conscious fictional return to the world of the short stories that had brought his first success, and also to his television play *The Imitation Game* of 1980, in which secret political history and espionage came centre stage and which also had a female protagonist, Cathy Raine. *Sweet Tooth* further invited a re-evaluation of *The Innocent* (1990) and *Black Dogs* (1992), the two novels which were produced at the time of the fall of the Berlin Wall in 1989 when the Cold War era ended, or at least took on a different shape. In doing so, *Sweet Tooth* not only reframed the earlier McEwan as a writer of the Cold War decades from the birth of the North Atlantic Treaty Organization (NATO) (1949) to the Fall of the Berlin Wall (1989), but also highlighted his use of certain typical features of that political era as metaphors for an ongoing exploration of human and sexual relations, the nature of fictional representation and the relationship between the writer and the reader in the new century.

To contextualize these concerns in McEwan's career, it is helpful to reconsider the introductions which he wrote to *The Imitation Game* volume (1981) and *A Move Abroad* (1989). The former began with his thoughts about the differences between writing for fiction and for television, and provided a number of insights about several topics: the typical procedure of the short stories (for instance, as 'chasing one or two ideas to logical, or even illogical, conclusions', *IG*, p. 9); the mathematical ideas in 'Solid Geometry' as well as the sexual censorship that frustrated the television adaptation of it; the backgrounds to *The Imitation Game* in the story of Alan Turing and the cracking of the Enigma code in wartime Bletchley that inform the play; and his interview with Sussex tutor Peter Calvocoressi, who had previously worked for Air Ministry Intelligence (*IG*, pp. 16–17). For McEwan, this was 'doing something completely different' (*IG*, p. 9), something different for him and, it might be added, for Cold War spy writing too. The Turing Bletchley story has since become more widely treated as the subject of the 2001 thriller *Enigma* and the 2014 film about Turing's life which was also called *The Imitation Game*, though it was not based on McEwan's work so much as on the biography of Turing by Andrew Hodges, which appeared in 1983 and focused especially on Turing's prosecution for homosexuality in 1952. In McEwan's 'Play for Today', as he explained, what was especially of interest to him was having Cathy Raine, a woman war worker, at the centre of the action where war secrets, the gender politics of the workplace and a failed sexual relationship might clash: 'at the centre would be a sexual relationship; its misunderstandings would be the consequence of the absurdity of the structure' (*IG*, pp. 17–18). The 'structure' he refers to here is one of wartime security and espionage, but also the structure of gender relations that might help to fuel war, a perspective that anticipates the ultra-feminist credo of *Or Shall We Die?* (*MA*, p. 23).

In the introduction to *A Move Abroad* (1989), containing the libretto for *Or Shall We Die?* and *The Ploughman's Lunch*, McEwan further recalls the period when, between novel projects in 1980–1, it seemed to him that a 'new cold war had begun' at the start of the Reagan presidency, and the 'two contestants were full of swagger' (*MA*, pp. xviii, xix). The argument for a radically feminized consciousness to overcome militarist swagger is somewhat reminiscent of the pacifist 'female' consciousness advocated by D. H. Lawrence in a well-known letter to Gordon Campbell written on the eve of the First World War,[1] though with the distinctive turn that it is a 'new physics' that is said to be required to reform dangerously binary oppositions here. Gender-inflected interest in physics feeds into McEwan's metamodernist novel *The Child in Time*, appearing in 1987, whose protagonist Thelma Darke is a physicist, much as Serena Frome in *Sweet Tooth* has trained as a mathematician. Cold War history comes to inform the two novels of the fall of the Berlin wall, *The Innocent* (1990) and *Black Dogs* (1992), the first of which captures the anxiety and intrigue of the early Cold War period and the second of which attempts to dig more deeply into the historical nightmares of the European past whilst recording some of the potentially optimistic transitions of the later moment. Both, as Dominic Head explains, address and unravel binary forms of thought.[2]

The situation of war and conflict enables McEwan to use his distinctive gift for relentlessly realistic, while also darkly gothic depictions of the violent and grotesque. It also permits him to develop his interest in the intensely private individual consciousness and his micro-mapping of the emotional tensions in sexual relationships, while at the same time developing an increasingly public and engaged kind of fiction. The particular pressure put on individuals by the profound ethical and intellectual ambiguities of Cold War situations informs his backward glance and resonates deeply with the intellectual anxieties of the rapidly changing and unstable present at the turn of the new century.

It might be said of the Cold War that among its powerful effects was the prevention or at least delay of a proper mourning of the Second World War, especially problematic for the generation born after it, but without direct memories of it, and with new perspectives of their own. For that reason, the adventure of reading Ian McEwan's fiction through the 1970s, 1980s and 1990s was in part an adventure of discovering the repressed memories of that wartime through changing Cold War circumstances. The fictions rewrote a political history as a generational coming of age for the baby boomer generation, whose historical significance was not, for once, marked by its military encounters so much as by its near utopian sense of the suspension of another total war, albeit under the shadow of the darker apocalyptic nuclear threat. For McEwan, as for his contemporary Martin Amis in the collection of stories *Einstein's Monsters* (1987), the 'thinkability' of the nuclear threat that so darkened the balance of power needed to be readdressed.[3] Intriguingly this coming of age is negotiated through stories of sex and gender that explore the Cold War experience in more depth than its more familiar genre manifestations could allow.

The Innocent (1990)

The Innocent tells the story of the naïve post office engineer Leonard Marnham, in his twenties, drawn into the intertwined secret worlds of espionage, adultery and murder in 1955 Berlin, where the immediate legacy of the Second World War, the special relationships of the recently formed NATO, and the new threats of the Cold War are keenly felt. Leonard falls for an older German woman at a night club and is led into murdering her husband and disposing of his body in the secret spy tunnels built under the Russian sector of the city to monitor communications to Moscow, just before their secrecy was betrayed by the notorious double-agent George Blake. The mixture of real history and spy fiction is key to the novel's impact and McEwan meticulously details the geography and experience of Berlin, hidden from many throughout the Cold War period, though familiar from a wide range of cultural representations in Graham Greene–style thriller noir, Christopher Isherwood's novel *Goodbye to Berlin* and the musical and film which followed it.[4]

In a strategy that has become familiar in his novels, McEwan provides a brief but fascinating 'Author's note' re-grounding the fiction in the historical facts of the CIA-MI6 'Operation Gold' Berlin Tunnel project, noting the involvement of George Blake (*I*, p. 247), acknowledging the help of particular individuals and significantly contextualizing early Cold War 1950s history in his personal end-of-the-Cold-War experience of a visit to the site in 1989, and citing David C. Martin's book *Wilderness of Mirrors* as a source. This eminently scholarly strategy of acknowledging sources was well-judged for a novel with a strong basis in historical fact and factional negotiation with Cold War spy thriller and gothic romance genres, even though in *Comfort of Strangers*, and later in *Atonement*, some commentators accused McEwan of plagiarism from the very works he cited.[5]

The novel invites the reader to investigate its source materials and to revel in the intertextual play they represent. The use that is made of such materials is part of the intrigue, *The Wilderness of Mirrors* being a case in point. It is at once the source of many authentic historical details of the tunnel project, whilst also providing a powerful metaphor in its title for the world of lies, secrecy and intrigue that the Cold War produced for political and for personal relationships in the novel.[6] As Leonard catches a glimpse of himself and his bespectacled face in the mirror in his new quarters, a rich sense of his 'innocence' is developed. This sense defines his professional and emotional situation, working on the secret spying project, but is also symbolic of a wider epistemological condition according to which his knowledge of facts, of other people, and of himself might be said to be distorted by his lack of worldly self-interest and clouded by reflections of his self and his illusions which not even his later retrospective vantage point in the final chapter may fully dispel. As readers, we share Leonard's innocent perspective, which, paradoxically, renders the wealth of historically informed detail all the more believable.

David C. Martin's title, *Wilderness of Mirrors*, thus resonates with a key constituent of McEwan's distinctive aesthetic. In one of the books he may well have ingested as a student of English in the later 1960s, *The Mirror and the Lamp* by the American critic Meyer Abrams, theories of literature are separated into the 'mimetic' and 'expressive' camps indicated by these two metaphors, Abrams's underlying point being to identify the shift from mimetic to expressive theories in Romanticism.[7] Subsequent literary theory deeply complicates such a move and arguably returns to theorizing in terms of the mimetic, though in ways which draw out the more complex inner logic of reflection as opposed to a representation that may be drawn from the image of the mirror.

Such a move might, at any rate, help us to see the relevance to his narrative strategies of McEwan's 'move abroad' to physics in his thinking about subject–object relations. In the introduction to *Or Shall We Die?*, he referred to the 'Theory of Complementarity' of Neils Bohr and Heisenberg's uncertainty principle (*MA*, pp. 13, 15), and the principle of the post-Newtonian quantum universe that 'reality is changed by the presence of the observer' and that 'the observer is a part of what he observes' (*MA*, p. 13). The presence of Thelma Darke, the female physicist who appears in *The Child in Time* (1987), provides a scientific context for the radical shifts in time and parent–child relations as well as gender perspectives which shape that novel. McEwan makes Serena Frome in *Sweet Tooth* a gifted but reluctant mathematician more enthused by the literary and cultural knowledge denied in her chosen educational pathway, yet mathematical concepts of probability (albeit poorly grasped ones) play an interesting role (*ST*, pp. 205–12).

McEwan's Tom Haley, the writer character in *Sweet Tooth,* whom Serena has to recruit as part of the Cold War strategy of covert cultural propaganda, is a highly self-reflexive character. He is the author of a number of short stories, several of which we are shown in detail during the course of the novel and many directly recall the short stories with which McEwan began his own writing career in the 1970s. Among them is the story 'Reflections of a Kept Ape' (*IBS*, pp. 19–35), which is recognizable here in the account of a story narrated by a talking ape given to 'anxious reflections' about his lover (*ST*, p. 193). McEwan revels in the mirror chamber of such self-reflexive literary trickery, drawing on it to create the experience of the unreliability of appearances in a world of espionage or in the potentially treacherous world of misunderstanding between sexual partners which he so excruciatingly explores.

Black Dogs (1992)

Black Dogs drew more directly still on the generation-defining experience of the fall of the Berlin Wall in 1989. It is a novel with a modernistic attention to its formal construction, jumping back and forward in five short sections between the Cold War bookend dates of 1946 and 1989. McEwan uses a personalized narrator, Jeremy, an independent book publisher compiling the memoirs of his parents-in-law, to simulate the historical and biographical curiosity of the reader as if we too were researching their history. From the start, it is a narrative where the presence of the observer is as prominent as that of the events narrated, sensational and powerfully symbolic as they are.

Jeremy's parents-in-law, June and Bernard Tremaine, have separated. He has been soliciting June's memories in a nursing home before she died and these accounts are corroborated or revised with information he elicits from Bernard on their shared trip to Berlin in 1989. By this technique, the reader is afforded a sense of objectivity and of the deep incommensurability there may be between two different accounts of the same events, arising from two different world views. Behind the implied division of political ideologies represented by the Berlin Wall and the Cold War, McEwan constructs a disjuncture between June's intuitive spiritual vision of symbolic evil that has informed her life and Bernard's rational scepticism. Clearly, gender is at stake as well as ideology in this, and a dynamic of gender conflicts and accords recurs throughout the novel. Jeremy sees two contrasting types of certainty emerging from their respective reactions to their wartime experience and, beyond that, a generational divide between himself and both of them. He sees them as certain in their respective beliefs, but himself as orphaned, believing in nothing, attached to no 'enduring principle' or 'fundamental idea' (BD, p. 18), born after the war and living a comparatively affluent, cultured and leisured life whose access to the nightmares of their history comes only through their witnessing and their certainties, which cause him to question his own. He is 'uncertain whether our civilization . . . is cursed by too much or too little belief, whether people like Bernard and June cause the trouble, or people like me' (BD, p. 20).

It is the gradual revelation of a horrific, previously suppressed historical atrocity that drives the evolving story across its various times and locations, and the episodic structure of five parts accentuates the alternation of perspectives between the generations and between the sexes that remains a key feature of McEwan's writing. The dramatic physical landscapes include June's nursing home in Wiltshire, 1980s Berlin, Jeremy's adolescence in Notting Hill, the sublime natural rift of the Gorge de la Vis, and the primeval Dolmen de la Prunarède and village of St Maurice de Navacelles in the Cevennes region of Southern France, where June's defining event has taken place and whose importance as actual as well as symbolic place is acknowledged by McEwan's brief endnote to this novel.

Highly significant also is the Cold War setting of one brief flashback interlude recounting Jeremy's first meeting with his wife Jenny in the Polish city of Lublin and the spontaneous birth of their relationship on a visit to the preserved structure of the Majdanek concentration camp. A feature of the ending of the Cold War division of Europe was the sudden revelation of much previously suppressed traumatic history of the Holocaust. This is vividly portrayed in the scene where the nightmare of the concentration camps, which has been concealed from the liberated Western Europe by the fact of the Cold War, proves to be still horribly visible in the urban landscape of Lublin–Majdanek. Jeremy's reactions are disturbing in their honest, disillusioned, first-hand, non-stereotypical account: 'they lay side-by-side, Lublin and Majdanek, matter and anti-matter' (*BD*, p. 109). He is, as he puts it, 'liberated from the usual constraints of selfhood' by the experience, and with striking results, finding a rare moment of spontaneity in which he does 'something uncharacteristically brilliant', kissing Jenny with whom he spends the rest of the day making love (*BD*, p. 112). Their relationship, bred out of the precariousness of post-war Europe, promises a life-affirming renewal.

In 2016 at a launch of *Nutshell* in Bristol when asked which of his novels a new reader should start with, he suggested *Black Dogs* as an enduring personal favourite. It is a novel whose prominence in the cultural memory is not (or not yet) supported by a widely known film adaptation (such as is the case with *Atonement,* the war novel that followed in 2001), but it remains important and impactful, powerfully concentrating so many of his distinctive narrative strategies, as well as psychological and political concerns.

Sweet Tooth (2012)
The Woman Intelligence Agent

The assured return to Cold War history in *Sweet Tooth* draws on these precedents, bringing the material up to date and closer to home. The novel uses the 1970s setting as a vehicle for the creation of one of McEwan's most complex and convincing women characters to date, for the exploration of conflicts between personal and public relationships, and as an opportunity for an unprecedented level of authorial self-reflection on his own work and on the relationship between readers and writers as it persists in the unnervingly transformed twenty-first century cultural world.

The outline history of the 1970s period is neatly sketched in a series of embedded contextualizing devices that begin with Serena's education in the 'concerns of the day' in leader articles from *The Times* (*ST*, p. 23), which she puts to good effect in her successful job interview with MI5 at the start of chapter 3 (*ST*, pp. 34–6), and then develops in her much better informed discussion with MI5 colleague Max Greatorex, with whom she debates the respective threats to national security in the 1970s posed by the Provisional IRA and the 'grisly factions' of terrorism, as against the hundred and five Soviet agents expelled as a result of the defection of Oleg Lyalin (*ST*, pp. 60–1). Historical detail provides a background of substance for McEwan's imagined private lives: American and Russian support for Israel and Palestine in the Middle East stokes fears of a 'new Cuban Missile Crisis'

(*ST*, pp. 161–2); Serena revives her 'newspaper habit' of reading the 'why-oh-why?' pieces on the state of the nation in the opinion pages (*ST*, pp. 189–90); and news reports of the social unrest of the winter of 1973–4 figure as the backdrop to the start of chapter 20 (*ST*, pp. 267–8).

McEwan's endnote to *The Innocent* cited *The Wilderness of Mirrors* as a key source; the equivalent list of acknowledgements in *Sweet Tooth* (*ST*, p. 323) lists fifteen titles, a substantial reading list for the construction of the novel's world, which includes histories of the 1970s by Dominic Sandbrook, Andy Beckett, Alwyn Turner and Francis Wheen.[8] McEwan acknowledges several of the works that have animated the discussion of the security services in the last decades, including Peter Wright's *Spycatcher* (1987) and histories of MI5 by Christopher Andrew and Thomas Hennessy and Claire Thomas.[9] He also cites R. N. Carew Hunt's *Theory and Practice of Communism*, which dates back to the early Cold War in 1951, and *Reluctant Judas*, a book by Geoffrey Robertson about the IRA informer Kenneth Lennon, found dead in mysterious circumstances in 1974, a book that provides details of the MI5 interest in the Provisionals' terror campaign (*ST*, p. 170).[10] Campaigning journalistic history such as Frances Stonor Saunders's *Who Paid the Piper? The CIA and the Cultural Cold War* is also acknowledged, which – along with studies by Paul Lashmar and James Oliver, Hugh Wilford and Carol Brightman on Mary McCarthy – underpin the heated controversy about the CIA funding of culture that informs the main plot.[11] The sensational headline vocabulary of these source texts – 'cultural cold war', 'writing dangerously', 'reluctant Judas' – charges the anxious atmosphere of the novel throughout, even where it deals with nuanced personal material and adopts an understated tone.

There is ample material here to spawn informed and acute studies by future literary researchers. Especially noteworthy is the explosion of espionage discourse itself, to which this list testifies, and two key texts which inform the novel and the new-century espionage world might be highlighted in this connection. The first is *Open Secret: The Autobiography of the Former Director-General of MI5* by Stella Rimington, the first woman Director General of MI5 from 1992 to 1996, whose name was publicized on her appointment, who has since taken to writing prolific spy fiction under her own name. She appears briefly in the novel as Millie Trimingham (*ST*, p. 39), rendering McEwan's reflection of the contemporary gender composition of the real world of the secret service as topical as was the casting of Judi Dench as M in the millennial James Bond movies from *Goldeneye* (1995) to *Skyfall* (2012).[12] McEwan's topicality goes further here, beyond the question of gender, to speak to the circumstances of the digital information world, rapidly transformed through the apparent digital availability of everything to everybody, in which the reputation of the free world for freedom may depend as much on the freedom of access to sensitive information for an informed public as on the concealment of such information from actual or supposed enemies.

The second key text is *Operation Mincemeat* by Ben Macintyre, the story of the successful disinformation hoax perpetrated by the British intelligence services during the Second World War to distract the Germans from the Allied invasion of Sicily, attributed by Macintyre to none other than Ian Fleming.[13] Added together, these two texts appear to allow McEwan to register a world in which women are no longer at the margins, but at the very centre of power, a world where the work of the secret services may no longer be to be 'secret' so much as to operate within and attempt to manipulate the world of publication and media publicity wherever possible.[14] It is also a world in which the comfortable assumed divide between the real world of the secret intelligence services and the worlds of fiction – whether of James Bond, Stella Rimington, or even of Ian McEwan himself – may be unnervingly subverted, transgressed or lost.

Early in *Sweet Tooth*, Serena reminisces on 'those days', the 'Cold War years of binary thinking' (*ST*, p. 9). Such clear binary opposition between the capitalist west and communist Russia in the early Cold War years, already unsettled in *The Innocent* and *Black Dogs*, is further complicated in the retrospective view on the world of the 1970s in this novel. Along with the destabilized macropolitical binary of America and Russia, the recent history of the cultural sphere is precisely one of destabilized binaries of gender, of race and ethnicity, of social class, between the arts and sciences and between elite and popular cultures. An aspect of McEwan's interest in changing East–West relations may be found in the complex character of the Polish housekeeper Maria in his libretto for the Michael Berkeley oratorio *For You* in 2008.[15] To plot the history of such change in more detail, much of *Sweet Tooth* is given over to an account of the cultural, political and sentimental education of Serena Frome. The character of Tom Haley does not enter until the eleventh of twenty-two chapters and, even then, much of his early function is to continue Serena's literary education. (She is an observant reader and notes a similar strategic use of character in one of Haley's stories, *ST*, p. 105). Much of this material in the novel has a powerful nostalgic quality for any (presumably most) of McEwan's readers who have themselves enjoyed an education in the humanities during the last quarter of a century. For those who may not have done so it provides its own crash course in contemporary literary and cultural history, especially that of the novel.

As significant, then, as the official reading list provided on the acknowledgments page is the extensive reading list indicated in this densely allusive novel itself, a 'polyreferential' work, as Peter Childs has called it.[16] Serena discovers herself through a cultural education that includes such diverse Cold War reference points as Aleksandr Solzhenitsyn's *One Day in the Life of Ivan Denisovich* and Ian Fleming's *Octopussy*: the transition from the latter to the former initiates her decline, as she puts it, (*ST*, p. 8). She imagines herself in the language of an Austen heroine (*ST*, pp. 42–3), and the Camden where she lives as that of the *Dombey and Son* that Tom Haley can quote by heart (*ST*, p. 175). Closer antecedents for her type of character might be found in the works of Doris Lessing, Margaret Drabble, or Iris Murdoch, whose characters she acknowledges as part versions of herself in her bedsit life (*ST*, p. 65); closer still may be those of Muriel Spark, a writer (among others) she later discusses with Haley (*ST*, p. 184). Serena's literary education closely follows the sentimental education of her affair with her first boyfriend's history tutor Tony Canning, then the relationship she initiates with her colleague Max Greatorex (*ST*, pp. 58–62) and then the most intense one that develops with Haley. Her sex life and literary life progress through these three degrees. We might observe that Frome, which (we are told more than once) rhymes with plume (*ST*, pp. 1, 139) – as in *nom de plume?* – also rhymes with James Joyce's narrator of her own sentimental and self-taught literary education, Molly Bloom.

The novel is credibly about an educated intelligence community and draws characters who are marked by their intelligence, so the reader is made aware of the depth and diversity of their intellectual enthusiasms, ranging from Dante (*ST*, p. 8), how to identify edible ceps (*ST*, p. 19), the Elizabethan mathematician John Dee (*ST*, p. 21) and the Saavedra endgame position in chess (which is known for its strategic underpromotion to rook instead of queen *ST*, p. 36). McEwan includes a host of literary references to the literary journals and personalities of the day, including *Encounter* and Stephen Spender, at the centre of a CIA funding scandal in 1967, Ian Hamilton of *The New Review*, Tom Maschler and the iconic Bloomsbury Pillars of Hercules pub (*ST*, p. 258), among a variety of famous meeting places, Fitzrovian literary pubs and restaurants from the era. Avant-garde novelists such as William Kotzwinkle (*ST*, p. 193) and Alan Burns (*ST*, p. 184) are discussed. A list of just the *B*s on the contemporary literature bookshelf, would include J. G. Ballard, A. S. Byatt and Elizabeth Bowen (*ST*, pp. 184–5), as well as Anthony Burgess (*ST*, p. 267) and McEwan's UEA tutor Malcolm Bradbury (*ST*, p. 68). The American agents also boast impressive academic credentials. For example, Pierre, the CIA man who comes to talk on the Sweet Tooth project to the MI5 officers, is an expert on the Spartan Hegemony and on Agesilaus the Second and the beheading of Tissaphernes (*ST*, p. 240).

Sweet Tooth travels lightly through this intimidating world of elite education where even the most contemporary of social symptoms has a Latin or a Greek name. The early McEwan imagined the Cold War as a collective madness presented as sanity (*MA*, p. 4). In this post-millennial re-evaluation, Serena notes Tony Canning's use of the term *akrasia* (acting against one's better judgement), registering a stage beyond *akrasia*, not just in a single character, but in society at large, at least according to the language of the news media in 1972: 'But there *was* no better judgement, nothing to act against. Everyone had gone mad, so everyone said' (*ST*, pp. 23–4).

The character of Serena makes for lightness in McEwan's presentation of such learning: the innocent narrator can carry a huge burden of necessary knowledge and awareness without threatening, excluding or patronizing the reader. Among her many fictional analogues, Charles Highway the comic adolescent narrator of Martin Amis's *The Rachel Papers*, who 'crams' literary knowledge in his attempt to get into Oxford, comes to mind. McEwan highlights the connection, in fact, including a scene in which Tom Haley and Amis share the same platform and Amis reads from this very novel (*ST*, p. 254). In *Sweet Tooth*, the power of innocence is one of the many paradoxical points of resemblance – and also a point of symbiotic relationship – between the worlds of the intelligence services and of cultural knowledge that the novel is able to exploit. Max Greatorex advises her when their relationship breaks up, and her friend Shirley has lost her job, and Serena suspects that she is under surveillance by someone in the service, to 'stop acting as though you know more than you do. You'll end up getting followed' (*ST*, p. 133). Mostly this is advice she hardly needs. In her first briefing for the Sweet Tooth project, she is described by Harry Tapp as being 'awfully well read and quite in with the scene' of contemporary literature, to which she modestly responds: 'I like reading in my spare time, sir' (*ST*, p. 88). Throughout, her straightforward Alice-in-Wonderland curiosity guides her into the strange worlds of the secret service, and of literary learning, where her agency as a bearer of cultural intelligence and the values of civilization can succeed at different complex levels. The innocent narrator can be a strategy in fiction as effective as the underpromotion of the pawn in the Saavedra ending in chess.

Reader–Writer Relations

It is an engaging paradox of Serena's situation, and that of Tom Haley as he begins to enter and gradually become more prominent within the narrative, that they seem to represent the best values of civilization and intelligence when they are least attempting to do so. This deftly understated defence of Western Civilization is apparently ingested by Serena during her affair with Tony Canning, even before she knows she is being drawn into the world of Defence. 'Thanks to Tony', she thinks, 'I now knew with what trouble it had been assembled, Western civilisation, imperfect as it was' (*ST*, p. 38). Though he turns out to have been a double agent, Tony's civilizing values remain a positive force in her education and prepare the reader for the idea which gradually emerges in *Sweet Tooth*: that in the longer term, intellectual freedom is its own best defence, the best creative writer or artist being a witting or unwitting 'secret agent' of freedom, whether funded by the state or not.

The first chapters of *Sweet Tooth* chart Serena's education, but it is in chapter 7, when her mission becomes clear, that 'the story began' (*ST*, p. 86), as she puts it, and from this point (after she cannily negotiates a work promotion on the strength of it), the scrutiny of Haley's work and the assessment of his suitability as an MI5 agent – or to put it another way, the construction of McEwan's portrait of the artist as a young man – begins. Haley is a splendidly judged creation of a writer of that period, who has traces of McEwan himself, but also many features that make him a plausibly representative figure for a moment when a new generation of writers was emerging, and a renaissance of serious literary fiction in England was in the offing.

Chapter 8 comprises Serena's study of an invented short story by Haley, a conscientious combination of plot summary, inserted quotation and a mix of personal and professional reflections on the story that construct, just as tellingly as the figure of an author, the figure of the reader of, and in, the text. The chapter is thus a clever double-parody by McEwan: on the one hand, we have a certain type of story, of marital complication amongst the English middle classes, containing elements indicative of a number of the more serious novelists of the era; and on the other hand, we have a certain kind of literary reader response, genuine and intelligent, if not always informed by the latest academic literary criticism. Had, for example, Serena been a real student of literature at degree level in the early 1970s, she might well have encountered (along with the postmodern writers her 'sophisticated friends' press on her, *ST*, p.77) that classic essay by Roland Barthes 'The Death of the Author', first published in 1967, which steers the academic critic away from authorial determinants of meaning and the figure of the author.[17] Serena, by contrast, feels herself a 'born empiricist' (*ST*, p. 76) and allows her experience of reading to be 'skewed' by being about to meet the author in person (*ST*, p. 109). The title of Haley's story, 'This is Love', is a richly ironic title (noticeably unlike the sensational Cold War titles of McEwan's acknowledged sources for the novel), and it might well gesture towards another well-known work by Barthes from 1977, *A Lover's Discourse*.[18] Barthes's later work did not address the reader–writer relations as directly as the earlier one, but it certainly worked to efface the binary relationship between the reader and the writer at a theoretical level and so seems an appropriate point of reference for a novel in which we see the relationship of reader and writer develop from a professional relationship into a love relationship. McEwan's version of this relationship is also suggestive in being a Cold War relationship of secret lovers and collaborators in the narrative that follows. At the end of the chapter, Serena thinks, 'if I hadn't wasted three years being bad at maths at Cambridge, I might have done English and learned how to read. But would I have known how to read T. H. Haley?' (*ST*, p. 109). This is a good literary-critical as well as an autobiographical question for her, as the reader of the teasing *mise-en-abyme* or wilderness of mirrors that is *Sweet Tooth* might well be thinking, at some self-reflexive level, about 'how to read' and what makes or does not make a good reading of such a nuanced literary text.

As the novel continues, Serena's self-conscious reading of Haley's fiction, and the reader's self-conscious reading of both, become a fascinating experience. Indeed, the reader–writer relation is something that she tries to articulate: 'writers owed their readers a duty of care, or mercy' she thinks at one point (*ST*, p. 105), hoping that the author will not be too hard on his main character, despite his weaknesses. Later on, she distrusts the 'fictional trick' embodied in the story of the kept ape, believing that there is an 'unwritten contract' with the reader that the invented world 'had to be as solid and self-consistent as the actual' (*ST*, p. 193).

The application of legalistic language to the writer–reader 'contract', subject to a 'duty of care' stems from Serena's embroilment in government officialdom, but it also ironically foreshadows a key episode in Haley's career: the mini-crisis that results from his departure from politically innocuous brief fictions of bourgeois life, to his first foray into a longer novel conceived as an anti-capitalist post-apocalyptic dystopia entitled *From the Somerset Levels*. Haley's ability to convince and engage Serena as a reader is supported by the basic kind of contract she describes. At a subtler level, *Sweet Tooth* establishes a more sophisticated kind of contract with its readers, always being on the verge of revealing the 'open secrets' of its own construction, of the fact that its fictional world, and perhaps even also the supposedly real worlds of politics and public life, have a necessarily fictive dimension. Max Greatorex attempts to warn Serena that the line between imagination and reality is blurred 'a big grey space', where you imagine things 'and you can make them come true' (*ST*, p. 134).

In the novel's denouement, Serena's deepening dilemma revolves around her inability to reveal her identity as an MI5 agent to Tom without, she fears, destroying the unwritten contract on which their love affair has been based. Her innocence consists in her fear that their love may not survive the collapse of this basic contract. Suffice it to say that, in plot terms, this innocence is challenged by the final chapter in which the dynamic of innocence and experience, the reader and the writer, the spy and the spied upon, the narrator and the narrated, and the blurred grey space between the fictional and the real, are called into question, and where there is some suggestion that a deep emotional relationship may thrive on the excitement of betrayals and deceptions as much as on contractual literalism.

That chapter is written in the form of a letter and, like so much in *Sweet Tooth*, plays on intertextual resonance both within and beyond Mc-Ewan's earlier writing. The retrospective epilogue to *The Innocent* comes immediately to mind as a precedent for a mode of closure which offers a temporally distanced perspective on the action we have witnessed. The narrative technique of the final chapter in the novel may also be an acknowledgment of D. H. Lawrence's *Lady Chatterley's Lover*, which ends with a chapter in the form of a letter from Mellors to his absent lover Connie which gives some readers a new perspective on his character. McEwan here adds a radical twist of perspective indicating that Haley may not have been an entirely innocent party in their relationship, but was potentially using Serena for his purposes as much as she has used him for hers. Cold wars between the sexes, between ideologies, between reader and writer, literature and politics and fiction and reality have been the stuff of McEwan's fiction from the 1970s and he returns to them in this remarkable, self-reflexive fiction of his maturity. Early in the novel the learned CIA man Pierre floats the widely resonant idea that the more interesting part of the Cold War is that it is a 'war of ideas' (*ST*, p. 240). He also says that the Cold War is not over (*ST*, p. 244), which has proved true in the historical context, and recurs as a disturbing thought for our political times once again, and as an intriguing one for the reader of McEwan's fiction, speculating on how it might resurface and in what guises in his work somewhere, in another time.

NOTES

1 *The Letters of D.H. Lawrence Volume II*, eds. George J. Zytaruk and James T. Boulton (Cambridge: Cambridge University Press, 1981), p. 218.
2 Dominic Head, *Ian McEwan* (Manchester: Manchester University Press, 2007), pp. 91–119.
3 Martin Amis, *Einstein's Monsters* (London: Jonathan Cape, 1987).
4 See Richard Brown, 'A Wilderness of Mirrors: The Mediated Berlin Backgrounds for Ian McEwan's *The Innocent' Anglistik: International Journal of English Studies* (Heidelberg), 21 (September 2010), 2, pp. 49–56.
5 McEwan responded to the claims that he had plagiarized from *No Time for Romance* by Lucilla Andrews in an article in *The Guardian*, 27 November 2006. His adaptation of a line by Craig Raine at the close of *A Comfort of Strangers* is recalled in a reference by Mark Lawson in his review of *Saturday* in *The Guardian* (22 January 2005) to the use of lines by Raine for the poetry of Daisy Perowne.
6 McEwan did not just draw on the historical details in Martin's book. For example, he also borrows an anecdote about a dog named George, the warehouse mascot, mistaken for a soldier who might be compromised. See David C. Martin, *Wilderness of Mirrors* (1980; Guilford, CT: The Lyons Press, 2003), p. 82.
7 M. H. Abrams *The Mirror and the Lamp* (Oxford: Oxford University Press, 1953), pp. 30–5.
8 These historical works are: Dominic Sandbrook, *State of Emergency: The Way We Were Britain 1970–1974* (London: Allen Lane, 2010); Andy Beckett, *When the Lights Went Out: What Really Happened to Britain in the Seventies* (London: Faber, 2010); Alwyn W. Turner, *Crisis? What Crisis? Britain in the 1970s* (London: Aurum Press, 2008) and Francis Wheen, *Strange Days Indeed: The Golden Age of Paranoia* (London: Harper Collins, 2008).
9 Full details of these works are: Peter Wright, *Spycatcher: The Candid Autobiography of a Senior Intelligence Officer* (Australia: Heinemann, 1987); Christopher Andrew, *The Defence of the Realm: The Authorized History of MI5* (Canada: Penguin, 2009); Thomas Hennessey and Claire Thomas, *Spooks: The Unofficial History of MI5* (London: Amberley Publishing, 2010) and R. N. Carew Hunt, *The Theory and Practice of Communism: An Introduction* (1951; London: Penguin Books, 1973).
10 Geoff Robertson, *Reluctant Judas: Life and Death of the Special Branch Informer Kenneth Lennon* (London: Maurice Temple Smith, 1976).
11 See Frances Stonor Saunders, *Who Paid the Piper? The CIA and the Cultural Cold War* (London: Granta, 2009); Paul Lashmar and James Oliver, *Britain's Secret Propaganda War: 1948–1977* (London: Sutton Publishing, 1998); Hugh Wilford, *The CIA, the British Left and the Cold War: Calling the Tune?* (London: Routledge, 2003) and Carol Brightman, *Writing Dangerously: Mary McCarthy and Her World* (New York: Clarkson Potter, 1992).
12 Stella Rimington, *Open Secret: The Autobiography of the Former Director-General of MI5* (London: Hutchinson, 2001).
13 Ben Macintyre, *Operation Mincemeat* (London: Bloomsbury, 2010).
14 Christopher Andrew describes Rimington's agenda as 'the demystification of the Service and the creation of a more informed public and media perception' (*Defence of the Realm*, p. 30).

15 Ian McEwan, *For You* (London: Vintage, 2008).

16 Peter Childs 'Ian McEwan's *Sweet Tooth*: "Put in Porphyry and Marble Do Appear"', in *Ian McEwan*, second edition, ed. Sebastian Groes (London: Bloomsbury, 2014), pp. 139–43 (p. 139).

17 Roland Barthes, 'The Death of the Author', in *Image, Music, Text* (London: Fontana, 1977), pp. 142–8.

18 Roland Barthes, *A Lover's Discourse*, trans. Richard Howard (London: Jonathan Cape, 1979).

6

PETER CHILDS

The Construction of Childhood

McEwan's most common representation of childhood is arguably one of threatened vulnerability. Actual children frequently also feature in his novels as potential victims or endangered innocents (the opening chapter of *Enduring Love* is exemplary in this regard, with its arresting image of an escaped helium balloon containing a solitary child). Even when there is a portrayal of a violent and aggressive child, such as Henry in McEwan's film script for *The Good Son* or 'The Bully' in *The Daydreamer*, it is the harm posed to other children that is the main focus of interest.

This chapter outlines how the depiction of childhood and the treatment of children appears to serve throughout McEwan's fiction as a barometer for social care in its broadest sense: from the concern with child neglect and abuse in the early stories of the 1970s, through the loss of children and the pointed childlessness of adult protagonists in the middle works of the 1980s and 1990s, to the centrality once more of vulnerable children, one of them unborn, in his most recent works, *The Children Act* and *Nutshell*, which touch on the role of the state in the twenty-first century.

As this summary suggests, the chapter points up how the concept of childhood in McEwan's work is steeped in innocence and absence as recurring touchstones. With the exception of his writing for child readers, after *The Cement Garden* in 1978, children hardly appear as anything other than minor characters in McEwan's novels up until *Atonement* in 2001. Despite this, the figure of the child is a perennial missing presence in his work. Similarly, references to literal or figurative surrogates ('science was Thelma's child [Charles was another]' in *The Child in Time* [*CT*, p. 43]) or to adopted children (as when Adam asks Fiona to adopt him in *The Children Act*) recur throughout the fiction. We can also see the importance of the child as metaphor in McEwan's fiction, exemplified in Katherina Dodou's focus on figurative uses of the child and on childhood imagery across McEwan's fiction, including novels such as *Saturday*.[1]

However, before trying to understand childhood further in relation to McEwan's writing, it needs consideration as a concept. For example, in her essay on 'The Historical Construction of Childhood', Diana Gittins notes that 'childhood is a more general and abstract notion than the concept of the child' and is 'used to refer to the status ascribed by adults to those who are defined as not adult'.[2] Gittins observes that 'childhood' is a modern invention (arguably dating from the sixteenth century) that, though deemed universal, has changed over time. Understanding of the concept has also varied with, for example, gender – childhood for boys traditionally ended with entry into the world of work and childhood for girls traditionally ceased with marriage, at whatever age. Childhood, she concludes, is 'a fiction interwoven with personal memories', which is amplified in LuAnn Walther's argument that as a concept childhood is not just the invention of adults, but 'reflects adult needs and adult fears quite as much as it figures the absence of adulthood'.[3]

McEwan's understanding of childhood is undoubtedly modern, indebted to a degree to the conception of the child popularized by Rousseau (of innate innocence only corrupted through experience of the world),[4] but exemplified in the Romantic poets' portrayal of the innately good child whose innocence is corrupted by adults, as subsequently dramatized in the images of child labour and exploitation pervading the industrial settings used by myriad nineteenth-century novelists, from Hugo (for example, in *Les Misérables*) to Dickens. If the presence of a right and proper childhood became a Victorian concern, the effect on the child of its absence might best be noted in Mayhew's *London Labour and the London Poor*, first published in 1861. At one point, Mayhew meets an eight-year-old street seller, the Watercress Girl, who seems to be a child physically but not mentally. When he speaks to her of what he assumes to be childhood staples, such as going to the park, or toys and friends, he finds she has no experience of them – or of 'play' more generally. Mayhew associates childhood with the right to indulgence in carefree pleasures, during which the child should be protected from the adult world of work and responsibility – a viewpoint epitomized in *The Child in Time* through Charles Darke's regression to playing in the woods in a novel as much concerned with the lost child within the adult as lost children *per se*. When the novel's protagonist Stephen Lewis recalls his stolen daughter Kate, he fondly remembers 'her lessons in celebrating the specific', and asks himself: 'wasn't that Nietzsche's idea of true maturity, to attain the seriousness of a child at play?' (*CT*, pp. 105–6). McEwan's focus on lost childhood innocence echoes the perceived loss of a state of natural grace since the industrial revolution that is associated with the transfer of workers and their families from the country to the city, the field to the factory – hence the title and *mise-en-scène* of his first novel, *The Cement Garden*, as if the ideal of an Edenic childhood is itself encased in concrete. Yet, as suggested, McEwan's view of childhood has broadened over the course of his writing, from the emphasis on the neglect and abuse of innocence in the early work, through a concern with childcare in families in the middle period, to a fuller consideration of the subject against a social canvas typical of his novels in the twenty-first century, as in *The Children Act*, which couches welfare in childhood in terms of preparation for the ideal features of adulthood, based on a judicial definition embracing 'economic and moral freedom, virtue, compassion and altruism', as well as 'satisfying work', the 'esteem of others' and 'at the centre of one's life a small number of significant relations defined above all by love' (*CA*, p. 15).

This essay looks at examples from each of these three periods of McEwan's career to suggest both continuities and changes in his perspective on the construction of childhood. His early writing, such as the short stories, together with *The Cement Garden* and its micro-community of abandoned siblings, gave rise to the impression that McEwan was interested in how children might behave differently when isolated from their elders, particularly in relation to sex and aggression.[5] Mary Kehily argues that 'the idea of childhood innocence in the West retains its strength as an adult ideal, something which adults would like children to be.'[6] This is maintained by boundaries and taboos that both reinforce symbolic distinctions between adults and children and create the conditions for the acts of transgression which McEwan's early work sought to explore. Six of the eight stories in the first collection, *First Love, Last Rites*, contain examples of mistreated and exploited children. 'Homemade' is an inaugural tale of abuse as a brother determines to rape his sister in order to lose his virginity; 'Last Day of Summer' concludes with a child drowning after a boat capsizes; 'Butterflies' ends with a dead girl floating in the water, after the story's narrator sexually abuses her beside a canal; 'Conversations with a Cupboard Man' recounts a story of infantilization and arrested development, leaving the narrator wanting 'to be one year old again' (*FL*, p.87); 'First Love, Last Rites' features child neglect; and 'Disguises' closes with the assault of a child.

Only with his third novel *The Child in Time* does McEwan really begin to place concerns for child safety and care into a broader social and philosophical context, while asking what significance childhood and children play in the psychological well-being of adults: 'Kate's growing up had become the essence of time itself ... without the fantasy of her continued existence he was lost, time would stop. He was the father of an invisible child' (*CT*, p. 8). Since the abduction of his daughter Kate, Stephen Lewis feels her constant absent presence as a parent, but, as a participant member of one of the

subcommittees in the government's Childcare Commission, he is simultaneously involved in impassioned debate over the upbringing of children and
the role of the child in the future of society. Here he is dismayed to find that
'there was no richer field for speculation assertively dressed as fact than
childcare', a field defined by shifting ideologies: 'for three centuries, generations of experts, priests, moralists, social scientists, doctors – mostly men –
had been pouring out instructions and ever-mutating facts for the benefit of
mothers' (CT, p. 80).

Stephen is struck by the persistently assertive and yet contradictory advice
given to parents, including 'how children should be allowed to do whatever
they want so that their divine natures can blossom, and how it is never too
soon to break a child's will' (CT, p. 80). This image of guidance oscillating
from one viewpoint to another is also McEwan's starting point, and he
imagines a fresh intervention by the state: The *Authorised Childcare Handbook*, published by Her Majesty's Stationery Office and aimed to counter
'the pallid relativism of self-appointed childcare experts' (CT, p. 7). A key
pejorative term here is 'self-appointed', implicitly asserting that direct advice
should be regulated as well as consistent and prescriptive; also, that the
giving and receiving of guidance in parenting is not a matter for individuals,
but that recommendations should be sanctioned by institutional authority.

As a novelist, McEwan's entrance to this discussion is partly through the
position of the writer in relation to children's literature. Just as childhood is
an invention of adults, Stephen finds the publisher Charles Darke explaining
to him 'as though to a child' that there is no distinction between fiction for
children and for adults. Darke goes on to assert that 'the greatest so-called
children's books were precisely those that spoke to both children and adults,
to the incipient adult within the child, to the forgotten child within the adult'
(CT, p. 31). An implication, underscored by Darke's later behaviour, is that
childhood is timeless, lived in the present moment, but also a way of being
that is not the sole province of children (CT, p. 33).

In *The Child in Time*, McEwan portrays a late twentieth-century British
society in which the control of childhood is deemed by the state to be integral
to the production of self-reliant citizens. The *Authorised Childcare Handbook* thus aims at the reduction of play and dependence, emphasizing that
'childhood is a privilege', and that every child should remember the economic cost and consequent social obligation of this privilege 'as it grows
older' (CT, p. 93). The purpose of the Handbook is, therefore, to provide a
template for the education of children in responsibility and authority, and to
naturalize this perspective, so that (for example) the duties dictated by the
clock 'are as incontestable as the tides' (CT, p. 27). The ultimate analogy
used by the Handbook makes plain that childhood is seen as debilitating, a

'disease ... from which growing up is the slow and difficult recovery' (*CT*, p. 179).

Neil Postman had argued in 1982 that, exposed to the same images and media influences, children were increasingly similar to their parents, losing special status in terms of their vulnerability, innocence and dependency. Postman also pointed to the creation in the age of digital media of the adult-child as the only category in between infancy and senility, an individual characterized as 'a grown-up whose intellectual and emotional capacities are unrealized and, in particular, not significantly different from those associated with children', which Postman attributes to the flourishing of television and a decline in literacy beside the rising tide of information, stressing the 'minimal role ideological premises, logical consistency and force, or adeptness with language play in the assessment of a television image'.[7] McEwan arguably sees the new category more as a consequence of authoritarianism, re-creating citizens as children in response to social control and political patronage. Watching television, Stephen berates the audience on a daytime television show 'as infants who longed for nothing more than to be told when to laugh', while the text portrays him as similarly infantilized, sucking at a bottle and imagining summary justice for these 'enfeebled souls' (*CT*, pp. 124–5).

Through such comparisons, McEwan postulates that a generation is inescapably reflected in its attitude towards the nurturing and education of children. This goes some way to explain the novel's title, which is in part an allusion to the various designs on and desire for childhood that run throughout the narrative.[8] The title additionally embraces the idea of 'childhood across time', not least because it has a major concern with the ways in which the concept of 'the child' is created and positioned by adults, so that childhood becomes 'an historical construction'.[9] This involves not just reinvention, but historicization as well. It has been argued that in medieval times there was no concept of childhood in contrast with a contemporary view that the child is a nascent individual who at least needs to be nurtured and educated for adulthood. The period in between crucially saw the evolution across the seventeenth to nineteenth centuries of modern schooling and the privatization of the family, segregating children from wider society and characterizing them primarily in terms of innocence and investment. McEwan explains that he was partly inspired by reading Christina Hardyment's book *Dream Babies*, which first suggested to him the idea that childcare manuals accurately indicate 'the spirit of an age': 'You have the intense regulation of the Victorian notion of breaking a child's will, followed by a rather sentimental child-centred Edwardian view, followed by the rather grisly pseudo-scientific notion of childcare that predominated in the 1920s and '30s, with a lot of input from behaviourists, and then in 1948 ... Spock'.[10]

In *The Child in Time*, the childcare handbook secretly commissioned by the Prime Minister's office is leaked anonymously to the press while the Official Commission on Childcare is still deliberating its report. Its aim is to address 'falling standards of behaviour and lack of civic responsibility', especially in young people (*CT*, p. 181). However, while the handbook intends to illustrate how the nation can be 'regenerated by reformed child-care practice' (*CT*, p. 162), McEwan aims to show how little decisive control those in authority can exercise over their children's future, from the micro-level of Kate's loss under Stephen's care to the macro-level of nation building.

The Child in Time begins with the disappearance of a little girl and ends with the birth of a baby in an analogous private example of renewed responsibility for childcare. The sex of this newborn child is unknown, leaving the reader with a sense of open-endedness (the baby could be the child 'in time' to save its parents' relationship). The reason for this indeterminacy is made explicit in other work McEwan undertook in the 1980s while drafting *The Child in Time*, which he began in 1983. In particular, he developed his thinking while working on the 1981 libretto for Michael Berkeley's oratorio *Or Shall We Die?*, in which McEwan pitches a masculine aggressiveness against the need he then perceived for what he termed 'womanly times'.[11] In *The Child in Time*, he consequently paints a society rooted in 'masculine times' and nuclear threat where authoritarianism is exemplified in the state-licensing of beggars. Pitted against this are the different Einsteinian temporal possibilities offered by the scientist Thelma Darke and a belief in the alternative of 'constant flux' advocated by the grieving mother Julie, for whom hope lies 'in endless mutability, in re-making yourself as you came to understand more' (*CT*, p. 54). This expresses the life-affirming 'feminine' possibility that McEwan opposes to patriarchy and is perhaps most clearly dramatized by Stephen's pregnant mother's decision not to abort the baby she is carrying when she sees his adult self in a moment of premonition across a curve in time. As in the womanly times of *Or Shall We Die?*, this is an assertion of life against the threat of destruction, and McEwan writes in his introduction to the libretto how 'love of children generates a fierce ambition for the world to continue and be safe, and makes one painfully vulnerable to fantasies of loss' (*MA*, p. 5).

It is *The Child in Time*'s concern with the meaning of childhood that has attracted most attention, yet its equally important preoccupation with children becoming adults and adults turning into children is common in

McEwan's novels since *The Cement Garden*. The focus on transformation is most evident in McEwan's novel for children, *The Daydreamer* (1994). The conceit of the seven interlinked stories in this book is that daydreaming is an out-of-body experience where the imagination takes the mind far from the individual's physical environment – a theme revived in *Atonement*. Each of the stories in *The Daydreamer* concerns metamorphosis: the daydreamer's projection into another kind of body, such as a doll or a cat, a baby or a grown-up; or the transformation of others from mother's boy into bully or old lady into burglar. It is in the final story that McEwan confronts childhood's uneasy relationship with the adult body. In the daydreamer's twelfth year, he begins 'to notice just how different the worlds of children and grown-ups were' (*D*, p. 86). It is here that McEwan makes explicit his debt to Kafka by transforming the famous first sentence of *Metamorphosis* into this premise: 'The following morning Peter Fortune woke from troubled dreams to find himself transformed into a giant person, an adult' (*D*, p. 89).

By alluding to Gregor Samsa's overnight metamorphosis into a huge insect, McEwan is suggesting both the importance of imagination and (day)dreaming to the inventions that underpin fiction and the inevitable, painful transformation of adolescence resisted by his protagonist.[12] Drawing on another key intertext, McEwan quite likely chose the name Peter because of the eponymous character in J. M. Barrie's 1904 play *Peter Pan, or The Boy Who Wouldn't Grow Up* and the well-known opening to the subsequent 1911 novel *Peter Pan*, which begins: 'all children, except one, grow up'. Hence, Peter Fortune is positioned as a boy who wishes to revel in childhood play and whose nightmare is to be turned into an adult, 'a giant person', as though this transformation itself were something grotesque.

Echoing the sentiments of Charles Darke, McEwan's 'Preface' says that *The Daydreamer* was written as 'a book for adults in a language that children could understand'.[13] McEwan's other work in a language that children can understand is *Rose Blanche*, a story book illustrated by Roberto Innocenti, originally with French-language text by Christophe Gollaz. For his story set in Germany in the Second World War, Innocenti chose as his protagonist a blonde-haired, blue-eyed German girl who he called Rose Blanche in tribute to a youthful German resistance movement *die Weisse Rose*. The book was published in Britain with an English-language text by McEwan, whose attraction to the tragic story of a young girl who brings food to Jewish children in a concentration camp and is herself killed in crossfire when the Russians invade, was almost certainly partially because of its depiction of the barbarous ways in which children can be mistreated, and also the ways in which, as McEwan observes right up to *The Children Act*, the welfare of children can be ignored by feuding adults.[14]

Such a thematic concern throws a sidelight on McEwan's most celebrated work, *Atonement*, in which three children of divorcing parents are shipped out to the relatives at the heart of the story only to encounter further threats: two of the children, nine-year-old twin boys, run away into the night under fear of punishment while the other, their fifteen-year-old sister, is sexually assaulted in the search for her brothers. At the heart of the narrative is Briony, a thirteen-year-old girl trying to understand the adult world, which is most frequently presented in the novel as one of threat, neglect, violence and menace.

Prefiguring the extreme example of *Nutshell*, *Atonement* recalls such novels as *What Maisie Knew* and *The Go-Between* in depicting adults' sexualized behaviour from the perspective of a child. When a girl, Briony feels that she will mature through experience of real life, in which the process of becoming involves cutting away 'the sickly dependency of infancy and early childhood' until 'real events, not her own fantasies, rose to her challenge, and dispelled her insignificance' (*At*, pp. 74, 77). Thinking that she is emerging from her childhood, Briony has yet to encompass the breadth of adult comprehension at this point. Stationed symbolically on a bridge, she stands poised between possibilities such as inexperience and experience, pre- and post-adolescence and imaginative fiction and quotidian reality. Consequently, she misses the truths of adults' experience, conjuring the world for herself through 'a trick of her imagination' (*At*, p.177), such that her mother thinks she is 'always off and away in her mind', oblivious to the 'self-evident world' (*At*, p.68).

In Briony, McEwan presents the child and the writer together, in the sense that her story is fictionalized by Briony herself, but also in the sense that the child and the novelist both fashion narratives from imagination, are both 'daydreamers' in the novel's terms, curious how the 'arena of adult emotion and dissembling' in others' lives might benefit their writing (*At*, p.113). Briony thinks her childhood has 'ended' (*At*, p. 160), meaning that she has moved from mere stories to what she takes to be an adult conception of life, 'strange and deceptive' (*At*, p.158). In words that describe both his and Briony's position well, McEwan says in an interview that, 'on the whole, it doesn't suit novelists to be collaborators. We are so used to playing God by ourselves'.[15] It is notable that he puts Briony in a similar position where her imagination may run wild, largely unfettered by the society of siblings and peers. The ten-year age difference between Briony and her sister Cecilia is important in this regard (their brother Leon is several years older again) because McEwan effectively presents Briony as an only child. There is the considerable age difference but also, on the pivotal day on which the novel opens in 1935, Cecilia is newly returned from university and, while her sister has been at Cambridge, Briony has grown from a pre-pubescent girl into an adolescent asking herself questions of selfhood and sexuality. The opposite of Peter Fortune, she cannot wait for the end of childhood and yearns to be transformed.

McEwan's most recent inquiry into childhood is *The Children Act*, in which he debates the legal arena where responsible adults arbitrate over the 'bitterly contested destinies of children'.[16] Fiona Maye, a childless sixty-year-old High Court Judge in the Family Division, repeatedly weighs up the question of the care of other people's children, always asking what is in the best interests of this boy or that girl. The short novel/novella opens with an epigraph that is a quotation from Section 1(a) of the 1989 Children Act: 'when a court determines any question with respect to ... the upbringing of a child ... the child's welfare shall be the court's paramount consideration'. The Children Act is the legislation covering the protection of children in Britain and it places the child's welfare over and above the parents' wishes and the state's interests. In light of this emphasis, McEwan's narrative concentrates on the effects on Fiona of taking responsibility, judicial and personal, for the lives of others.

In a novel concerned with the different questions of what is moral and what is legal, what is deemed to be 'right' and what is sanctioned by law, the first lives to come under Fiona's consideration are those of conjoined twins, Matthew and Mark, who share only one organ but who will die within six months if not separated.[17] If a surgical intervention is allowed, Mark alone could live a normal healthy life. The hospital's request to operate is opposed by the twins' Catholic parents who believe only God may make decisions of life and death. The medical threat to Mark from this perspective is thus not so much from Matthew, which can be ameliorated, as from their parents. The counter perspective is that Matthew is at threat from the hospital. Proceeding from the overriding principle of the welfare of the children, Fiona's concluding argument in favour of intervention is one of intent: that the surgery is not intended to kill Matthew, but to save Mark, who is under threat of fatal harm (*CA*, p. 28). The twins' parents would similarly argue that their position seeks to do no harm to Mark and that their stance is the moral one because it does no harm to Matthew. However, Fiona concludes that Matthew has no interests, from a legal point of view, and only Mark's welfare can be reasonably taken into consideration.

Fiona is deeply troubled by the case and lies awake at night going over the judgment while turning over in her mind both thoughts of her childlessness, together with her husband's declaration that he is going to have an affair, and of the letters she has received from those such as the Archbishop of Westminster, who declare it wrong to interfere with God's purpose. The experience leaves Fiona emotionally numb, squeamish about bodies, and desirous of a purely mental existence (*CA*, p. 31). Fiona is still disturbed by the case when she encounters another in which religious principle seems to gainsay secular rationality. A hospital in Wandsworth needs to transfuse a cancer patient to save his life, but both he, an only child of seventeen, and his parents, Jehovah's Witnesses, refuse. Fiona reflects – in the process drawing a distinction between this novel's twenty-first century setting and the time of McEwan's early fiction – that 'back in the 1980s a judge could still have made the teenager a ward of court and seen him in chambers or hospital or at home'. This was a time when 'a noble ideal had somehow survived into the modern era'. The old method may have been 'slow and inefficient', but it 'preserved the human touch', whereas now 'the lives of children were held in computer memory' (*CA*, pp. 35–6).

This train of thought, largely about changes consequent upon the 1989 Children Act, spurs Fiona to make a hospital visit to meet the boy with leukaemia, Adam Henry, while still reflecting on her own situation; she feels she has sacrificed the chance of raising children to a successful law career, culminating in 'rueful thoughts of adoption', vacillations about 'surrogate mothers', before she realizes that her profession is her sole vocation (*CA*, p. 45). Such reflections highlight the way in which McEwan pits reason against emotion, which is in part a consideration of the competing claims on human beings of religion and science, but they also personalize the responsible duty of care towards children shared by parents, society and those entrusted with power over children's welfare, such as Fiona.

Playing repeatedly with the title's dual concern with legal guidance and personal agency, the narrative from now on hinges on a prolonged consideration of Adam's welfare in the light of a series of Fiona's deliberations. The first concerns a formulation of 'Gillick competence' by Lord Scarman, which maintains that a minor may consent to medical treatment 'if and only when the child achieves sufficient understanding and intelligence to understand fully what is proposed' (*CA*, p. 83). On the one hand, Adam is an intelligent, thoughtful, assertive seventeen-year-old. On the other hand, he does not fully appreciate the ordeal that awaits him if a transfusion is denied – though, without extensive briefing and counselling, neither would he if he were a year older. A second consideration is introduced by Fiona, who decides she is not finally influenced by whether Adam fully comprehends his situation, but by what his welfare dictates: she makes her judgement following the precedent of a very similar case (a famous real-life case that McEwan is drawing on);[18] and she shows how this precedent aligns with 'the clear injunction of the Children Act of 1989' with its emphasis on 'the primacy of the child's welfare' (*CA*, p. 121).

Fiona therefore overrules the wishes of Adam and of his parents to refuse a transfusion, concluding that Adam 'must be protected from such a decision. He must be protected from his religion and from himself' (*CA*, p. 123). In terms of McEwan's narrative concern, the most significant aspects to this ruling are not only Fiona's adherence to the guidance of the Children Act, but also the personal impact on her of a professional position of authority over the life of another. For example, Fiona subsequently receives letters from Adam explaining, first, that his actual parents are delighted that he has been saved without them having to go against their faith, and second that he himself wishes Fiona, with her clarity of thought, her *authority*, to tell him what to make of this new turn of events.

It is here that Fiona's personal responsibility for Adam's welfare, as opposed to her judicial responsibility as a High Court judge in the Family Division, reaches a peak of intensity. Adam follows her when she leaves London on circuit to hear cases that would otherwise themselves need to travel to the law courts in the capital. Fiona is at dinner in Newcastle, when Adam, who has pursued her from King's Cross, suddenly arrives, drenched from the rain.

McEwan here introduces a major intertext that he also alluded to in *Saturday*, James Joyce's 'The Dead'.[19] Just as Adam and Fiona shared together at his bedside a musical performance of Yeats's 'Down by the Salley Gardens', in Joyce's story Gretta is haunted by the memory of Michael Furey singing 'The Lass of Aughrim' during their courting days in Galway. Though only seventeen, Adam's age, Michael Furey died when Gretta left for her convent in Dublin. She was in love with him (more than she is in middle age with her steadfast husband Gabriel) and believes that Furey's passionate insistence on walking out in the rain to see her while already sick led to his death. When Gabriel asks if Furey died of consumption, Gretta replies that she thinks he died for her.[20] In middle age, Gretta assumes a responsibility for Furey's death that parallels Fiona's responsibility for Adam's welfare. In McEwan's novel, Fiona turns Adam away into the rain again, but also, as the boy leaves to depart in a car, moves to kiss his cheek. At the last moment, he turns his mouth towards her: 'if it was possible to kiss chastely full on the lips, this was what she did' (*CA*, p. 169).

McEwan's narrative ends just before Christmas with Fiona preparing a recital for the annual court Revels in the Great Hall. She receives from Adam a poem, 'The Ballad of Adam Henry', pointedly stating that 'Her kiss was the kiss of Judas' (*CA*, p. 181), and, in one of several parallels, written in imitation of the rhythm as well as the 'young and foolish' theme of 'Down by the Salley Gardens'. At the concert Fiona accompanies a colleague, as she accompanied Adam in hospital, in a performance of a poem put to music:

Mahler's setting of the German Romantic Friedrich Rückert's '*I am lost to the world*': '*Ich bin der Welt abhanden gekommen*'.[21] Its words are reminiscent of Adam (and of Michael Furey):

> *I am lost to the world*
> *with which I used to waste so much time,*
> *It has heard nothing from me for so long*
> *that it may very well believe that I am dead!*[22]

The words suggest the choice of death over life made, it transpires, by Adam Henry, of whose death by refusing further medical treatment Fiona learns that evening, posing the question as to whether Adam in some sense dies because of Fiona. Echoing the final scene of 'The Dead', and even its dialogue, Fiona dwells on a memory of the deceased boy as her husband Jack talks to her of the party they have just attended; when she explains about Adam to Jack, he asks if she was in love with him, to which she replies: 'he was just a child! A boy. A lovely boy!' (*CA*, p. 210).[23]

Fiona concludes to herself 'she offered nothing in religion's place, no protection' for Adam, effectively failing to support the Children Act's emphasis on welfare by neglecting his social needs: 'no child is an island' (*CA*, pp. 212–13). Adam's welfare was broader that the matter of the transfusion and Fiona failed to give him sufficient meaning, through art or reason or love. In this harsh light, Adam might be said to have died for Fiona's desertion of him: for Adam, it would appear that emotion and love, wellsprings of mental well-being, proved more important than physical welfare.

The Children Act advances McEwan's views on childcare from *The Cement Garden* and *The Child in Time*. There is a loss of intimacy and of belief in the paramountcy of the parents' wishes evident in the rulings that have followed from the Children Act, but the novel suggests McEwan's support for Fiona's view that it is 'a significant marker in civilisation's progress, to fix in the statutes the child's needs above its parents' (*CA*, p. 4). This is drawn out in the passages that dwell on divorcing parents, as when Fiona is said to feel the need to suppress, in her judicial judgements, 'a puritan contempt for the men and women who pulled their families apart and persuaded themselves they were acting selflessly for the best' (*CA*, p. 133). Arguably, it is this judgement of others, and her conviction that her decisions remain unaffected by these buried thoughts, that returns to haunt Fiona after her encounters with Adam. McEwan evidently wishes to do more than one thing with Adam's liminal status between childhood and adulthood, as he did with Briony's adolescent position on the bridge in *Atonement*. On the one hand, Fiona's chaste connection with Adam forms a parallel relationship to her husband's rather more considered desire to have an affair with a woman thirty years his junior. On the other hand, it is also a quasi-parental relationship; and in this respect it is important that Fiona is undergoing a marital crisis bordering on separation. Fiona's comments on the damage caused by divorcing parents is thus in part a verdict passed on the effect of her own private life on her seemingly dispassionate and disinterested treatment of Adam; as a professional she has acted in one way, but her encounters with Adam have also acted on her personally. Having begun with the Children Act's injunction to make judgements in the best interest of the child, the narrative ends with the complex question of whether Fiona as a person has acted in Adam's best interest.

McEwan proposes that the assumption of responsibility for child welfare, whether by parent, state, or High Court judge, weighs as heavily as ever since the turn in law marked by the Children Act. While in the 1980s, in the context of British authoritarian government policies, McEwan condemned interventionist state authority over childcare practice in *The Child in Time*, it is hard not to see *The Children Act* in the context of the neglect by official authorities of their responsibility for safeguarding children, which has been repeatedly exposed in the twentieth-first century in the starkest ways.[24]

With *The Children Act*, and also, though to a lesser extent, with the police investigation of *Nutshell*, McEwan's interest has also seemed to move to the juridical and procedural in the social debate over children, his particular concern focusing on welfare in its broadest sense. The social positioning of the child in law stands as his most recent point of attention after the construction of childhood concentrated upon in earlier work, particularly *The Child in Time*. However, alongside his emphasis on families and relationships, an interest in the importance of the well-being of children remains a perennial concern, illustrating the care society accords its members more generally. Yet, it must be remembered that *The Child in Time* is also a deceptively childless narrative, like much of McEwan's mid-career work where the construction of childhood is largely explored in and through the absence of children. With *The Daydreamer* and *Atonement*, the personality and perception of the child, placed at the centre of the text, brings to McEwan's work a re-evaluation of childhood, intimately bound up with imagination. In *The Children Act*, where the legal construction and well-being of the child becomes the fulcrum of a debate over morality and agency, McEwan's eye has alighted on a tangential dimension of concern, and, like much public debate in recent years, he has arguably moved the most direct focus of his attention from the mid-career emphasis on the protection of childhood, to once again concentrate on the protection of children.[25]

NOTES

1 See Katherina Dodou, *Childhood without Children: Ian McEwan and the Critical Study of the Child* (Uppsala, Sweden: Uppsala Universitet, 2009). Dodou examines the significance of childhood as a thematic approach to questions of society and identity in works by McEwan that do not themselves foreground child characters.

2 Diana Gittins, 'The Historical Construction of Childhood', in *An Introduction to Childhood Studies*, second edition, ed. M. J. Kehily (Milton Keynes: Open University Press, 2009), pp. 35–49 (p. 37).

3 Ibid.; LuAnn Walther, 'The Invention of Childhood in Victorian Autobiography', in *Approaches to Victorian Autobiography*, ed. G. Landow (Athens: Ohio University Press, 1979), pp. 64–83 (p. 64).

4 See Jean-Jacques Rousseau, *Émile, or On Education* (1762).

5 This is underscored by his essay on *The Lord of the Flies*: see Ian McEwan, 'Schoolboys', in *William Golding: The Man and His Books*, ed. John Carey (London: Faber, 1986), pp. 157–60.

6 Mary Jane Kehily 'Understanding Childhood: An Introduction to Some Key Themes and Issues' in *An Introduction to Childhood Studies*, second edition, ed. M. J. Kehily (Milton Keynes: Open University Press, 2009), pp. 1–16 (p. 7).

7 Neil Postman, *The Disappearance of Childhood*, second edition (New York: Vintage, 1994), pp. 99, 102.

8 The title is also an allusion to Michael Tippett's 1930s oratorio *A Child of Our Time* with which McEwan became acquainted while writing his own oratorio *Or Shall We Die?* (1983).

9 Michael Wyness, *Childhood and Society*, second edition (London: Palgrave, 2012), p. 14.

10 Margaret Reynolds and Jonathan Noakes, *Ian McEwan: The Essential Guide* (London: Vintage, 2002), p. 11. At the end of this quotation, McEwan is referring to Dr Benjamin Spock (1903–98), an American paediatrician whose influential theories encouraged mothers to show greater attention towards, and freedom of expression for, their children.

11 McEwan said in 1989 that from this work he 'carried over a belief in the insufficiency of the intellect alone in understanding ourselves or our world', which is a comment that militates against attempts to rationalise all the events of *The Child in Time* (*MA*, p. xxvi).

12 The subject matter, McEwan says in his 'Preface' to the Vintage edition, is 'imagination'; the theme 'transformation' – hence the book's epigraph from Ovid's *Metamorphoses*: 'My purpose is to tell of bodies which have been transformed into shapes of a different kind'. See *The Daydreamer* (London: Vintage, 1995), p. 6.

13 Ibid., p. 9.

14 *Rose Blanche* (1985; London: Red Fox, 2004).

15 Richard Morrison, 'Opera gets between the Sheets with Ian McEwan's *For You*', *The Times*, 9 May 2008, p. 2.

16 Ian McEwan, 'The Law versus Religious Belief', *The Guardian*, 5 September 2014, pp. 38, 57, 60–1, 62. Retrieved from: www.theguardian.com/books/2014/sep/05/ian-mcewan-law-versus-religious-belief (accessed 3 January 2018).

17 McEwan's choice of names is seemingly made to remind the reader of the continued influence of religion in private and public life, but also of the Gospel writers themselves and the simultaneous mutual reliance and distinctiveness of their accounts, whose individuality sometimes puts them in opposition.

18 'Re E (A Minor) (Wardship: Medical Treatment)', *Family Law Reports* (*FLR*), 1993, 1, 386.

19 From the collection *Dubliners* published in 1914, exactly 100 years earlier than *The Children Act*. From at least this point on in the novel, McEwan strongly sounds echoes of Gretta Conroy's memory of Michael Furey, the doomed boy from Joyce's story, knowledge of which suggests the import of the encounter between Fiona and Adam in *The Children Act*.

20 James Joyce, 'The Dead', in *Dubliners* (London: Grafton, 1977), p. 252.

21 Fiona planned to end her performance with a piece by Schubert, but she plays instead 'Down by the Salley Gardens'.

22 *Ich bin der Welt abhanden gekommen, / Mit der ich sonst viele Zeit verdorben, / Sie hat so lange / nicht von mir vernommen, / Sie mag wohl glauben, ich sei gestorben*!

23 McEwan also incorporates the symbolism of Joyce's story, juxtaposing the Christian imagery of Christmas with the pagan emphasis on the regenerative cycles of nature to underscore the rival claims of the secular and religious in his own story.

24 Perhaps especially since Operation Yewtree, the police investigation begun in 2012 into nearly 600 historical allegations, predominantly the abuse of children, against the radio and television broadcaster Jimmy Savile and others, including well-known British personalities. Led by the Metropolitan Police Service, the operation became a full criminal investigation, broadening to involve many public figures, with politicians, including cabinet ministers, coming under intense media scrutiny as well as becoming the subject of police inquiries.

25 He was not one of the 200 teachers, academics, authors, charity leaders, and other experts who wrote a letter to the *Daily Telegraph* newspaper in 2011 calling for measures to 'interrupt the erosion of childhood', a follow-up letter to the one which was written under the name of more than 100 similar authorities in 2006 berating the way in which school testing, advertising, bad childcare, computer games, and television were encouraging children to grow up too fast. See: www.telegraph.co.uk/education/educationnews/8784996/Erosion-of-childhood-letter-with-full-list-of-signatories.html (accessed 3 January 2018).

7

DAVID MALCOLM

The Public and the Private

I

There is a critical consensus that, since the writing and publication of *The Child in Time* (1987), McEwan has been a public author, a species of latter-day Condition-of-England novelist, his work oriented towards topics of social substance and contemporary relevance. He has certainly seen himself as such, if not exactly in those terms.[1] The force of this argument is augmented by McEwan's willingness to play the role of a public man of letters (a Victorian sage for the late twentieth and early twenty-first centuries), commenting in essays and interviews on public affairs (nuclear threat, the role of science in society and culture, and war and terrorism).[2] Indeed, the arc of his career that is often drawn is one that rises from the murderous and poisoned solipsism and the exploration of a near hermetic psychology and psychopathology in the early short stories and novellas (from *First Love, Last Rites* to *The Comfort of Strangers*), to the social and political maturity and broad perspectives of post 1987 fictions and other writings.[3] It is certainly true that McEwan has shown a readiness to tackle large public issues in his fiction: the creeping authoritarianism of the dystopic Thatcherite Britain of *The Child in Time*; Anglo-American relations and the Cold War in *The Innocent* (a later Cold-War Britain is also the action-engendering chronotope of *Sweet Tooth*); pre-Second World War and wartime British social and political mores in *Atonement*; the modern city, war (the imminent invasion of Iraq in 2003), medicine and class conflict in *Saturday*; the relationships of science and society in *Solar*; and the interstices of law and social conduct and policy in *The Children Act*. Even the fiction that precedes *The Child in Time* can be seen as, at a certain level, focusing on the social and not just on the a-social personal (if such a distinction is actually viable): the collapse of moral, social and generational authority in *The Cement Garden* and the interplay of gender roles, constraints, and apostacies in *The Comfort of Strangers*.

It is striking how much public institutions play a role in McEwan's fiction: government in *The Child in Time*; journalism in *Amsterdam*; state medicine and medicine in general in *Saturday*; the committees, lecture circuits, research and development projects, publication procedures and funding activities of contemporary science in *Solar*; the intelligence and security apparatus of *The Imitation Game, The Innocent* and *Sweet Tooth*; and courts of law in *The Children Act*. In this respect, it is particularly telling with what frequency the police and police personnel recur in McEwan's work. These may only be in the form of a synecdoche, an imminent *deus ex machina* at the conclusion of *The Cement Garden*, but they keep turning up in other fictions: *The Comfort of Strangers, Enduring Love, Amsterdam, Atonement* and *Nutshell*. The Condition-of-England focus on public institutions, so prominent in Elizabeth Gaskell's, Charles Dickens's, or George Gissing's novels, is augmented by quotations from and allusions to relevant predecessors. References to nineteenth-century and early twentieth-century fiction abound in *Saturday* (*S*, pp. 58, 66–8, 276), as do allusions to the iconography of Victorian socially engaged painting (*S*, pp. 262–3). When Perowne sits at Baxter's bedside, he is echoing Sir Luke Fildes's image of the Victorian medical practitioner's care.[4] Serena Frome avidly reads George Eliot and Anthony Trollope (*Sweet Tooth*), and *The Children Act* begins with an improvization on the opening of *Bleak House*.

The narrational shift of perspective, the movement to a broad social or national perspective, a summation of *Zeitgeist* and its artefacts, a *résumé* of the state of public things, that is embodied in the opening of *Bleak House*, or in the sweeping national perspective that occurs in the opening paragraph of chapter 19 of E. M. Forster's *Howards End*, is also a mark of McEwan's fiction. There is, for example, a broad purview in *Black Dogs*, which recreates in a single paragraph the sights, the smells, the customs, the social atmosphere and the *mentalité* of the mid-1940s (*BD*, p. 54). Similarly, insouciant but glittering riffs on different aspects of the early 1960s can be found in *On Chesil Beach* (*CB*, pp. 24–5, 31–2, 119–21). In *Nutshell*, the as-yet unborn narrator is able to do something similar by listening to and summarizing the podcasts that her or his mother listens to (*N*, pp. 25–9). The echoes of the beginning of *A Tale of Two Cities* are unavoidable. McEwan emulates aspects of the nineteenth-century and social novelist: the public social apparatus is his subject matter.[5]

The social focus of McEwan's work is apparent in works that are at the margins of his output, as well as in those that are central. *Amsterdam* may have won McEwan the Booker Prize in 1998, but it has always enjoyed a stepchild's position among critics and commentators. The texts collected in *A Move Abroad* and *The Imitation Game* are neither novels or short stories (for which McEwan is most celebrated), but excursions into other forms – oratorio and film script.[6]

I think *Amsterdam* more interesting than most commentators concede, and, in any case, it is germane to the subject of my essay. It is manifestly a piece of social satire, a dissection of persons functioning within social institutions and contexts. The action of *Amsterdam* is played out among journalists and in the milieu of newspaper publishing. Vernon Halliday is editor of *The Judge*, and several sections of the novel present the meetings, staffing and policy decisions and office intrigues that are part of the work of the newspaper and the doings and structures of the press (e.g. *Am*, pp. 29–37). Clive Linley is part of the establishment of culture, an environment of commissions, performances, broadcasts and celebrity (e.g., *Am*, pp. 18–24, 156–62). These circles – journalism and culture – intersect with institutions of government and politics. Clive's millennium symphony has been commissioned by an official committee (*Am*, pp. 20–1). At Molly Lane's funeral, he and Garmony, a government minister, exchange barbed remarks. Vernon seeks to destroy Garmony's political career and is defeated by the superior skills of Conservative Central Office (*Am*, pp. 121–5). Public relations and its manipulations and power are also a focus of the novel (*Am*, pp. 126–8). Clive is called into a Manchester police station to identify a suspect (*Am*, pp. 151–4). In addition, the narrator offers, like several other of McEwan's narrators, a concise and insightful broadening of perspective on Clive's and Vernon's generation. Clive looks round the mourners at Molly's funeral and reflects on the development of what he sees as a successful and prosperous post-1960 elite, still doing well despite political changes that they disdain (*Am*, pp. 11–12). Clive's rail journey northwards through the cityscape of North London involves a typical broad perspective on the haphazard urban sprawl he sees (*Am*, pp. 63–4).

McEwan's text for Michael Berkeley's oratorio *Or Shall We Die?* is a very public work indeed. Its subject is the threat of nuclear war in the early 1980s (a predominant concern at the time of writing and performance). Its focus is on what it sees as the terrible danger to the world embodied in thousands of missiles in their silos, on the insanity of war plans, and on the public policies that have made such a danger possible. It even suggests the development of a different kind of female science, a world view that might prevent Armageddon. Public, too, is the fine screenplay for *The Imitation Game*. The Second World War provides setting and subject matter for a study of social attitudes towards women and the restriction of their roles even in such an important national struggle. Bletchley is a man's club serviced by women. Cathy is kept in a subordinate role in the war, and when she breaks a social code that restricts women she is relegated further. In fact, she ends the screenplay in confinement, having been manipulated and betrayed by men, in a manner that is no more than an extension of her father's disdain for her aspirations, her government's patronizing contempt for women and her society's suspicion and hatred of independent women. McEwan's screenplay for *The Ploughman's Lunch* takes a similarly social perspective. James is a radio news editor purveying an account of current events. Jeremy works for a national newspaper doing the same. Susan is a television editor producing programmes on recent history. James is commissioned to write a book on the British invasion of Suez in 1956, and the reader/audience learns a lot about that conflict and its centrality in post-war British history. While James is investigating the crucial colonial conflict that was Suez, the build up to the Falklands War of 1982 is taking place. James, Jeremy and Susan even visit the Conservative Party Conference in Brighton in 1982. The screenplay uses documentary material to emphasize its focus on Britain and its polity in 1956 and 1982. Further, the massaging or excision of social memory and the dangers attendant on those form a central topic of the text (*MA*, scenes 47 and 65, pp. 76–7, 91–2). The ploughman's lunch itself is taken as a metaphor for the creation of tradition, a lie that is so manufactured and presented as to become unquestioned truth.[7]

II

At the same time, McEwan is a writer concerned to delineate the minutiae of the physical and the personal, and their interrelation. In *The Cement Garden*, Jack masturbates and meticulously describes his ejaculate (*CG*, p. 17). He is similarly detailed about the acne on his face three pages later (*CG*, 20). Some thirty years later, in *On Chesil Beach*, McEwan has a similar (but ultimately radically different) episode, in which Edward erupts in detailed ejaculation over the unhappy Florence (*OCB*, pp. 104–5). This incident has been preceded by the agonizingly itemized account of the stuck zip on Florence's dress (*OCB*, pp. 82–3), and the particulars of the itinerary of Edward's fingers over Florence's groin and the sensations they produce (*OCB*, pp. 86–7). Something comparable, in terms of close observation, can be found in Perowne's physically detailed self-scrutiny in *Saturday* (*S*, p. 20). McEwan's novels are also full of denotations of small movements of emotion and small physical movements that mark the configuration and development of a relationship between two people. This is apparent in the early fiction: see, for example, the depiction of Colin and Mary in their hotel room in *The Comfort of Strangers* (*CS*, pp. 15–19). It is there, too, in *The Children Act*, as Fiona and Jack edge towards a reconciliation among the seeming trivia of making morning coffee, laying down a cup, moving or not moving away

(*CA*, p. 144). McEwan is a novelist of the microscopically physical and personal, as well as of the public and grand.

Indeed, like so many high Victorian novelists (and their successors), the action of McEwan's fiction constantly centres on the interrelation of the public and the personal. In an interview in *The Paris Review* in 2002, McEwan remarks that 'I've always been drawn to situations in which events on the large scale find a reflection in the private life'.[8] In *The Child in Time*, Stephen's malaise is Britain's, and not just metaphorically, for his depression and inertia are partly generated by the politics and governance that surround him. Charles is in flight from roles that the social world imposes on him. The Prime Minister's emotions and actions are constrained by the demands of public office. In *The Innocent*, Leonard's and Maria's love affair and its outcome would have been impossible under any other circumstances than the Berlin of the Cold War in 1955. The outcome of their love gives a kick to history (in the discovery of *Operation Gold*). June's dogs in *Black Dogs* may have been the hounds of hell, but they may also have been Gestapo-trained beasts run wild. Her bravery in 1946 and the bravery of the girl by the Berlin Wall in 1989 might just redeem history. In *On Chesil Beach*, Florence's and Edward's unfortunate relationship is set about by the demands and prohibitions of a particular time and place (*OCB*, p. 96). In *Amsterdam*, Clive perceives the Manchester police station, to which he has been summoned, as 'the family living room' (*Am*, p. 153), inhabited by policemen, criminals, social workers and unfortunates, trying to solve or mitigate the seemingly intractable problems of people and society. This moment reflects one from *Enduring Love*, in which Joe, too, visits a police station and sees it in both personal – domestic and social – and institutional terms, as a place where 'the human need for order meets the human tendency to mayhem' (*EL* p. 153). The personal and the public intersect and interpenetrate each other. Institutions shape, constrain and enable the personal; the personal affects and at times directs (or at least nudges) the course of the public.

This interpenetration of private and public realms is especially notable in *Amsterdam*. The minutiae of consciousness and bodily functions are ever present: the details of Molly Lane's lapse into dementia are given (*Am*, pp. 3–4); Clive's worries and imaginings about his health are particularized (*Am*, p. 25); the narrator enters the complex intuitions of death and non-existence, physical as much as emotional, that flow through Vernon's mind and body as he sits in his office (*Am*, pp. 31–2); the details of Garmony's fantasy transvestite existence are set forth (*Am*, pp. 69–71); the reader is given the physiological grounds, velocity and contents of Lanark's vomit (*Am*, p. 165), and Clive's and Vernon's dreams and illusions as they are murdered by the medical team each has hired to kill the other are rendered in convoluted detail (*Am*, pp. 166–73).

But all this personal particularity inhabits, intersects with, and much of it is shaped by and shapes the broader civic and institutional frameworks in which characters exist. All the major characters are part of the meritocratic elite of their generation. Molly's decline is particularly poignant (and discussed) because of her previous glamour and success. Clive and Vernon are undone, in part, because of the self-serving ambitions of their kind and their environment. Clive's symphony fails because he believes (or tries to convince himself) that artistic success is more important than human responsibility (*Am*, pp. 88–9). Vernon's decision to publish the photographs of Garmony in drag is occasioned as much by egoistic desire for fame as by political distaste (and public duty) (*Am*, pp. 56, 116, 74). Lanark vomits because he is afraid of exposure as a paedophile. No knighthood for him under such circumstances. Garmony must be a closeted cross-dresser, because of his public role. In addition, private impulses have material social consequences. Vernon loses the editorship of *The Judge* through his miscalculations, and the newspaper takes a new shape under his perfidious successor. Garmony's career is ruined by Vernon's publication of Molly's photographs, and his challenge for the leadership of his political party comes to nought.

The intersection of public and private is apparent, too, in *Or Shall We Die?*, as McEwan notes in the preface to the volume.[9] The text of the oratorio begins with a woman relating how she leaves her home and watches the night sky. But this personal idyll is disturbed by her awareness of the men who watch their screens for nuclear attack (*MA*, p. 17). The man's voice is that of the agents of the institutions that will bring destruction on all (*MA*, p. 19). The voice of the woman in segment Five is that of someone who experiences the personal consequences of history as her child dies in agony in her arms (*MA*, p. 21). Such intersections are clear, too, in *The Imitation Game*. The war makes Cathy vibrantly alive, eager for new things and new experiences (*IG*, Scene 11, p. 90). But she is brought low and damaged by the institutional and public framework (patriarchal, woman-hating) in which she must work. This is a cultural apparatus that extends from family and personal relations to the state in an almost seamless fashion. In turn, *The Ploughman's Lunch* is an admonitory and searing exposure of how private corruption and public corruption, personal lies and social untruths, intersect and augment each other. James is ambitious to have an affair with Susan, seduced by her social glamour. He is equally seduced by Gold and his offer of a chance to rewrite history. He lies to obtain information from Ann Barrington, purporting to be a socialist (*MA*, Scene 45, p. 75). James denies the existence of his dying mother to pursue his professional, social and sexual ambitions (*MA*, Scene 24, p. 57, and Scene 71, p. 97). The moment in which he glances at his watch during her dismal funeral is an index of individual but also wider public corruption (*MA*, Scene 103, p. 118). The lessons of Suez have not been learned; mutatis mutandis, the British are off doing something similar in the Falklands.[10] Ann Barrington indulges in a lie: James is clearly a substitute for her long-dead brother. Her husband Matthew has foisted and continues to foist well-paid lies on people. The newsreader whose marriage is collapsing pulls himself together to fulfil his social role (*MA*, Scene 61, pp. 89–90). The personal and social constantly intertwine in McEwan's fictional world.

III

There is, then, a marked consistency in McEwan's depiction of the relationship between the public and the private throughout his writing. There is a similar consistency in his configuration of the interpersonal throughout his career, something that has not been emphasized by most commentators.[11] Accordingly, in what follows I set out a typology of interpersonal relationships within McEwan's work as a whole, with particular emphasis on those seemingly marginal texts discussed earlier (*Or Shall We Die?*, *The Imitation Game* and *The Ploughman's Lunch*).

Six broad and thematic categories of the interpersonal can be observed in McEwan's work from the late 1970s to the present, and these can be grouped in two larger categories. The two larger categories mutate at times one into the other; the smaller categories overlap and meld at certain points, but they can be distinguished from each other. They are as follows:

I. Relatively positive relationships involving allegation and juncture –
   1. closeness;
   2. care, intimacy, security, pleasure; and
   3. obsession.
II. Negative relationships involving disjunction –
   1. cruelty, savagery, violence;
   2. manipulation, use; and
   3. failure, fragility.

The first of these categories is closeness, which identifies how McEwan has been a chronicler of interpersonal attachment throughout his career. We can see this in the motif of childbirth, which is present in two texts from different ends of the oeuvre, *The Child in Time* and *Nutshell*. The incest motif belongs here too, present in the short story 'Homemade' from *First Love, Last Rites*, in *The Cement Garden* and in *Jack Flea's Birthday Celebration*. More broadly, McEwan's interest in the family and the couple indicates a strong interest in very close personal relationships. The family is central to *The Cement Garden*, *The Child in Time*, *Black Dogs*, *Saturday* and *The Children Act* (in which the reader is offered several families, with children and without, to consider). Couples (some of which are potential families) are also central to his work. This is the case in, for example, *The Comfort of Strangers* (where Colin and Mary and Robert and Caroline are both close couples and also form a quasi-family unit), *The Innocent* (Leonard and Maria), *Enduring Love* (Jake and Clarissa), *On Chesil Beach* (Florence and Edward) and *Solar* (Michael and Patrice, and Michael and Masie and Darlene).

Care, intimacy, security and pleasure – my second category – is a conglomerate of motifs apparent over a wide range of McEwan's work. It is there in the lyrical early piece 'To and Fro' from *In Between the Sheets*, for example. The children in *The Cement Garden* look after each other and care for their mother, both when she is alive but ailing, and when she is dead. Their methods may be unorthodox, but their actions are born of close association. The incest at the novel's end is a sign of love not abuse and is surrounded by an image of family cohesion. Examples of this kind of closeness abound: the Prime Minister in *The Child in Time* clearly loves Charles; Leonard and Maria have a close and exciting relationship in *The Innocent*; the Perowne family in *Saturday* is an ideal of familial closeness and support; and Fiona and Jack work out their problems in *The Children Act*. The intense – and at times dangerous – intimacy of the Chareidi family and the Jehovah's Witness family is foregrounded in this novel.

The final category of this group is obsession, another frequent preoccupation of McEwan's: an unconquerable fascination for a shop-window mannequin drives the narrator of 'Dead As They Come' from *In Between the Sheets*; Jack is obsessed by his sister in *The Cement Garden*; and *Enduring Love* is a case study of obsession (quite literally, with the conceit of Appendix I). McEwan returns to the theme in the figure of Adam Henry and his feelings for Fiona in *The Children Act*.

Much more negative features of interpersonal relationships are also explored consistently throughout McEwan's work. As I have indicated, the relatively positive aspects of such relationships that interest McEwan frequently overlap with or morph into more destructive ones. My first category in the more overtly negative aspect is cruelty, savagery and violence. Many of McEwan's interpersonal relationship throughout his output are savage: obsession turns to murder in 'Butterflies' in *First Love, Last Rites*; the relationship between Colin and Mary, on one hand, and Robert and Caroline, on the other, is an occasion and veil for violence and perversity, which the relationship of Robert and Caroline embodies in any case in *The Comfort of Strangers*; Leonard and Maria find occasion enough for murder when Maria's husband makes an unexpected appearance in *The Innocent*; and in *Enduring Love* Parry's and Joe's connection turns violent on the part of both protagonists. In *Saturday*, Baxter and the Perowne family have a relationship fraught with threat and violence, ultimately on both sides. Baxter breaks into the Perowne mansion and promises violence, while Perowne and his son contrive to throw the intruder down the stairs. And a grisly family murder is one of the central elements of the story material of *Nutshell*.

In the category of manipulation and use, I place the McEwan characters that are depicted exploiting each other. Such manipulation cuts both ways in 'Pornography', from *In Between the Sheets*, when Pauline and Lucy take their revenge on the vile O'Byrne. Glass does a good job controlling and manoeuvring Leonard in *The Innocent*. *Atonement* is an exploration of different forms of manipulation through the persona of Briony. Clouded by misunderstanding at the age of thirteen, Briony uses Lola and Cecilia and Robbie to make a satisfying melodramatic fiction with appalling consequences; and, when older, she choreographs them (or their fictionalized selves), now in an attempt to expunge her guilt. Serena's and Tom's affair in *Sweet Tooth* embodies and engenders several levels of calculation. Manipulation, too, is what the unsavoury lovers in *Nutshell* are engaged in throughout the text. Even the unborn narrator intervenes on occasion to make his mother do his bidding (*N*, pp. 192–9).

The last of the six categories, failure and fragility, registers the frequency with which interpersonal relationships in McEwan's work fracture and fail. In *The Comfort of Strangers*, Colin and Mary go looking for trouble, get lost and find horror and grief. Stephen's and Julie's relationship (*The Child in Time*), Leonard's and Maria's (*The Innocent*), and June's and Bernard's (*Black Dogs*) crumble under the weight of guilt, negligence and circumstance. In the more recent fiction, there are relationships that almost fail: Serena's and Tom's in *Sweet Tooth*, and Fiona's and Jack's in *The Children Act*.

This classification does not exhaustively identify the appearance of these separate motifs in particular texts (for example, *Enduring Love* could supply evidence for all of the categories), but it does indicate the way in which McEwan's *oeuvre* is marked by a strong degree of coherence and consistency in its configuration of the interpersonal. The relatively marginal texts that I have been discussing also supply ample evidence of this. Clive and Vernon in *Amsterdam* are neither a couple nor a family, but they are old friends. Their relationship – at times close and valuable (for example, *Am*, pp. 46–50) – degenerates into one of manipulation and violence.

Indeed, each engineers the other's death. Garmony's transvestite obsession, which he is able to indulge with Molly, but which must otherwise be hidden, is central to the action of the novel. The Conservative Central Office defeats the campaign against Garmony in *The Judge* by portraying the Garmony family as close and loving. But interpersonal relations in the vile world of the novel are generally those of use and violence. Characters snarl at each other and look out for themselves. See, for example, Garmony's and Clive's conversation at Molly's funeral (*Am*, pp. 13–17). George Lane's visit to Vernon's widow at the novel's close is clearly an act of exploitation of her grief for his sexual ends (*Am*, p. 178). Only Molly herself and Mrs Garmony seem beyond or above such conduct, in a work that implicates society at large: Clive sees the police station in Manchester with its mayhem and casual cruelty as Britain's 'family living room' (*Am*, p. 153).

The same configuration of the interpersonal is apparent in the oratorio and screenplays contained in *The Imitation Game* and *A Move Abroad*. In *Or Shall We Die?*, the horror of nuclear war is made vivid in the woman figure's apprehensions about the death of her child and in the harrowing account of the death. Intense closeness and care are disfigured and disrupted. *Jack Flea's Birthday Celebration* is about the manipulations and intimacies of a son, a mother and a lover. In *Solid Geometry*, Albert's and Masie's relationship has soured into violence, disdain and point scoring. In the penultimate scene, Albert inflicts an ultimate manipulation on Masie by folding her into nothingness. *The Imitation Game* creates a world in which Cathy has little real closeness with anyone (even with her sister and Mary). McEwan suggests that, like all women in wartime Britain, she is used, abused and disdainfully cast aside by the men who run things (father, publican, Cambridge genius). *The Ploughman's Lunch* offers a panoply of obsessions and abuse on a personal and social level, from private life to the conduct of the state.

McEwan does allow for redemptive interpersonal relationships. This is apparent in the children's care for one another and their mother in *The Cement Garden*, in what Leonard and Maria (in *The Innocent*) and Florence and Edward (in *On Chesil Beach* pp. 154–6, 160–1) might have had, and been, under different historical and cultural circumstances. Reader's familiar with McEwan's fiction will be able to generate other examples that underscore the point: it is the fragility of potentially positive relationships that the reader takes from McEwan's work. We are constantly made to feel that closeness produces fragmentation, and to recognize the corrupting effects of violence and manipulation. These effects occur at all stages of his work, although the balance at different times is various – so that, for example,

Amsterdam is vilely sad, while *The Cement Garden* is strangely and paradoxically moving and redemptive.

IV

A further broad category that illustrates McEwan's thoroughly coherent view of the relation of the personal/interpersonal and the public has to do with intrusion. This is a category that encompasses the other categories, and it is one of the master motifs in McEwan's fiction. The motif of intrusion comprises three constitutive and connected motifs: enclosure, occlusion and interruption.

Images of enclosure abound in McEwan's writing, from the early short story 'Conversation with a Cupboard Man', from *First Love, Last Rites*, in which the protagonist and narrator literally encloses himself and is enclosed throughout the text: in a cupboard, in an oven, in a wardrobe. In *The Cement Garden*, the children shut themselves off from most of the rest of the world, secreting their mother's body in a trunk. In *The Child in Time*, Charles seeks to seal himself off from the adult world in his wood, his tree house and his fantasy of boyhood. Leonard, in *The Innocent*, thinks of the circumscription of the tunnel under Berlin as a 'confined and private space' (*I*, p. 205). Indeed, he and Maria imitate the tunnel when they create a warm and vivid sensual world within the confines of the quilts and clothes they pile up to stave off the outer cold (*I*, pp. 77–8). This strategy works until Otto is discovered in Maria's closet (*I*, p. 144). The Perowne family in *Saturday* form a warm, ideal, supportive family unit with a rich inner life, almost completely sealed against the threats and breakdowns of life outside their home. This secure enclosure is reflected in Henry's splendid Mercedes (*S*, p. 75) and in the locks on the doors and windows of the Perowne home (*S*, pp. 36, 238). In *Nutshell* we find perhaps the most complete evocation of this preoccupation with enclosure, with a protagonist and narrator protected by the amniotic fluid of her/his mother's womb.

Occlusion is often a complicating feature of enclosure in McEwan's fictional worlds, because enclosure almost always implies concealment. (*Saturday* is an exception to this rule. The Perowne family are not hiding but are protecting themselves and their way of life from what lies beyond the home.) The world beyond the family does not know what the children are up to in their hermetic communion in *The Cement Garden*. Charles hides in the woods in *The Child in Time*. The tunnel is a secret in *The Innocent* (or is supposed to be), just as Blake's treachery is. *Sweet Tooth* is about lies, deceit and pretence. The narrator in *Nutshell* is hidden from her or his surroundings, and the other characters are unaware of her or his attention to and participation in events. A recurrent motif of disguise and cross-dressing in McEwan's work is related to this concern with occlusion and concealment. Certainly, there is a lot of transvestism in McEwan's *œuvre*. Little brother Tom in *The Cement Garden* goes around in a girl's dress, plays outside in it and no one seems to mind (*CG*, pp. 42–3, 71–2). Charles in *The Child in Time* is not a transvestite, but he does dress up. The dissembling in 'Disguises' (from *First Love, Last Rites*) has principally to do with Henry wearing girls' clothes; and in *The Innocent*, Maria urges Leonard to slip into one of her dresses (*I*, p. 116).[12]

The motifs of enclosure and occlusion are always susceptible, however, to interruption. At the end of *The Cement Garden*, the lights of police cars intrude into the children's perverse and perversely loving communion, as their private era of enclosure and occlusion comes to an end. Robert suddenly walks into Colin's and Mary's private sphere in *The Comfort of Strangers*. In *Saturday*, Baxter is a violent intruder in the privileged Perowne home, while at the end of *The Children Act* a related disruption of domestic space comes with the news of Adam Henry's suicide, shattering the mood of success and joy at Fiona's concert (*CA*, p. 197). The police arrive in *Nutshell* to break up Trudy's and Claude's feelings that they have pulled off a perfect crime, and at the text's end the protagonist/narrator is about to get herself or himself born and cause yet another interruption. Coitus interruptus, and the failure of coition, emerges as a special case of interruption in McEwan's work: there is Edward's premature ejaculation in *On Chesil Beach*; Otto's intrusion on Leonard's and Maria's love-making in *The Innocent*; and the moment when Bernard's telephone call about the fall of the Berlin Wall ends a moment of intimacy between Jeremy and Jenny in *Black Dogs* (*BD*, pp. 67–8).

The configuration of this motif underscores McEwan's method for making us see the interrelationship between the public and the private. In *Or Shall We Die?*, the nuclear missiles threaten to intrude on domestic idyll and personal love, as they have already, in Japan in 1945. *The Imitation Game* is obviously about national secrecy, hidden messages (which Bletchley must decode) and hidden purposes (the women involved must not know what they are doing nor tell anyone ever about it). Yet gender oppression is a central aspect of this secrecy, figured emphatically in the confinement of Cathy at the end of the text. In *The Ploughman's Lunch*, the invasion of Suez is based on deceit, and the image of the family created by advertizing occludes the reality we observe in the text.

Amsterdam clearly belongs within the overall configuration of motifs in McEwan's work in this respect too. In the episodes alluded to above, the dynamic of enclosure and interruption recur. For example, Clive's composing is an act of hermetically sealing himself off, enclosing himself, from outer distractions (*Am*, pp. 23–4, 143–4), and it is twice interrupted, once by the attempted rape that he witnesses, and once by the police who visit his home. Ultimately, death comes to both the protagonists as an interruption to their fantasies of fame and status. Garmony is a transvestite, and his cross-dressing drives the action of the novel. It is also presented in some detail (*Am*, pp. 69–71), with a running commentary of Clive's inner appreciation where the cross-dressing is more successful or 'feasible' (*Am*, p. 71). The exposure or continued occlusion of Garmony's sexual and identity/gender affiliation is one of the central moral dilemmas of the novella: the intrusion on his cross-dressing idyll epitomizes McEwan's insistence on the interpenetration of the private and the public, but also conveys the keenly felt sense of trespass we see so often in his work, when the public intrudes on the personal and the interpersonal.

NOTES

1 See the 'Preface' to *A Move Abroad: 'Or Shall We Die?' and 'The Ploughman's Lunch'* (London: Picador, 1989), especially p. xii and pp. xvii–xxi.

2 See in this respect the essays in *Ian McEwan: Art and Politics* (Heidelberg: Universitätsverlag Winter, 2009), ed. Pascal Nicklas, especially Nicklas's own essay, 'The Ethical Question: Art and Politics in the Work of Ian McEwan', pp. 9–22, and those of Erik Martiny, '"A Darker Longing": Shades of Nihilism in Contemporary Terrorist Fiction', pp. 159–72, and Helga Schwalm, 'Figures of Authorship, Empathy, and the Ethics of Narrative (Mis-)Recognition in Ian McEwan's Later Fiction', pp. 173–85. For the complexities of this issue, see also two recent studies of McEwan's work: Johannes Wally's *Secular Falls from Grace: Religion and (New) Atheism in the Implied Worldview of Ian McEwan's Fiction* (Trier, Germany: Wissenschaftlicher Verlag, 2015), and Tomasz Dobrogoszcz's *Family and Relationships in Ian McEwan's Fiction: Between Fantasy and Desire* (Lanham, MD: Lexington Books, 2018).

3 I have written about this understanding of McEwan's work elsewhere. See: *Understanding Ian McEwan* (Columbia: University of South Carolina Press, 2002), pp. 4–5, and 'The Media-Genic and Victorian Mr McEwan?', *Anglistik*, 21 (2010), 2, pp. 13–22 (pp. 14–18). See also Peter Childs, *The Fiction of Ian McEwan: A Reader's Guide to Essential Criticism* (Basingstoke: Palgrave Macmillan, 2006), pp. 2–4, and Dominic Head, *Ian McEwan* (Manchester: Manchester University Press, 2007), pp. 1–2, 7.

4 See Sir Luke Fildes's 'The Doctor' (1891), The Tate Gallery. Retrieved from: www.tate.org.uk/art/artworks/fildes-the-doctor-no1522 (accessed 19 January 2018).

5 The sudden broad purview also occurs in fiction that is strictly outside some of the conventions of the nineteenth-century social and psychological novel, of course. For example, similar effects can be found in chapter one of Virginia Woolf's *Mrs Dalloway*, and the last paragraph of her story 'Kew Gardens'.

6 In what follows, I do not discuss two scripts contained in *The Imitation Game*. They deserve some attention, but are less relevant to my topic than the other text in the volume, 'The Imitation Game' itself. If any text supports the argument that McEwan's early work tends towards the hermetically psychopathological, *Jack Flea's Birthday Celebration* – with its focus on maternal obsession and struggle – is it. This introversion is much less so in *Solid Geometry*, in which the sexual dynamics of Maisie's and Albert's relationship have a social and historical dimension. Maisie is a woman of the 1960s, we are told. Albert has inherited a legacy of patriarchal attitudes (embodied in the pickled penis on his desk). However, the relationship between public and private is much more powerfully exhibited in the other text in the volume, as they are in the texts in *A Move Abroad*.

7 In McEwan's screenplay, the Ploughman's Lunch is 'exposed' as an invention of a 1960s advertising campaign, rather than the traditional English fare it purports to be (*MA*, scene 82, pp. 106–7). Martyn Cornell shows how this argument points the finger at the Milk Marketing Board. However, in the testimony of interwar rural novelist Adrian Bell, Cornell also uncovers evidence of a traditional 'Ploughboy's lunch', with the same components, available in pubs before the Second World War. See Cornell's 'Zythopile' blog, '*The Ploughman's Lunch* – Guilty or Innocent?', 16 July 2007. Retrieved from: http://zythophile.co.uk/2007/07/16/the-ploughmans-lunch-guilty-or-innocent/ (accessed 19 January 2018).

8 Adam Begley, 'Interview with Ian McEwan', *The Paris Review*, (2002), 162, pp. 30–60 (p. 45).

9 *A Move Abroad: 'Or Shall We Die?' and 'The Ploughman's Lunch'* (London: Picador, 1989), p. xviii; see also pp. 5–6.

10 The Falklands War and the invasion of Suez are not the same (as McEwan points out persistently in *The Ploughman's Lunch*; see also the 'Preface' to *A Move Abroad* [*MA*, p. xxv]). But both military campaigns have partly to do with assertions of British world importance and national pride.

11 See Kieran Ryan's classic (and nuanced) formulation of the matter, *Ian McEwan* (Plymouth: Northcote House, 1994), pp. 2–5. Exceptions include: Peter Childs, *The Fiction of Ian McEwan*, p. 6, and Tomasz Dobrogoszcz, who, in *Family and Relationships in Ian McEwan's Fiction*, convincingly discusses interpersonal relationships in McEwan's *œuvre* (from a different perspective to mine). Head, too, observes a character-centred continuity over McEwan's work as a whole, but it is a different, although related one to that which I propose here (see *Ian McEwan*, pp. 13–15, 17–18).

12 The subject of cross-dressing in McEwan's work can be considered on a higher fictional level, that of the implied author. McEwan is remarkable for his adoption of the voices and points of view of female characters, and for a recurrent focus on the details of female dress and bodies. There is a sense in which – as a reader – one must be aware of McEwan's performance of female roles. Examples run from Mary in *The Comfort of Strangers* to Fiona in *The Children Act*. For a full discussion of the phenomenon of cross-dressing, see Peter Ackroyd's seminal *Dressing Up: Transvestism and Drag – The History of an Obsession* (New York: Simon and Shuster, 1979). For gender performance, see Judith Butler's *Gender Trouble: Feminism and the Subversion of Identity* (1990; rep. London: Routledge, 2006).

8

BEN KNIGHTS

Masculinities

Ian McEwan's early story 'Disguises' broaches several themes which are intertwined through his work and are the subject of this essay. Recently retired from the stage (her final role the 'bad daughter' Goneril in *King Lear*), Mina adopts her orphaned nephew Henry. 'Always on stage even when alone an audience watched' (*FL*, p. 101), she inducts him into a world of tableaux, alcohol and dressing up – latterly as a girl. Frequently humiliated, Henry finds himself playing along with her erotically-charged fantasies. Then one day when he has upset Mina by staying out late, and terrified of her fury, he suddenly finds himself comforted as he dresses up as his new friend Linda, and feels 'free of Mina's anger, invisible inside this girl' (*FL*, p. 114). Descending into a phantasmagoric, breathlessly unpunctuated scene of incipient abjection, this story encapsulates several key elements for the examination of McEwan and masculinities which follows: performance and staging, the instability of gender, cross-dressing, occupation of another's text, and the lost child. In a way that recalls some of Angela Carter's earlier work (*The Magic Toyshop* [1967], for example), the story condenses an anxiety that all the conventional securities of identity and desire might turn out to be theatrical counterfeits.

An attempt to discuss McEwan's narratives of masculinity needs to sketch, however baldly, key elements of context. McEwan belongs to a generation of British male novelists (born in the mid- to late 1940s) who emerged into prominence in the late 1970s. They developed their skills during a period when normative masculinity was increasingly questioned and estranged as a phenomenon not simply to be taken for granted. Very different writers from this period have in common the tendency to be self-reflexive about their roles as male novelists, and preoccupied by male self-fashioning through discourse. James Kelman, Graham Swift, Martin Amis, McEwan himself, Julian Barnes, Salman Rushdie, or the slightly younger Kazuo Ishiguro engage in extensive metafictional reflection on the roles and gendered performance of men and male story tellers. All search for a vocabulary and narrative repertoire for male experience and for the wider social implications and impacts of that experience. All negotiate a treacherous and shifting boundary between conventional realism and elements of the fantastic. In their work, the vagaries and motivations of the unreliable narrator and his indirect relation to (or implied disjunction from) his author can subsume the narrative into a metafictional drama into which the reader is – however obliquely – enlisted. In this spirit, David James argues that McEwan's narration implicates readers 'as they shift between ironic and complicit readings'.[1] In terms of literary history, this emerging group of self-consciously male novelists can be set against an earlier generation, in particular those US novelists widely read and admired on both sides of the Atlantic and who for many (not least through the more advanced syllabuses within university English departments) had come by the 1970s to stand for 'the modern novel', or even, in some sense, for modernity itself: Saul Bellow, John Updike, Norman Mailer, William Styron and Philip Roth. For those novelists and their audiences, signature tales of male *Bildung* from Mailer's *The Naked and the Dead* (1948) to Bellow's *Humboldt's Gift* (1975) take for granted and perpetuate the centrality of the male experience, and heterosexual male authority to impose symbolic order on a centrifugal social world.

At the same time, the British group were learning their trade in a world where understandings of gender and gendered roles, parenting conventions and norms of initiation and career, were becoming increasingly conflicted. To stress the national context, these novelists were born just too late for National Service, an institution which played a significant role in shaping British masculinities between the end of the War and the early 1960s.[2] McEwan's own service upbringing endows him with particular insight into the militarization of the British male, and the forms of resistance to hierarchies and bullying which arose as a result. Further, the group referred to came of age as novelists during a period of gender ferment and interrogation of conventional roles propelled forward by second wave feminism. Simultaneously, the Campaign for Homosexual Equality and, more radically, the Gay Liberation Front were beginning to chip away at conventional hostility towards nonconforming sexualities. The Achilles Heel men's collective, formed in 1978, can stand for an explosion of consciousness-raising 'men's groups' drawing their models and their gender politics from feminism.[3] In the same historical moment, the revived anti-nuclear movement which took shape at the end of the 1970s and burgeoned in the 1980s promoted an analysis in which patriarchy and competitive masculinities bore a large share of responsibility for the arms race and the deteriorating condition of international politics. In the moment of the Greenham Common peace camp,

McEwan was rhetorically to summarize the argument: 'Shall there be womanly times, or shall we die'.[4] But it was not enough to hope that women could redeem a world perilously perched on the brink of thermonuclear and environmental catastrophe. Key to both intersecting movements was the widely-shared conviction that, rather than pin the responsibility for salvation on women (a scenario queasily reminiscent of aspects of the nurturing 'angel in the house'), men urgently needed to do their own work on their relationships to women, to children, and, above all, to each other.[5] The scope and simultaneous ambiguity of McEwan's contribution to a model of thinking about gender (one with which the twenty-first century is rapidly becoming unfamiliar) is the subject of this chapter.

Forty years ago, in his 1981 introduction to *The Imitation Game*, McEwan revealed the influence of 'The Women's Movement' on his thinking at that time, and his intention to write a novel that responded to that current of thought, which increasingly tended to subordinate class to gender and patriarchy as lens for analysis, and programme for political action (*IG*, p. 16).

The new men's movements understood hegemonic masculinities as stabilized and reinforced through language and narrative culture. Manhood and patriarchy were increasingly seen not as given, immutable templates, but as plural, vulnerable and fluid conditions, perpetually reassembled (and hence, potentially, subverted) through social and cultural conditioning. The point was to take advantage of what Ross Chambers referred to as 'room for maneuver', that space for play within any system where opposition or change could emerge.[6] In a related spirit, McEwan captured from Bellow's protagonist Herzog his epigraph for *Saturday*. 'For instance? Well, for instance, what it means to be a man'.[7] One account of McEwan's rich *oeuvre* might see it as a series of narrative experiments in the ethics and formation of masculinity. Delineating very different routes for male *Bildung* from those you would be likely to carry away from Bellow or from Updike, McEwan sets about exploring subjectivities as given shape, perspective and meaning through cultural acts. In one way or another, all his stories and novels constitute metafictions, in the sense that they draw reflexive attention to the ambiguities of the male-authored narrative and the production of masculine styles. Such metafictions of the male author transmute into metafictions of masculinity, confronting and ironically reframing the repertoire of symbolic gestures and narrative tropes through which tales of masculinity and male agency are told. Thus, while McEwan is acknowledgedly fascinated by forms of evolutionary narrative, the occasions when related ideas surface in his work are shot through with ambiguity.[8] Perowne's reflection (meditating on the psychic low of the early hours of the morning) that there 'must have been a survival advantage in dreaming up bad outcomes and scheming to avoid them' is only tangentially borne out by the novel (*S*, p. 39). And as we shall see, the narrative trope of (sometimes extreme) physical violence occurs in most of his novels, often forming a pivotal point in the narrative. Whether through violence or its sublimation into ritual male competition (Perowne and Strauss's squash game ironically recapitulates Perowne's earlier encounter with Baxter [*S*, pp. 108–16]), the obsessive recurrence of this motif both draws attention to and questions the role of violence and the violent encounter with another man in the formation of hegemonic masculinity. Men can be victims of patriarchy, too.[9]

In this spirit of Caroline Levine's understanding of literary texts 'as sites, like social situations, where multiple forms cross and collide', rather than as fixed 'reflections or expressions of prior social forms', this chapter seeks to suggest that masculinity (in or out of novels) is a narrative project, a recurrent, socially-sanctioned, effort to author and authorize an unconditioned story.[10] Specifically, this chapter argues that McEwan repeatedly trials colliding versions of the structural devices around which such narratives are spun. Now, in a moment when debates about gender have gravitated towards identity wars, it is important to remind ourselves that, in the 1980s and 1990s, arguments about masculinity were not restricted to the formation and experience of identity, or the structures of feeling occupied by men.[11] The wider debate took as its imperative for enquiry the formation or questioning of patriarchy, and thus of the dynamics of power at every level.

The dialectical relation of proximity and distance, the management of boundaries and exercise of power preoccupy the next stage of this chapter, and I flesh out some of my assertions by examining McEwan's first full-length novel/novella, *The Comfort of Strangers* (1981). In this work, McEwan's variation on Thomas Mann's *Death in Venice*, the setting is one of those Kafka-esque, slightly dream-like cities that we also find, for example, in Jim Crace's *Six* (2003). The novel sheds much of the metonymic compulsion of the realist tradition to create a faintly surreal, and curiously affect-less scene, in which the instability of space chimes with the volatility of relationships and unexpectedness of outcomes. Almost from the beginning, inadequate maps allude to disorientation arising from the poverty of the available codes and narrative resources. The available city maps, we gather, are largely useless, yet the failure to bring out with them any map (however inadequate) when they leave the hotel results in Colin and Mary getting thoroughly lost and thus to their fateful encounter with Robert (*CS*, pp. 22–6). How do you know your way around a domain which, Adrienne Rich, quoted in the epigraph, refers to as 'the kingdom of the sons'? Disorienting contexts and hallucinatory events interrelate and reinforce each other. Given that texts constitute invitations to readerly improvization, the challenge to the reader is to summon up sufficient agency to defend the self against the nightmare of the text, or against passive dissolution into someone else's sadistic fantasy, which is also the process to which Colin and Mary are subject. The implosion of Colin and Mary into a kind of Lawrentian victim-hood takes place through and within the choreography of their dependent relationship to Robert. In essence, they (and Colin in particular) find them-selves unable to detach or distance themselves from him, and their boundaries break down in his presence.[12] Uncritically internalizing his childhood trauma, they find themselves subsumed into a transferential drama of his making. Robert, the dominant figure within the narrative, externalizes and re-enacts his own trauma ('real' or imaginary) of paternal bullying, and humiliation by his sisters by casting others as players in a drama where he holds the keys to the script. We are moving closer here to putting a finger on the metafictions of masculinity. Robert's ensnaring of the hapless couple begins with mesmeric monologue and escalates by stages (the invitation to his apartment, the introduction to Caroline) to acts of grotesque violence. From the moment he begins to tell his story in the underground bar to which he has lured them, the couple physically enter into his reality. He 'seemed to be holding his breath, and this caused Colin and Mary, who watched him closely, to breathe with difficulty' (CS, p. 31). The voyeurism of Robert's illicit photography (of Colin) brings into relief an underlying identity between representation and stalking: the obsessive pursuit of an object of desire treated as an object, rather than a sentient being with their own inner world and their own dignity. Colin has become the object of the photo-graphic male gaze. We can discern in *The Comfort of Strangers* a suggestion of features which stalker, narrator and novelist have in common, each a collector of illicit images, each arraying others on a chessboard of their own fantasies. Here, in *The Comfort of Strangers*, the sadistic male contriver stands in for and constitutes an exaggerated version of the manipulative novelist.

Stalking – the perversion of intimacy into an obsessive pursuit of proximity – is one of the pivots of McEwan's self-reflexively fictional fictions. His stalkers include the abductor of Kate in *The Child in Time*; Jed in *Enduring Love*; Baxter in *Saturday*; and Adam in *The Children Act*, all of whom refuse to leave the object of desire alone or respect their wishes (explicit or implied) not to be pursued. The motif casts an oblique light on the process of narration. Through the narrative trope of stalking, McEwan foregrounds the ambivalence of the act of self-authorship – moulding others to fit to your fantasy. At the same time, the implicit and sometimes explicit violence of stalking expresses in exaggerated form the dynamics of the formation of desire and identity. The motif symbolizes an almost colonial presumption that the object of such harassment has lost their right to enjoy the security of their own boundaries. McEwan is questioning the ethics of his own departures from narrative convention, his own undermining of the codes which have been trusted to sustain coherence, and upon which pacts between texts and readers are founded. This search for a new vocabulary of forms harbours its own dangers. From the rag and bone shop of outworn forms, the hankering for a heroic role and heroic storylines leads in potentially divergent directions. One route tends towards Colin's becalmed implosion, or the ignorance of how to 'do' masculinity, which results in Leonard's infatuation with the style and panache of his American colleagues in *The Innocent*. Another harks back to the archaeological ruins of another and potent set of masculine scenarios, exemplified in *Enduring Love* in the attempts of Joe Rose to ground himself as he confronts the effects of Jed Parry's obsession.

With the exception of *The Children Act* (where the violence takes place off stage), McEwan's novels seem unable to escape the pervasive narrative trope constituted by acts of physical violence. These allusions to the 'hard-boiled' school of masculinity and masculine initiation may constitute an examination of the hardened boundaries and the serious commitment to conventional norms of the male narrator (or his novelist). Jago Morrison considers the 'close identification with the problems of their male narrators' in McEwan's texts, but suggests that 'what we see in them is far from an attempt to rehabilitate some older, masculinist mode of authorship'. Rather, we may encounter 'a narrative voice that is self-conscious in its refusal of full coherence', but which is also 'unable or unwilling to disguise the extent of its own instability and unease'.[13] And yet, scenes of brutal violence (the murder and dismemberment of Otto in *The Innocent*, Joe's purchase of a gun and shooting of Jed in *Enduring Love*, the retreat to Dunkirk in *Atonement*, the toppling of Baxter in *Saturday*, murders from *The Comfort of Strangers* to *Nutshell*) recur in McEwan's work. Just as several of his novels experiment with recognizable genres – thrillers and the spy novel (*The Innocent, Sweet Tooth*), gothic, magic realism, the country house novel and the war memoir – so these often pivotal violent episodes seem to be an allusion to a stereotypical way of punctuating the story of male lives, that warrior conflation of courage, physical prowess and heroism. Ordeal inflicted or endured has been (and across multiple cultures) a recurrent, and often defining element in the male genre. While usually abrupt and isolated within the narrative of each novel, such episodes inflect the direction and reception of the individual novels in which they occur. Like the threat of Jed's or Baxter's poised knives, they leave a trail of menace. At the same time, McEwan's physical attention to damaged or ruined bodies undermines attempts to expunge the horror by writing off or diluting the shock value of such episodes simply as metafictional allusions to conventional narratives, because we are implicitly invited to go on recontextualizing and making sense of such episodes. Without new maps, without radically new narrative forms, novels (in dialogue with their audiences) may be doomed to go on re-enacting competitive and violent masculine codes.

Attempts to decentre masculine narratives may, then, result in the suscep-tibility of narratives to colonization by stereotypical structuring motifs. Experimental narratives may lack defences against invasive intertexts. But this is not in itself a reason to dismiss McEwan's persistent experiments in decentring and remapping tales of masculinity. Violent episodes do not constitute the only way in which McEwan's novels are shadowed by intertextual allusions to the canon. Such intrusions of other potential or proto-texts represent a leakage of alternative symbolic potential, of variant registers, of other glimpsed routes. The simulated scientific article which is presented as an appendix to *Enduring Love* and the Nobel presentation speech which concludes *Solar* have antecedents in the *Authorised Childcare Handbook*, which is threaded as a sequence of epigraphs through *The Child in Time* (1987), and in *Lemonade*, the children's novel purportedly written by the protagonist, Stephen Lewis.[14] *The Child in Time* is McEwan's earliest and, in a way, his most programmatic critique of patriarchy, a critique conducted especially through the portrayal of Stephen and Charles Darke (Stephen's dark side): these two are in many ways complementary doubles. Where Stephen painfully, with Julie's and Thelma's help, learns how to mourn his lost daughter, it is Charles's inability to integrate his child self into his public life as successful publisher, politician and cabinet minister which results in his breakdown and re-enactment of himself as a ten-year-old schoolboy out of an imagined 1950s. In a literal rendering of the 'inner child' motif prevalent in the counselling discourse of the time, Charles externalizes his lost 'inner child' in the adopted persona of a 'Just William'-type school-boy.[15] After Charles' death, Thelma reflects on how public life provides no outlet for the qualities learned in childhood, and that 'Charles's case was just an extreme form of a general problem' (*CT*, p. 204). Within a futuristic novel whose setting is a projection of Margaret Thatcher's Britain into an era of worsening environmental degradation and an increasingly authoritarian polity, the co-presence of alternative routes hints at the optimism provision-ally symbolized by the birth of the child – like the Prime Minister, unassigned to a gender – with which the novel ends. The motif of the plasticity of time recurs in the 'hanging' ending, 'before the beginning of time' (*CT*, p. 220). Throughout the novel, the passage of time is not totally inexorable, and alternative possibilities are not irretrievably lost: this is one implication to be drawn from Thelma and Stephen's conversations about the physics of time (*CT*, p. 117). The redeemable potential of time is also implied by the hallucinatory time-slip moment where Stephen finds himself transported back some forty years to make a wordless appeal to his parents at the moment when they are discussing whether his mother should abort the child that will become himself (*CT*, pp. 55–60). In laying claim to a male role in nurture, Stephen becomes the guardian of his own birth, and then subsequently presides over the secular nativity scene with which the novel concludes. A novel which sets about disrupting the hierarchies of authority and masculine centrality foregrounds and in a sense becomes its own act of nurture. In essaying this act of narrative healing, McEwan opened himself to the charge of colonization of the female, wittily (if unfairly) levelled by Adam Mars-Jones in his polemical essay 'Venus Envy' (1990).[16] It is hard to resist the feeling that, acute as the essay is, Mars-Jones (perhaps understandably exasperated by a wave of paternal sentimentality) has landed McEwan and his other target Martin Amis in something of a Catch-22 situation. What McEwan has continued to dare is precisely that double bind: that if as a man you make a point of articulating your vulnerability or capacity to nurture you can be accused not only of colonizing the female, but of finding ever more sophisticated ways of making yourself the centre of attention. *The Child in Time* remains a challenging and important experiment in the negotiation of this dilemma: to surrender patriarchal authority over its material and its reader, while at the same time taking responsibility for initiating metamorphosis and healing. In that spirit one might suggest that its failures are irretrievably entangled with its strengths.[17]

Masculine behaviours and identities (like the identities and behaviours of any other group) are not, so to speak, indigenous, but take shape, meaning and potency in dialectical relation with other groups. McEwan is in tune with that growing tendency which in the 1990s was to turn into a performative account of gender as (in Judith Butler's terms) 'an identity tenuously constructed in time, instituted in an exterior space through a stylized repetition of acts'.[18] In McEwan's early television play *The Imitation Game*, Cathy is used as a spokesperson for a position that is more than an analysis of the gendering of warfare, proposing that the 'morality' of war hinges on the defence of women, a 'morality' that would dissolve 'if girls fired guns, and women generals planned the battles' (*IG*, p. 174). Shorn of a supposedly passive and defenceless body of women to shelter and protect, warfare in Cathy's analysis would be deprived of its ideological defences and much of its justification, a principle we might extend beyond warfare and military spectacle: this speaks also (for example) to the grotesque rivalry of Halliday and Linley in *Amsterdam*, and their mutual destruction, which is conducted over and around the memory of Molly.

As practitioners of prestigious cultural forms (a broadsheet editor and a classical composer), both Halliday and Linley use their arts as media of influence and seduction. Through these prestigious forms, they also compete with each other over Molly and over their audiences. There are echoes of Elisabeth Bronfen's (then recent) study of the paradoxical meanings of the dead or dying woman in western representational discourse. Bronfen suggests that the 'construction of masculinity and of the masculine artist is made not only in opposition and in precedence to a feminine body caught in the process of fading ... but also in opposition and in precedence to absent femininity, because the feminine functions as a sign whose signified is masculine creativity'.[19] For all the disappointment voiced by many critics, *Amsterdam* can perhaps better be understood as an engagement with that important and arresting paradox. The making of symbolic and narrative forms and thus the making of the identities and behaviours which are stabilized and normalized through those forms is not the expression of the pre-existing character of an individual or a group. It arises dialectically in the dialogue between communities. External discursive habits feed back into ways of being, inside and outside, in perpetual mutually-influencing interchange. While the stereotypical binary within which gender is formed is female/male, McEwan's work suggests a complication of this dualistic scheme.

The Child in Time is not his only novel to be haunted by a lost child, or by children. Somewhere in the margins of *The Comfort of Strangers* are the children whom Mary has left behind. The postcards she has bought to send them are a recurrent motif, until, at the end, packing to go home, she 'put the postcards between the last pages of her passport' (*CS*, p. 163). In novels (as, perhaps, in life) messages which fail to arrive are often as significant as those which do. In terms of the metafictional analysis which underpins this chapter, they may represent, as Peter Brooks suggests, a fear that narrative will fall on deaf ears or drop into oblivion. For Brooks, 'most narratives' express 'anxiety concerning their transmissibility', a desire 'to become the story of the listener as much as of the teller'.[20] In this light, the children who are not there, but whose absence is foregrounded, represent failures of creation or nurture. From the margins, these glimpsed and vanished children are subsumed into the narrative journeys of the adult characters. We have already seen how the disappearance of Kate is the starting place for Stephen's voyage of self-discovery, and that the disappearance is symbolically redressed in the birth at the end of the novel. A variant on this disturbing motif propels both *Enduring Love* and *The Children Act*, where the mourning of unborn children is projected onto women. In *Enduring Love*, Clarissa, unable to have children herself, becomes a godmother to many, her desk a 'tracking station for godchildren' (EL, p. 104). And her academic field – the letters of John Keats, dead at twenty-five – embodies an investment in another human absence, in a kind of resonating allusion (EL, p. 71). As Joe and Clarissa try to make sense of the balloon episode and of Logan's death by talking to friends, they find themselves telling 'shivering and shaking stories' to each other (EL, p. 34). As 'so often in these talks, childhood was central', and Clarissa contributes the story of how once on a family holiday her five-year-old cousin went missing (EL, p. 34). Embedded within the narrative, such fragmentary proto-stories create semiotic flickers, a ghostly glow colouring and adding their own shadows to the reader's reception of the plot. Absent children are the precondition of the story and thus also of Joe's narrative role. Mourning motherhood is at one and the same time to mourn fatherhood: 'It was with a touch of sadness that Clarissa sometimes told me that I would have made a wonderful father' (EL, p. 118).[21] Adopting as a science journalist the voice and persona of others, Joe invents his own version of paternity.

In The Children Act, the mourning of lost children becomes a central focus. As a High Court judge in the Family Division, Fiona, the scholarly author of weighty and learned judgments, intervenes in and takes charge of the lives of families. The role of judge parallels (though with more immediate real-world consequences) the role of narrator. Fiona harks back to the role of the judiciary in the 1980s, standing in 'for the monarch' and acting as 'the guardians of the nation's children' (CA, pp. 35–6). At the same time, the novel repeatedly returns to the children that Fiona and Jack have not had. In a dejected mood, Fiona reflects on 'her childlessness' as 'a flight from her proper destiny' (CA, p. 44). The 'almost existing children' become voices in her head, the flat (like that of Clarissa and Joe in the earlier novel) a hospitable haven for all the nephews and nieces who are welcomed there. These ever-present absences (like the little girl abducted by her own father – CA, p. 47) propel the narrative. The trauma of the case of the Siamese twins obsesses Fiona and the narrative which she carries: 'some part of her had gone cold, along with poor Matthew. She was the one who had dispatched a child from the world' (CA, p. 31). And the horror of the case echoes at the climax of the novel in Fiona's grief-stricken reception of the news of the death of the young Adam, and Jack's failure to grasp the meaning of her tale (CA, p. 210).

The relationship between the novel's lost children and the question of masculinity and its narratives requires further consideration in the work of such a self-conscious author. It is difficult to resist the implication that the absent children make space for the narrator's, or the author's, creative acts.

An absence so insistently foregrounded bespeaks not only the loss of the child in self-identified male narratives, but also a space to father your own textual children. *The Child in Time*, observes Adam Mars-Jones, 'is a narrative of pain and loss, but it is also a suppressed drama of symbolic ownership . . . only in the absence of the child does it become possible for the father's claims to be heard so favourably'.[22] This critique is acute: the narrative text – banishing rivals for maternal affection – does in some ways present itself as the inner space within which a self-consciously male author carries out his acts of creation and nurture.

There is also a long history of male novelists occupying the subject position and point of view of women. Many of the most celebrated, most highly canonical novels work on this formula. (While far from being unknown, it is much less common for female novelists to adopt male personae.) There are of course many problems attaching to glib recourse to authorial gender or biography; but, nevertheless, a reader's awareness of a disjunction between the gender of a novelist and that of his subject compels, as a form of cross-dressing, attention to the asymmetrical gendering of representation.[23] As so often in McEwan's work, the responsibility for narrative and for the veracity of narrative is a core subject.[24] By positioning the narrator of *Atonement* close to and later within the viewpoint of Briony, McEwan foregrounds the self-interestedness, and illocutionary, persuasive effects of fiction. Briony's unshakeable conviction that her reading of events is accurate has real-life effects in the text world. Here again, a paratext intervenes with a variant reading. The male critic and attributive reviewer of Briony's story *Two Figures by a Fountain* asks (inadvertently highlighting a key dynamic of the novel): 'if this girl has so fully misunderstood or been so wholly baffled by the strange little scene that has unfolded before her, how might it affect the lives of the two adults? Might she come between them in some disastrous fashion?' (*At*, p. 313). In some ways a mutation of L. P. Hartley's *The Go Between* (the country house as scene of sexual and class secrets, the naiveté of the child caught in the middle), the first section of *Atonement* revolves around Briony's self-conscious dramatization of herself as observer and writer. Having opened and read Robbie's obscene message, Briony feels confirmed in the view 'that she was entering an arena of adult emotion and dissembling from which her writing was bound to benefit' (*At*, p. 113). The burden of self-interested narrative, misleading through its very aesthetic coherence, is placed on the shoulders of a female narrator; and the rest of the novel consists in Briony's long-drawn out attempt to atone for what she has done.

By 'dressing up' as Briony, McEwan is enabled to test a thesis about the unreliability and self-interestedness of narration. In the end, the conclusion rests on the horns of a dilemma: given Briony's form in telling convincing but meretricious stories, which version of the fates of Robbie and Cecilia should we believe? 'But what *really* happened?' she imagines a 'certain kind of reader' saying. Her answer emphasizes the power of fiction: 'as long as there is a single copy, a solitary typescript of my final draft, then my ... sister and her medical prince survive to love' (*At*, p. 371). Briony's re-running of the story is close in spirit to Hillis Miller's extension of the theory of repetition to implicate the reader: 'if, in Lockwood's dream the air swarms with Catherines, so does this book swarm with ghosts who walk the Yorkshire moors inside the covers of any copy of *Wuthering Heights*, waiting to be brought back from the grave by anyone who chances to open the book'.[25] In *The Child in Time*, appraising Stephen's novel *Lemonade*, Charles tells Stephen: 'you've given [children] a first, ghostly intimation of their mortality' (*CT*, p. 33). The novelist in *Atonement*, disguised as Briony, has the power to give back to the characters the life that she has taken away.

As this essay has shown, in their treatments of masculinity, McEwan's texts seek to occupy sites and forms of cultural and symbolic prestige. This is not just an intertextual matter: in a more general, institutional sense, these prestigious sites and domains include not only the anonymized Venice of *The Comfort of Strangers*, but also law and the High Court in *The Children Act*; a wide swathe of science – Joe's profession as a science journalist, and especially the neurosurgery of *Saturday*; the broadsheet newspaper and symphonic composition of *Amsterdam*; and the performance of classical music (from Julie's violin in *The Child in Time* to Fiona's piano playing in *The Children Act*). There is also the re-investment of prestigious verbal texts, notably the ghostly presence of Virginia Woolf's *Mrs Dalloway* in *Saturday*. Matthew Arnold's 'Dover Beach', recited from memory by Daisy, so mesmerizes her assailant in *Saturday* as to enable the family's successful act of joint self-defence. Such foregrounded intertextuality can lead in different ways: in one direction, as we have seen, towards the ultimately fatal competition for superiority in *Amsterdam*, carried on over the dead body of Molly; in another, towards the playful and liberating reinvention of the cultural monument.

McEwan's acts of intertextual nesting find an analogy in the drive to enter other bodies: appropriating the body of the text parallels the symbolic occupation of human bodies. Women, reflects Stephen in *The Child in Time*, because of their 'faith in endless mutability, in re-making yourself as you came to understand more, or changed your version', were not so easily taken in than men 'by jobs and hierarchies, uniforms and medals'. In Stephen's estimation, 'women upheld some other principle of selfhood in which being surpassed doing', and so 'enclosed the space which men longed to penetrate' (CT, pp. 54–5); or, perhaps, to usurp. As the embryonic narrator of *Nutshell* jovially remarks while forcing his way out through the birth canal, 'no casual cock can compete' (N, p. 196). *Nutshell* bears some resemblance to *Amsterdam* in presenting as a kind of *jeu d'esprit*. But perhaps in its very playfulness it acts as another parable of creativity, its narrator unfettered by any 'inner censor', and freed to pursue, in a kind of intellectual game ('You may never have experienced, or you will have forgotten, a good burgundy ... or a good Sancerre ... decanted through a healthy placenta' N, p. 6), an exploration of what within the still potent constraints of normative masculinity might constitute inner space.

As seems to be the case with Charles Darke, men are represented as containing their childhoods, and irreparably damaged by their own attempts to suppress or deny them. *Nutshell* brings to the surface a homology between the reoccupation of the symbolic body of another text and the attempt of the imaginary male to occupy at once the imagined body of the female and of the lost child. *Nutshell* is simultaneously an elaborate intertextual engagement with *Hamlet* – Hamlet's words are foregrounded from the epigraph onwards – and another attempt to colonize female internal space. Like *The Child in Time*, this narrative ends in childbirth, this time complicated by the enclosure of another bounded 'nutshell', the carceral world in the form the incipient imprisonment of mother and child ('I'm thinking about our prison cell – I hope it's not too small' N, p. 199). The fact that McEwan goes to the lengths of re-writing *Hamlet* and inhabiting Trudy's body only to come up with a narrator who sounds like a perky, show-off-y male undergraduate (a little like Hamlet himself?), may constitute an act of self-criticism, an elaborate charade of self-awareness about the challenging task he has set himself.

The grounds of argument about gender have shifted substantially since the 1980s. The interest of McEwan's future writing might arise from how he comes to engage in these new paradigms. Nevertheless, social, political and ethical responsibility still rests on attempts to remake the narratives of masculinity. Despite efforts to divest himself of hierarchical authority, the male-identified writer or narrator still risks reasserting a superior narrative position. Writing back to the discourses and stories which have shaped you is likely to involve the recapitulation of an inherited narrative. Yet the shadows cast by patriarchy do not supply a reason for abandoning the project. McEwan's Perowne, like Virginia Woolf's Richard Dalloway at the end of his wife's day, thinks admiringly of his daughter.[26] The pregnant Daisy is not only naked, but (incited by her poet grandfather) recites from memory the words of Matthew Arnold in a last-ditch attempt to distract the abject Baxter and his accomplice. Perowne hears her reciting Arnold's verse, believing it to be her own. Yet Arnold himself is, in turn, engaged in his own existential struggle with the reproving paternal voice of Thomas Arnold. Patriarchy sets men up for a fall, the dream of autonomous power engendering both imposter syndrome and a constant battle to prove oneself the real thing. The king will almost certainly, like Claude/Claudius, turn out to be a usurper. Yet, finally falling asleep, Perowne starts to dream that 'he's a king, he's vast, accommodating, immune' (*S*, p. 269). McEwan's persistent preoccupation with masculinity and patriarchal authority vivifies his novels as the scene – an infinite space – of a restless search for alternatives.

NOTES

1 David James, '"A Boy Stepped Out": Migrancy, Visuality, and the Mapping of Masculinities in the Later Fiction of Ian McEwan', *Textual Practice*, 17 (2003), 1, pp. 81–100 (p. 86).

2 A valuable recent study is Richard Vinen's *National Service: A Generation in Uniform 1945–63* (London: Penguin, 2014).

3 This is usefully summarised in Victor J. Seidler, 'Men, Sexual Politics and Socialism', in *The Achilles Heel Reader: Men, Sexual Politics, and Socialism*, ed. Victor J. Seidler (London: Routledge, 1991) pp. 1–16.

4 *Or Shall We Die* (1983), with Michael Berkeley; printed in *A Move Abroad: 'Or Shall We Die?' and 'The Ploughman's Lunch'* (London: Picador, 1989).

5 Some sense of the range of work on masculinities stemming from the 1980s can be gained from: David Cohen, *Being a Man* (London: Routledge, 1990); David Jackson, *Unmasking Masculinity: A Critical Autobiography* (London: Unwin Hyman, 1990); Lynne Segal, *Slow Motion: Changing Masculinities, Changing Men* (London: Virago, 1990); Jonathan Rutherford, *Men's Silences: Predicaments in Masculinity* (London: Routledge, 1992) and Victor J. Seidler, ed., *The Achilles Heel Reader: Men, Sexual Politics, and Socialism* (London: Routledge, 1991).

6 Ross Chambers, *Room for Maneuver: Reading the Oppositional in Narrative* (Chicago: University of Chicago Press, 1991).

7 Saul Bellow, *Herzog* (1964; London: Penguin, 2001), p. 201.

8 See: McEwan's own website: www.ianmcewan.com/science.html; Dominic Head, *Ian McEwan* (Manchester: Manchester University Press, 2007), pp. 121–9.

9 This question is examined by Jonathan Rutherford in *Men's Silences: Predicaments in Masculinity*, pp. 173–94.

10 Caroline Levine, *Forms: Whole, Rhythm, Hierarchy, Network* (Princeton, NJ: Princeton University Press, 2015), p. 122.

11 Raymond Williams summarises his own use of 'structure of feeling', which he first used in the 1950s, in *Marxism and Literature* (Oxford: Oxford University Press, 1977), pp. 128–35: 'because all consciousness is social, its processes occur not only between but within the relationship and the related' (p. 130).

12 In this reading, I am drawing on Eve Kosovsky Sedgwick's classic mapping of homosocial relations, itself derived from a reading of René Girard's influential work on the imitative nature of desire. See René Girard, *Deceit, Desire, and the Novel: Self and Other in Literary Structure* (Baltimore: Johns Hopkins University

Press, 1972); Eve Kosofsky Sedgwick, *Between Men: English Literature and Male Homosocial Desire* (New York: Columbia University Press, 1985).

13 Jago Morrison, 'Narration and Unease in Ian McEwan's Later Fiction', *Critique*, 42 (2001), 3, pp. 253–68 (pp. 267–8).

14 Stephen's *Lemonade* is in a sense brought to birth in McEwan's own children's book *The Daydreamer* (London: Jonathan Cape, 1994), illustrated by Anthony Browne.

15 The allusion to Richmal Crompton's stereotype of the 'outlaw' schoolboy is quite explicit. Among the items in the regressed Charles's treehouse there are 'some William books' (*CT*, p. 112).

16 Adam Mars-Jones, 'Venus Envy', in *Blind Bitter Happiness* (London: Chatto and Windus, 1997), pp. 128–56.

17 Criticising Mars-Jones, Berthold Schoene-Harwood suggests that McEwan subverts the traditional male *Bildungsroman* through a form of *écriture masculine*. See Schoene-Harwood, *Writing Men: Literary Masculinities from 'Frankenstein' to the New Man* (Edinburgh: Edinburgh University Press, 2000), p. 168.

18 Judith Butler, *Gender Trouble: Feminism and the Subversion of Identity* (London: Routledge, 1990), p. 140.

19 Elisabeth Bronfen, *Over Her Dead Body: Death, Femininity, and the Aesthetic* (Manchester: Manchester University Press, 1992), p. 174.

20 Peter Brooks, *Psychoanalysis and Storytelling* (Oxford: Blackwell, 1994), p. 50.

21 The appendix to the novel slips in a compensatory reference to the couple adopting.

22 Mars-Jones, *Blind Bitter Happiness*, p. 148.

23 On this topic see Ben Knights, *Writing Masculinities: Male Narratives in Twentieth-Century Fiction* (Basingstoke: Macmillan, 1999), pp. 134–66.

24 A related instance is Jeremy's attempts to tell the tale of his wife's parents in *Black Dogs*. We must ponder which of his parents in law he sides with, and whose version of the original story emerges as the dominant, or, in the novel's terms, 'true' version.

25 J. Hillis Miller, *Fiction and Repetition: Seven English Novels* (Cambridge, MA: Harvard University Press, 1982), p. 72.

26 'He had looked at her, he said, and he had wondered, who is that lovely girl? and it was his daughter!' Virginia Woolf, *Mrs Dalloway* (1925; Harmondsworth: Penguin, 1964), p. 215.

9

DOMINIC HEAD

The Novellas

One aspect of McEwan's celebrated status as a stylist is his distinctive contribution to the novella, a genre that arguably reached its pinnacle in the late nineteenth and early twentieth centuries, especially in the work of Henry James, Joseph Conrad and D. H. Lawrence. Novellas like *Amsterdam* (1998), with its focused critique of the left-leaning elite who did well in the Thatcher era, and *On Chesil Beach* (2007), with its (apparently) precise anatomy of sexual mores, reveal how McEwan uses the novella as an incisive instrument of cultural analysis. Embracing, as well, *The Cement Garden* (1978) and *The Comfort of Strangers* (1981), this chapter considers what it means to be an accomplished contemporary novella writer by making the case that, throughout his career, McEwan has continued to work with great skill in an overlooked literary form, once thought to be the most sophisticated mode of shorter fiction.

Defining the novella is a notoriously difficult business: it is an elusive form, which means that any useful working definition will always be incomplete. Yet the attempt to pinpoint its characteristics can help to identify what is distinctive about the effects of the novella, effects that authors often exploit quite deliberately. In pursuit of a definition we must, inevitably, start with the question of length. E. M. Forster's assertion in 1927 that 'any fictitious prose work over 50,000 words' constitutes a novel has provided a rough basis for distinguishing novels from shorter forms of fiction ever since;[1] Mary Doyle Springer, though wary of the limitations of a taxonomy based on the word count alone, observes the empirical fact that 'a count of any anthology of novellas . . . will attest to a common length between 15,000 and 50,000 words'.[2] My word count estimates for McEwan's works suggest that *Amsterdam*, *On Chesil Beach*, *The Comfort of Strangers* and *The Cement Garden* fall into this range, with *Nutshell* at or just over the upper limit.[3] The exclusion of *The Children Act* is justified by its length which, at around 55,000 words is slightly longer than the novella's notional limit. It still has some of the qualities of a novella, however, and in the round of interviews for that work, McEwan reasserted his interest in the form, explaining that 'originally I saw *The Children Act* as a novella, max 40,000 words', confessing uncertainty as to whether or not 'there's a difference between a short novel and a novella'. He also points out that the closing pages of *The Children Act* contain an explicit homage to James Joyce's greatest short story/novella, 'The Dead'.[4] (This homage is discussed in more detail in Chapter 11.)

The rough and ready taxonomy of fictional prose forms implied above – up to 15,000 words for a short story, over 50,000 for a novel, with the novella occupying the middle ground – can be usefully supplemented by Judith Leibowitz's range of narrative effects: for her, the narrative task of the novel is 'elaboration', while that of the short story is 'limitation'. The midground, narrative purpose in the novella, is conceived as combining the two in such a way as to give a 'double effect of intensity and expansion'. This apparent contradiction is explained by the novella's dependence on a 'theme-complex', the rich development of interrelated motifs and ideas which produce an expansion of a work's thematic concerns, within a narrative with a limited focus.[5] Gerri Kimber's authoritative overview of critical accounts of this 'complex mode' identifies a couple of additional characteristics that will be relevant here[6]: Tony Whedon's understanding of how 'novellas work through refracting and splicing time'[7]; and Leibowitz's identification of a quintessentially modernist capacity in the novella's propensity to 'crystallize a large segment of experience, often a whole lifetime, by selecting important moments of that life or by selecting an event which alters its total pattern'.[8] The temporal compression described by Whedon is a comparable feature, revealing how novellas 'are often concentric, onion-like', so that 'one reads them by peeling away layers of scenes and exposition and time (and meaning) until one has a revelation of character'.[9] Novellas, then, share common ground with other narrative modes – the temporal compression of the modernist novel, for example – through such features as the 'theme-complex', which generates ideational richness within a limited narrative range of action and perspective.

Making the case for the significance of the novellas in the oeuvre is made more credible by the author's own enthusiasm for the form. Kimber, for example, has identified McEwan's 'almost messianic zeal' for the novella.[10] This is evident in his short piece for *The New Yorker*, 'Some Notes on the Novella', in which the novella's relationship to the novel is conceived as that of 'the beautiful daughter of a rambling, ill-shaven giant (but a giant who's a genius on his best days)'.[11] McEwan emphasizes the technical demands of the novella ('it lays on the writer a duty of unity and the pursuit of perfection'), the self-consciousness it induces ('the smoke and mirrors, rabbits and hats are more self-consciously applied than in the full-length novel'), and the importance of its tradition in the Western canon ('the means by which many first know our greatest writers').[12] Perhaps the most significant observation emerges from McEwan's comparison between novella and screenplay, 'both operating within the same useful constraints of economy – space for a subplot (two at a stretch), characters to be established with quick strokes but allowed enough room to live and breathe, and the central idea, even if it is just below the horizon, always exerting its gravitational pull'.[13] The technical characteristics and formal features I have been identifying will guide the readings of McEwan's work that follow. I am interested in the paradoxical effect of intensity and expansion, the refraction of time, the revelation of character and the centripetal force of a main idea or organizing principle. Most important, perhaps, is McEwan's understanding of the novella writer's (and reader's) self-consciousness, in the pursuit of economy and a kind of 'perfection' in which a central idea is richly embellished.

McEwan's defence of the novella, like much of his non-fictional writing, is complicated when one turns to his fiction. In that essay, McEwan addresses his own experience of finding his shorter fiction over the years dismissed by critics, suspicious that 'you're trying to pass off inadequate goods and fool a trusting public'.[14] In *Amsterdam*, however, he baits his critics by inviting that response. *Amsterdam* is often considered to be an inferior Booker winner, the prize (so this line of thinking goes) being awarded for his cumulative effort and, perhaps, to right the wrong that *Enduring Love* did not even make the shortlist in the previous year (just as *The Child in Time* was overlooked a decade earlier). Did McEwan write *Amsterdam* in quick time for the next prize as a 'spoiler' in the hope of defeating the ambitions of other contenders?[15] And does the book's preoccupation with the 'spoiler' in professional life – and, especially, in publishing – signal this arch ambition? If so, McEwan stretched the novella's tendency to underscore its self-conscious effects to breaking point, implicating himself and his work in its own telling satirical condemnation.

That idea of the 'spoiler' embodies a 'theme-complex' in the novella, at the heart of which is the demonstration of how the pursuit of professionalism outweighs ethical considerations. The term is used when newspaper editor Vernon Halliday's front-page coup is 'spoiled', his photograph of the foreign secretary in drag revealed before it's published (*Am*, p. 124); it also figures in the dénouement of the plot when Halliday realizes that he and his composer friend Clive Linley have hatched the same plan to have each other killed, exploiting the relaxed Dutch laws on euthanasia. Here, Halliday acknowledges 'reverentially' this 'spoiler' (*Am*, p. 173). The satirical message is

obvious enough: in a world where the activity of spoiling is revered, professional excellence has become an end in itself, and thus facilitates mutual
destruction between competitors. McEwan implicates literary prize culture
in this purview, prompting one reviewer to feel 'a satisfying irony in knowing that this is exactly the kind of book that the society McEwan satirizes
would pick as the best book of the year'.[16]

A quick impression of the novella's richness can be gleaned from a
comparison with the short story McEwan published on the occasion of his
seventieth birthday, *My Purple Scented Novel* (2018). This is a very short
piece about literary rivalry in which a novelist explains how he contrived to
steal his best friend's novel by means of a fiendish plan that makes his act of
plagiarism rebound on the victim.[17] McEwan makes an arch reference to
himself, and to *The Information* (1995) by Martin Amis, a novel with a plot
that hinges on literary rivalry (*MP*, p. 21), but McEwan's story is essentially
a short conceit about an ingenious literary theft. In *Amsterdam*, by contrast,
the implications of the rivalry become multifaceted, exploiting the novella's
paradoxical propensity to combine intensity and expansion. The satire
extends to the world of literary culture, implying an authorial self-critique;
and there is also a wider political resonance suggesting that the entrepreneur-
ial spirit of the Margaret Thatcher/John Major era inescapably infects the
wider culture. *Amsterdam*, as a literary event, embodies McEwan's response
to the paradox that a political era vilified in much of the literature it
provoked, also produced a renaissance in English fiction. Illustrating this
paradox in the wider professional sphere, McEwan paints a portrait of those
who 'had flourished under a government they had despised for almost
seventeen years' (*Am*, p. 12). Acknowledging the inevitability of compromise, he invites us to reflect on the difference between such accommodation
and capitulation, bravely asking us to consider his novella as an example of
the problem, a work on the cusp.

Structurally, McEwan capitalizes on the novella's limited range, focusing
on the careers on his two central protagonists, compressing the significant
aspects of their careers as he uncovers the kernel of each one's social identity.
Vernon Halliday and Clive Linley each face an ethical dilemma, which will
expose a fatal lack of substance in their professional conduct. For Halliday,
the key moment involves his decision to publish compromising photographs
of the xenophobic foreign secretary, Julian Garmony. He is trying to take his
paper *The Judge* downmarket, but he is out-manoeuvred by Garmony, and
the 'scoop' explodes in his face. There is an element of straightforward moral
come-uppance about this: Halliday, 'once an apologist for the sexual revolution', fails in his hypocritical attempt to cash in on a mood of moral
conservatism (*Am*, p. 73).

For Linley, the key ethical choice is starker. Blocked in his attempts to complete his commission – he is writing 'The Millennium Symphony' for the celebrations in 2000 – he goes hiking in the Lake District for inspiration, and duly finds the motif for his finale in the song of a bird. He ignores a disputing couple to keep the creative spark in mind, actually abandoning a woman being molested by a rapist. His moral come-uppance is as clear as Halliday's: the completed symphony is flawed by its final movement, derivative of Beethoven, and the performance is cancelled (*Am*, p. 176). McEwan, in the parallel portraits of his two principals, exposes the vacuity of a self-perpetuating professionalism, unresponsive to the contingencies of life.

Amsterdam, then, deploys the kind of overt patterning discernible in many classic novellas, concluding with an elegantly counterpointed dispensing of just desserts. Linley's major mistake in composing his symphony, apart from the plagiarism of Beethoven, is to reintroduce an earlier theme into his finale, as he races against the deadline, without achieving the 'significant variation' that is needed (*Am*, p. 142). For Craig Seligman (and probably for other readers too), Linley's failed composition is comparable with *Amsterdam* itself, which 'returns, at the end of the book, to the broad, troubling theme' that culminates in parallel murders, suggesting that 'McEwan is an aesthete like Clive, seduced by the beauties of symmetry, and he is undone, in the end, by his own exquisite craftsmanship: instead of betraying his structure, he betrays his book'.[18] As we have seen, this kind of patterning is actually a staple feature of the novella form, so that the apparent replication of Linley's failure might also be seen as an indicator of McEwan's formal accomplishment, even as he invites us to see the resemblance. The further risk is that Linley associates 'the absence of the variation [that] had wrecked his master-piece' with his plan to kill Halliday, which, he feels, 'had the amoral inevitability of pure geometry' (*Am*, p. 161). This anticipates the plot contrivance of the novella's conclusion, and taints it with both artistic failure and professional rivalry. To the extent that *Amsterdam* could be taken as a 'spoiler' prepared for the Booker panel, this is an arch joke indeed. But McEwan is also anticipating a critical environment in which the artistic virtues of the novella go unrecognized, so that the skilful use of novella techniques – doubling, patterning – actually reveal the formal literary accomplishment that they are notionally deployed to question, at the level of theme.[19]

A crucial aspect of the book is the ambivalent portrait of Linley, established as pompous and self-important in the opening pages – he believes he is 'Vaughan Williams' heir' (*Am*, p. 21) – yet he also reveals a populist, antimodernist conviction about art which resonates with McEwan, the epitome of the writer who combines popular and critical success (*Am*, pp. 21–2). Linley's conviction that traditional artistic virtues remain significant; or, in the specific case of music, that 'melody, harmony and rhythm were not incompatible with innovation' (*Am*, p. 22), may also encode McEwan's conviction about the enduring virtues of the novella tradition. The different moods and tones of the work produce images and ideas that contribute to the central theme-complex. For example, in one of the editorial meetings (these scenes are the highpoint of the satirical comedy in *Amsterdam*), the modernizing Halliday is enthused by the story of Siamese twins who have fallen out, and he wants to run a picture showing the bite marks on their faces (*Am*, p. 37), a crystallization of the idea of self-defeating antagonism. However, such a mood shift – the vacillation between knock-about satire and more earnest self-consciousness – wrong-foots the reader looking for clear signals about the book's moral dilemmas.

In relation to the decisive moments of moral quandary – Linley's failure to intervene at the rape scene, Haillday's decision to publish the compromising photograph – both characters seek to justify their actions, Linley by giving precedence to his 'creative excitement' (*Am*, p. 89), Halliday through the utilitarian justification that the humiliation of Garmony, a potential Prime Minister, will spare the country a term of disastrous government policy (*Am*, p. 74). Neither one is on sound ethical ground. Halliday's self-justification, in particular, shows how self-deception conceals the personal motivation: he is driven by professional success and personal vengeance, but wants to see a golden political age dawn as a consequence (*Am*, p. 111). It is the crystal-lization of an idea that inspired *Enduring Love* – that the human moral animal relies on self-deception to claim the moral high ground – which here also speaks to McEwan's formal accomplishment. The idea of writing a spoiler in the form of a work that will be perceived as 'slight' becomes a fascinating gesture of performance: is this authorial self-delusion, akin to the pretensions of the work's protagonists? Or is the presumption justified when the formal elegance of the piece is properly understood? McEwan relies fully on the self-consciousness that he feels novella readers are trained to recog-nize and to share.[20] Is *Amsterdam*, then, not a work of great seriousness? Phil Baker suggested that 'if, like Graham Greene, McEwan divided his books into "novels" and "entertainments", then there is no doubt into which category this one would fall'.[21] This also suggests some superficiality in the treatment of the book's ethical dilemmas, which, for Stuart Burrows, are displaced by 'McEwan's weakness for melodrama'.[22] Another way of accounting for these effects, as we have seen, is to see them as the self-conscious attributes of a well-written novella, archly adapted to the treat-ment of a superficial society. In this sense, to say the neatness of the book carries part of the critique is less a case of special pleading, more a recogni-tion of how novellas often foreground their technique.

As Baker's review of *Amsterdam* suggests, for some critics and readers McEwan's books can be divided into 'major' and 'minor' works, with the shorter, novella-length pieces comprising the group of minor works. It is worth noting, however, that McEwan learned his craft writing in the medium of short fiction with two short story collections, *First Love, Last Rites* (1975) and *In Between the Sheets* (1978), followed closely by his first novel/novella *The Cement Garden* (1978). It is clear that he found short fiction amenable to his purposes, with its concentration of theme, singularity of focus, and – especially – the absence of a dominant implied authorial voice. And in these early works it is possible to detect the first appearance of several of McEwan's major themes, including his engagements with masculinity, the 'new science' and his ecological concerns. McEwan made a rapid appearance in critical histories of the short story. In an account of the English short story of the 1970s, for example, Walter Evans rates McEwan as 'undeniably one of the decade's better writers'.[23] Discussion of him specifically as a novella writer, however, has been scarce. Clare Hanson is an exception. When her study of short fiction appeared, McEwan had published two longer works, *The Cement Garden* and *The Comfort of Strangers*, prompting her to observe that 'both McEwan's novels or novellas are organized around a central, compelling image: both deal with bizarre personal and sexual relations in a context far removed from everyday life'. Hanson recognizes McEwan's importance as a writer of short fiction because his 'adoption of the short fiction and novella forms is bound up with [his] focus on our most private and usually well-guarded feelings', revealing the 'implied social context' but without 'the weight of social commentary which seems inherent in the novel form'.[24]

A consequence of this technique can be the absence of a moral compass. While this is not unusual in twentieth-century fiction, it is especially apparent in works that present challenging views and behaviour. This has been keenly felt in readings of *The Cement Garden*.[25] Alternative forms of moral signposting are apparent, however. For example, McEwan makes an extended allusion to the writing tradition in which children are put into a situation in which they must fend for themselves.[26] A key reference here is to William Golding's *Lord of the Flies*, a novel with some novella-type attributes in its focus on a governing theme, explored and expanded without the elaboration of contextual markers. The opposition between the savage and the socialized individual is complicated in *The Cement Garden* in that McEwan's children are not entirely isolated from the social world. They are abandoned by the successive deaths of their parents and try to keep their sense of family together by entombing their dead mother in concrete in the cellar of their isolated house; but two of the children are on the cusp of adulthood, and all are influenced by adult codes of familial behaviour, which produces a distorted temporal compression in their independent existence, a process which culminates in the incestuous involvement of the eldest siblings.

This novella thus explores the region between social control and unfettered impulse, but also the perception that an extreme family imperative leads to a damaging neglect of socialization. In Jack's account, the parents had no friends outside the family, and the children have to conform to the 'unspoken family rule' that they should never bring friends home (CG, pp. 21, 19). Left to their own devices, the children's games result in the infantilizing and gender transformation of Tom, the promotion of Julie to the maternal role, and – in the culmination of the book's Oedipal theme – the eventual incest between Julie and Jack.[27] McEwan's claustrophobic novella invites us to speculate on the degree to which family life, in less extreme situations, might be in tension with the socialization of children. Equally, we are asked to ponder how growth to healthy sexual maturity requires a progression beyond the restrictions of the family unit: these are the chief resonances of this novella's central idea, and it has been carefully crafted to provide this focus. Indeed, McEwan has conceived of a situation in which their family dissolves at precisely the point where Jack and Julie are discovering their emergent sexuality. For them, there is no family left to move away from; so, to meet the psychological need that sexual maturity demands, they must reconstruct the bedrock of family security (to be rejected), by becoming 'mummy' and 'daddy'.

The children's distorted development is caught in McEwan's central image of the cement garden, which also suggests a wider context for the family's dysfunctionality. Following the convention of the novella, this contextual element is not developed, but its evocation demonstrates McEwan pushing at the frame of the literary form. The family house is isolated, but once stood in a row of other houses, demolished to prepare for a motorway that was never built (CG, p. 21). In a neighbouring street a few more houses remain, where most have been cleared to prepare for the building of four tower blocks: 'They looked even older and sadder than our house. All down their concrete sides were colossal stains, almost black, caused by the rain. They never dried out' (CG, p. 22). The urban desolation is more general, the predicament of Jack and his siblings suggestive of a broader social malaise. The father's cement garden – 'a fascinating violation' for Jack, (CG, p. 16) – is a metaphor for this association between familial collapse and social dissolution concealed as orderly planning. McEwan's concrete vista is a reminder of the dour, recession-hit Britain of the 1970s. (This is considered at greater length in Chapter 1.) There is also a literary context in that the metaphorical cement garden might also stand for the state of the British novel at the end of the 1970s, in a widely held view at that time.

The Comfort of Strangers (1981) is also tightly written and stylistically consistent, following the discipline of good novella writing. It bears comparison with *Amsterdam*, as an equally accomplished novella. Its central idea, and the locus of its theme-complex, is to explore the inner lack that results when individuals adopt value systems, or codes by which to live, having paid little heed to their own desires and needs. Simultaneously, it addresses the problematic relationship between values, ideas and literature. It is, arguably, McEwan's most disturbing book, and the culmination of his early 'shock lit' fiction. Set in Venice, the novella draws on a long literary tradition in which that city is a mysterious, claustrophobic and sometimes threatening place, and also the site of personal dissolution, as in Thomas Mann's *Death in Venice*. The two main protagonists, Colin and Mary, hold strong left–liberal political views – socialist and feminist – but seem lacking in conviction, or even understanding, about their private lives. They are stalked by the sinister Robert, whose wife is confined to their upstairs flat, having been invalided by Robert's sexual violence. The novella restricts its action to focus chiefly on the two contrasting couples, and the strange allure of the machismo Robert: Colin and Mary willingly go back to Robert and Caroline's flat, after an unnerving earlier visit, and Colin is murdered in front of a drugged Mary, who then, in her befuddled state, witnesses some kind of depraved sexual activity that involves the corpse, a disturbing scene that underscores the central idea that a psychological vacuum results when individuals order their lives according to codes of behaviour that are untested at a personal level.

The opening chapter establishes the principle by which the prose conveys both the mood and the theme. Little happens, and the languid expression conveys the strange state of limbo in which Colin and Mary find themselves 'not on speaking terms' without remembering why (*CS*, p. 9). Adrift in the 'oppressive' city they 'frequently become lost' (*CS*, pp. 12–13). They smoke marihuana in their hotel room, and seem without commitment or volition, yet they dress with great care each evening, as if preparing themselves for an anonymous 'someone who cared deeply how they appeared' (*CS*, p. 11). Of course, it is Robert who turns out to be this someone, the hint of prolepsis here marking them out as victims-in-waiting, made vulnerable through their own inadequacy. In David Malcom's account of the novella's narrative mode, he identifies a principle of 'limited omniscience' in which most of the observations are rendered through the focalization of Colin and Mary, but which can also avoid 'identification with any character's point of view'.[28] This results in a detached style that captures the characters' uncertainty about themselves and their predicament. In chapter four, Malcolm points out that Colin's view of St Mark's Cathedral, while sitting at a café table in St Mark's Square, is drawn from John Ruskin's *Stones of Venice*.[29] What is notable about this is the propensity for Colin's mind to wander from a drooling baby to the architecture the baby seems to be gazing at, as if his attention is random. In the paraphrase of Ruskin itself there is a hint of vacuity in the easy reliance on a second-hand appraisal. This limited omniscience, another feature of compression in the novella, is McEwan's chief method of characterization here.

The brooding setting is well-suited to this purpose of exposing psychological inadequacy since the status of Venice as a menacing and claustrophobic city is well established. The most obvious twentieth-century literary antecedent in which Venice is presented as a place of malaise is probably Thomas Mann's *Death in Venice*.[30] Like Mann's protagonist Aschenbach, Colin and Mary seem to be subconsciously seeking their own destruction. McEwan's novella has affinities also with Daphne du Maurier's story 'Don't Look Now', and the still more sinister film by Nicholas Roeg that it inspired.[31] There is, in fact, a long Western tradition of writing about Venice as a threatening place in which one can lose oneself, but it is the parallel with previous shorter fiction – and especially Mann's novella – that suggests McEwan's artful contribution to a tradition to which the novella is particularly suited, with its prioritization of mood over narrative omniscience.[32]

As the novella's theme about adopted gender identity develops, Robert's collection of his father's and grandfather's effects – which Colin ironically calls 'a museum to the good old days' – becomes important as a shrine of patriarchal control. After proudly showing Colin these artefacts – his grandfather's seal, and opera glasses, his father's brushes, pipes and razors, their favourite novels, in first editions – Robert waxes nostalgic for an age when men 'understood themselves clearly', and 'were proud of their sex' (*CS*, pp. 74–5). For Robert, feminism has caused confusion. Women, he feels, 'lie to themselves. They talk of freedom, and dream of captivity' (*CS*, p. 76). Robert's worldview is undermined by his gratuitous violence at the end of this scene, when he punches Colin in the stomach with 'a relaxed, easy blow' (*CS*, p. 77). Masculine assertion is of a piece with unmotivated aggression, we instantly recognize.

McEwan supplies several explanations – or, at least, causal effects – that have produced Robert's strange attitude to gender, so that Robert's psyche is governed by the inadequacy he feels at failing to live up to his own masculine ideal. His sexual violence is a form a reassertion – it began when he was diagnosed as infertile (*CS*, p. 116) – and it also manifests itself in a stereotypical form of macho homosexuality, embodied in his gay bar, another route through which his masculinity seems to be channelled into an aggressive urge. The novella's patterning sets the purposeless Mary and Colin against the assertive Robert, so that they are sexually reinvigorated after their encounter with him, discovering new levels of intimacy which brings with it sadistic and masochistic fantasies (*CS*, p. 86). In their dazed state, 'mesmerized' (*CS*, p. 54) by Robert, Colin and Mary's sexual imagination is bent to his will. McEwan's limited omniscience, giving access to his characters thoughts but not their motivation, ensures that readers are as uncertain about Colin and Mary's volition as they are themselves. When Colin and Mary go back to Robert and Caroline's flat, they go without having made a conscious decision to do so, apparently unable to resist. In this way, the novella demonstrates how desire can be shaped, or distorted, as in the case of sex murderer Robert whose identity is partly fashioned from the strictures about gender imbibed in childhood. In its presentation of gender extremes – from strict taboos to unfettered sexual violence – the novella shows how inhibition and stereotyping can distort or suppress the sexual imagination with disastrous consequences, unpredictable or violent. This is just as true of Mary's untested theoretical feminism as it is of Robert's inherited perception of traditional manliness, or his adopted aggressive homosexuality. In its theme-complex *The Comfort of Strangers* opens up its investigation of gender – which is rooted in the gender politics of its age – to a broader concern with the resources of the self.

On Chesil Beach makes full use of the novella's capacity, in a self-conscious treatment that involves highlighting its own formal procedures with a degree of reflexivity that makes it comparable with *Amsterdam*. The most obvious formal convention is signalled by the setting in the title. Deploying short fiction's cultivation of a dominant symbolic setting or motif – in the case of the novella, one thinks of the Congo in *Heart of Darkness*, the brooding London of Robert Louis Stevenson's *The Strange Case of Dr Jekyll and Mr Hyde*, or the floating city in *Death in Venice* – *On Chesil Beach* uses the idea of the seaside as a liminal space to symbolize its central idea: that one failed wedding night in 1962 can be taken as emblematic of the dividing line between the sexual liberation of the 1960s and the repression that preceded it. Chesil Beach, the long stretch of pebbles that separates the English Channel from the Fleet Lagoon, is the location for the events that epitomize this epochal change – or, at least, that is how the novella is set up vis-à-vis its contextual referent. As with the other novellas considered here, McEwan extends the capacity of short fiction to realize his larger social and historical purpose. He focuses chiefly on two characters, places emphasis on their state of consciousness and devises a plot that leads to a moment of crisis for both. That revelation, as I have indicated, implies that the experience of these characters is representative of an epochal change in social mores. In this manner, the context is evoked in the same way that a sense of epochal awareness emerges from the sense of malaise in *Death in Venice*, or the implosion of imperialism is figured in *Heart of Darkness*, or the inequality of Victorian London is suggested by Stevenson's motif of dualism in *The Strange Case of Dr Jekyll and Mr Hyde*. On *Chesil Beach* toys with a precise contextual location, as we will see; but it also complicates its apparently straightforward associations.

A quick reading of the book, then, might uncover a perhaps too-schematic attempt to summarize an epoch based on the representativeness of the principal figures; but while establishing this structure, McEwan also works assiduously to undermine it, so that each of his principals is revealed to have a skeleton in the cupboard, an element of dysfunctionality in their upbringing, so that their backgrounds disqualify them from representativeness. For in the lives of both protagonists, Edward and Florence, a degree of emotional and psychological disorder is discovered, so that the reader is apt to blame these personal aspects of their respective psyches for their failure to connect, rather than the puritanical social mores of their age. A brief resumé of decisive moments in each protagonist's life establishes this less public significance that we learn to attach to their lives. The Mayhew family life is dominated by the mental illness of the mother, brain-damaged after an accident on a railway platform when Edward was small (*OCB*, p. 70). The family muddles through, but the father's attempt to assert domestic order involves also an 'elaborate fairy tale' of normality (*OCB*, p. 67). The children are forced to collude in a collective secrecy; and when Edward is finally told of his mother's condition, at the age of fourteen, he is alienated, feeling a sudden sense of separation from his family (*OCB*, p. 72). His reactions are cloaked to the extent that they also have the semblance of the onset of adolescence. His upbringing, in short, has not given him a domestic model that he might take into a marriage. An indication of the emotional scars he bears is his fondness for getting into fights, when younger. This propensity for violence is something he has kept from Florence, but it makes him anxious on his wedding night: we read, 'he did not trust himself' because 'he could not be certain that the tunnel vision and selective deafness would never descend again' (*OCB*, pp. 91, 95).

The sexual failure of the unconsummated marriage is also signalled, and perhaps more obviously, in the compressed account of Florence's life, with its key defining moments: Florence, we deduce, has been the victim of an abusive father, so that her revulsion at the thought of sex seems to stem from this childhood trauma. Her memories of her father, and especially the trips the two of them made in his boat from Dover to France, indicate an effort of suppression which surfaces on her wedding night when the smell of the sea evokes an 'indistinct past', and a memory of 'lying still like this, waiting' in the cabin of her father's boat when she was twelve, trying to pinpoint the source of her shame (*OCB*, pp. 99–100). Her horror during the wedding night sex scene is a revelation based on the resurfacing of that which she has suppressed, her disgust at the feel of Edward's semen on her skin summoning 'memories she had long ago decided were not really hers' (*OCB*, p. 105). Edward and Florence, then, both seem to be classic cases for psychoanalysis, their peculiar backgrounds rendering them unsuited to an ordered domestic life, with a healthy sexual relationship at its heart. Here McEwan is doing something interesting with the novella form, and also with his readers' expectations. The novella's central action and setting – the failed sex scene and the couple's alienation from each other, in the liminal setting of Chesil Beach – invite us to see them as representative figures, on the cusp of the sexual revolution; yet, given their idiosyncratic personal histories, Edward and Florence are clearly mis-cast. The novella sets up a chain of signification, and a central idea, which is then under-mined by the complications of its theme-complex, in which familial dys-function is so particularized that it loses any straightforward social or cultural purchase.

The novella has affinities with both *Amsterdam* and *The Comfort of Strangers*, setting up a comparable main idea – in this case, as in *The Comfort of Strangers*, about sexuality – from which context-specific conno-tations can be extrapolated, only to undermine the epochal implication it sets up. McEwan is refusing the formal simplicity that is sometimes perceived in his shorter works, as he reasserts the self-consciousness that the novella demands from its readers; and here the reading pleasure depends partly on a knowledge of McEwan's career and the reception of his previous novellas. As McEwan well knows, the craft of the novella depends on a certain foregrounding of technique, and the novellas examined here reveal an accomplished deployment of the form's recognized features: the paradoxical combination of intensity and expansion; the compression or refraction of time; the economical rendering of character and the elaboration of a main idea. We are called upon to recognize how these formal features are utilized, but also how they can be resisted or enriched. In the interview with Robert McCrum cited above, McEwan said

> I think I will write, in my 70s, more novellas. I love the idea of sitting down to read something in three hours – about the length of an opera, or a long movie, or a play where all of its structure can be held in the mind. A novella is a great length, and it's a demanding genre in which things have to be settled quickly.

This attests to the seriousness with which he has approached the form, and also his sense of its stature and potential, something that has not always been recognized, perhaps, in the reception of these books.[33]

NOTES

1 E. M. Forster, *Aspects of the Novel and Related Writings* (1927; London: Edward Arnold, 1974), p. 3.
2 Mary Doyle Springer, *Forms of the Modern Novella* (Chicago: University of Chicago Press, 1975), p. 8.
3 By this reckoning, two slightly longer works, *Black Dogs* and *The Children Act*, then qualify as short novels.
4 Robert McCrum, 'Ian McEwan: "I'm only 66 – my notebook is still full of ideas"', *The Observer*, 31 August 2014 (Sunday). Retrieved from: www.theguar dian.com/books/2014/aug/31/ian-mcewan-children-act-interview-only-66-note book-still-full-of-ideas-robert-mccrum (accessed 18 January 2018). For the reviewer in *The Irish Times* the concluding 'homage to Joyce's masterpiece *The Dead*' is 'a brave if ill-advised parody' because 'the daunting emotional power Joyce reveals in that story is a quality absent from … McEwan's chillingly formidable repertoire'. See Eileen Battersby, 'Tried and Found Wanting: *The Children Act*, by Ian McEwan', *The Irish Times*, 28 September 2014 (Sunday). Retrieved from: www.irishtimes.com/culture/books/tried-and-found-wanting-the-children-act-by-ian-mcewan-1.1943142 (accessed 18 January 2018).
5 Judith Leibowitz, *Narrative Purpose in the Novella* (The Hague: Mouton, 1974), pp. 12–17.
6 Gerri Kimber, 'The Novella: Between the Novel and the Story', in *The Cambridge History of the English Short Story*, ed. Dominic Head (Cambridge University Press, 2016) pp. 530–46 (p. 530).
7 Tony Whedon, 'Notes on the Novella', *Southwest Review* 96 (2011), 4, pp. 565–71 (p. 566).
8 Leibowitz, *Narrative Purpose*, p. 52.
9 Whedon, 'Notes on the Novella', p. 566.
10 Kimber, 'The Novella', p. 530.
11 Ian McEwan, 'Some Notes on the Novella', *The New Yorker*, 29 October 2012. Retrieved from: www.newyorker.com/books/page-turner/notes-n-the-novella (accessed 1 January 2018).
12 Ibid. McEwan cites works by Thomas Mann, Henry James, Franz Kafka, Joseph Conrad and Albert Camus, and then extends his list of authors to include Voltaire, Tolstoy, Joyce, Solzhenitsyn, Orwell, Steinbeck, Pynchon, Melville, Lawrence and Munro.
13 Ibid.
14 Ibid.
15 Also on the short list were three established authors – Beryl Bainbridge, Julian Barnes and Patrick McCabe – who had not won the Booker Prize at that point (Barnes finally won in 2011), and who had also been short-listed before. The relative standings of the novel and the novella are succinctly conveyed in the words of Nicholas Lezard: the Prize, Lezard argued, is 'really is meant to go to

novels, not five-finger exercises'. See Nicholas Lezard, 'Morality Bites', *The Guardian*, 'Saturday Review', 24 April 1999, p. 11. When McEwan's next novella, *On Chesil Beach* was short-listed for the Prize in 2007, history did seem to be on the verge of repeating itself.

16 Juliet Waters, 'The Little Chill: Has the Booker Prize Chosen the Noveau Beaujolais of Fiction?' Retrieved from: www.montrealmirror.com/ARCHIVES/1998/120398/book.html (accessed 13 July 2005).

17 *My Purple Scented Novel* (London: Vintage, 2018). This story was published under separate covers on 21 June 2018, but had previously been published in 2016 in *The New Yorker*. Retrieved from: www.newyorker.com/magazine/2016/03/28/my-purple-scented-novel-fiction-by-ian-mcewan (accessed 2 July 2018).

18 Craig Seligman, review of *Amsterdam*, Salon.com, 9 December 1998. Retrieved from: www.salon.com/1998/12/09/sneaks_2/ (accessed 3 July 2018).

19 Fyodor Dostoevsky's *The Double* (1846) is perhaps the most famous instance of 'doubling' in the novella, using the motif of the doppelgänger as an economical way of investigating aspects of a single psyche.

20 Ian McEwan, 'Some Notes on the Novella'.

21 Phil Baker, 'Comfy Conspiracies', *TLS*, 4979, 4 September 1998, p. 9.

22 Stuart Burrows, review of *Amsterdam*, *New Statesman* 127 (11 September 1998), 4402, pp. 47–8 (47).

23 Walter Evans, 'The English Short Story in the Seventies', in *The English Short Story 1945–1980: A Critical History*, ed. Dennis Vannatta (Boston: Twayne Publishers, 1985), pp. 120–72 (p. 140).

24 Clare Hanson, *Short Stories and Short Fictions: 1880–1980* (Basingstoke: Macmillan, 1985).

25 See, for example, David Malcolm, *Understanding Ian McEwan* (Columbia: University of South Carolina Press, 2002), p. 44; and Kiernan Ryan, *Ian McEwan*, p. 13.

26 Jack Slay's list of novels based on 'the familiar plot of children suddenly abandoned and isolated' includes R. M. Ballantyne's *The Coral Island* (1857), Richard Arthur Warren Hughes's *High Wind in Jamaica* (1929) and Arthur Ransome's *Swallows and Amazons* (1930). See Slay, *Ian McEwan* (New York: Twayne, 1996), p. 36.

27 For a fuller treatment of psychoanalytical themes in McEwan see Christina Byrnes, *The Work of Ian McEwan: A Psychodynamic Approach* (Nottingham: Paupers' Press, 2002).

28 David Malcolm, *Understanding Ian McEwan*, pp. 67, 69.

29 Ibid., pp. 70–1.

30 Slay's list of earlier antecedents includes Dickens's *Pictures from Italy*, Byron's *Childe Harold* and Ruskin's *The Stones of Venice*. *Ian McEwan*, p. 73.

31 McEwan, responding to a question about this apparent influence, claimed not to have seen the film or to have read the du Maurier story when the novella was written. 'John Haffenden talks to Ian McEwan', *The Literary Review*, June 1983, pp. 29–35 (p. 32).

32 For a discussion of this literary tradition, see George B. von der Lippe, 'Death in Venice in Literature and Film: Six Twentieth-Century Versions', *Mosaic*, 32 (1999), 1, pp. 35–54.

33 Robert McCrum, 'Ian McEwan: "I'm only 66 – my notebook is still full of ideas"'.

10

JUDITH SEABOYER

Realist Legacies

Ian McEwan's novels, beginning with the taboo-breaking, gritty-realist romance *The Cement Garden* (1979), but excluding the surreal *Nutshell* (2016), are firmly embedded in the literary history of the shifting aesthetic mode that is novelistic realism. While this statement could imply either a rejection of the subversive linguistic play of the postmodernisms of the mid- to late-twentieth century or a reversion to the plot-driven novels of the Victorian period, it goes without saying that literary historical categorization is both subtler and more complicated than a case of one form either mimicking or neatly succeeding or 'supplanting' another.[1] The central features of McEwan's realism have remained constant, from the embedding of his fictions in the literary history of what Pam Morris reminds us is 'the technically demanding medium' that is novelistic realism, to his finely tuned observation and critique of 'public and private spheres and outer and inner worlds' paralleled with an ongoing dialogue about ethics.[2] What has changed is that the aesthetic shift in contemporary novelistic realisms that began in the last decades of the twentieth century and continues into the twenty-first has begun to be read and critiqued differently. Consilience, a suitably Victorian neologism, is a useful term for this shift as what 'jumps together' in McEwan's work is meaning-making postmodern strategies and the kinds of literary realism characteristic of the long nineteenth century. I illustrate my discussion of this move towards post-realism with three of McEwan's mid-career novels that share a historical, geopolitical context: *The Innocent* (1989), *Black Dogs* (1991) and *Atonement* (2001). *The Innocent* brings together postmodern parody and realist Cold-War espionage fiction and film, while *Black Dogs* and *Atonement* are strongly realist metafictions that depend on an intertextuality whose resonance invites a critique of individual and communal social violence, particularly as a crime against 'the innocent'. For *Black Dogs* and *Atonement*, the shared aspect of that context is loosely the Second World War, and in the case of *The Innocent*, the Cold War as it arose from the 'still-warm ashes of the hot one'.[3] Literary technique, together with their real-world context, make these three novels narrative vehicles for McEwan's long-standing ethical exploration of human violence across both public and private spheres. I situate them as broadly realist and specifically post-realist.

Jed Esty argues novelistic realism 'is always a diffuse and moving target, as difficult to define as it is properly to apply'.[4] However, it has persistent characteristics that can be traced throughout McEwan's novels, which conform to Stephen Arata's definition (with reference to Kate Flint), in which realism reveals a historical commitment to everyday life, to 'a valuation of ordinary people, events and experiences', and also 'a qualified belief in the power of language to mirror accurately the world without and the world within'.[5] McEwan's fictions are informed by the kind of close description and dependence on social and cultural contexts that characterize the canonical novels of the long nineteenth century – from Jane Austen to George Eliot to Henry James, and from Honoré de Balzac to Gustave Flaubert to Leo Tolstoy. At the same time, they exhibit the characteristic and persistent stylistic changefulness these writers' novels exemplify. A further marker of McEwan's fiction is the productive conjunction of a range of disciplines. Arguing for the importance of realism, he has said of his own work that 'things that never happened tangle with things that did', so that the 'imaginary' enters into a dialogue with 'the flesh-and-blood real' of 'science, math, history, law, and all the rest'.[6] Such interdisciplinarity signals the postmodern but, as Gillian Beer directs us to see, High Victorian realism was as shaped by the new science that was evolutionary theory as it was by the intersecting socio-political effects of the industrial revolution and urbanization.[7]

From its inception, novelistic realism has been diminished as '[lacking] the cultural capital or prestige of poetry and drama', and since the late nineteenth century it has been denigrated periodically as a retrograde formal copy of its precursors that makes nothing new in its nostalgia for a lost plenitude.[8] The negative critique of post-realisms like McEwan's is part of this pattern. For example, in 1996, Jeanette Winterson, with her signature bravado, scorned much late twentieth-century fiction as 'a modern copy of a nineteenth-century novel ... no better than any other kind of reproduction furniture'. A turning away from post-war modernist experimentalism, she argued, has condemned 'writers and readers to a dingy Victorian twilight'.[9] This irritation with what is perceived to be a refusal of experimentalism persists. Sean O'Hagan reports David Shields's impatience with 'well-wrought' contemporary novels, 'exemplified by Ian McEwan's *Atonement* and Jonathan Franzen's *The Corrections*': Shields considers such works to be 'antediluvian texts that are essentially still working in the Flaubertian novel mode. In no way do they convey what it feels like to live in the 21st century. Like most novels, they are essentially works of nostalgic entertainment'.[10] His comments could as easily refer to any number of other contemporary British and North American post-realist fictions, from Zadie Smith's *On Beauty* (2005), Julian Barnes's *The Sense of an Ending* (2011) and Alan Hollinghurst's *The Stranger's Child* (2011), to Barbara Kingsolver's *The Lacuna* (2009), Ruth Ozeki's *A Tale for the Time Being* (2013) and Jennifer Egan's *Manhattan Beach* (2017). Like *Atonement*, each of these novels is identifiably realist, but like *Atonement* each positions itself within the mode and adapts it in response to contemporary socio-political concerns and by means of postmodern literary strategies. It goes without saying that any perceived nostalgia might best be read with an awareness of the critical shift they achieve by bringing to bear postmodern irony, parody, hybridity, metafictionality and a dialogue that engages its precursors as well as future fictions. Such works can be considered 'post-realist', and transformative in ways that David Shields's manifesto may not account for.[11]

The shift from realism to post-realism is, then, structural, and it has to do with situating the novel in terms of both realism and postmodernism. Esty argues the recent realist turn in literary fiction became marked in the 1990s, but 'has surfaced as a visible literary-critical issue [only] in the last ten years'.[12] Post-realism is increasingly understood to be less a flight from modernist and postmodernist experimentalism than an attempt to communicate the urgency of real-world crises using 'language to communicate, not as verbal display'.[13] The novels discussed here are exemplary of historical realism in that they describe in fine detail geopolitical events from the Second World War and the Cold War that continue to haunt the twenty-first century. They also embrace and are inflected by what Linda Hutcheon terms the 'discursive strategies' and 'ideological critique' that are an ethical legacy of the postmodern.[14] These techniques function at both the public and the personal levels. With a typically ironic nod to the 'both/and' of postmodernism, Hutcheon famously remarks 'it's over', only to raise questions of a continuing politics of *postmodernity* at the start of the twenty-first century and its potential 'political efficacy'. She is, she says, 'convinced that the answers we might come up with' in response to those questions 'will have profound political implications for both the textual and the worldly dimensions of our culture in the future'.[15] If they are understood as post-realist, *The Innocent*, *Black Dogs* and *Atonement* illustrate the change Hutcheon predicts in their deployment of nineteenth-century realist and late twentieth-century postmodern effects in writerly ways that invite a re-visioning of the way we live now.

The Innocent and *Black Dogs* are companion pieces in that *The Innocent*'s focus is a historical joint US–UK surveillance operation and foreshadows the erection of the Berlin Wall, a concrete metaphor for the ugliness of the psychological and physical violence perpetrated on German citizens in the Cold War struggle for hegemony in the names of competing ideologies, while *Black Dogs* records the Wall's equally metaphorical collapse in 1989, with its suggestions of 'the triumph of capitalism'.[16] Both may be defined as realist in that they exhibit all the markers I have listed, but they are structurally different. *The Innocent* parodies Cold-War espionage fiction as it was unsettled by John le Carré, while *Black Dogs* is, like *Atonement*, and like McEwan's other espionage novel, *Sweet Tooth* (2012), overtly metafictional. As a fiction about the difficulties of writing memoir, *Black Dogs* self-consciously parodies 'the memoir boom' David Shields has attributed to 'reality hunger' and what he terms 'the generic edge, the boundary between … nonfiction and fiction', the turn to life writing symptomatic of a contemporary hunger for reality that is accompanied by a critical awareness that 'nothing … is so unreliable as memory'.[17] At the level of the fiction, the narrative is the result of the first-person narrator's process of recording his protagonists' memories and it makes clear what Shields terms the deceptions of memory at the same time as it interrogates the ethics of writing the lives of others.[18]

Black Dogs questions the ethics of responding to human violence in the private and the public sphere – but its metafictionality means it also questions the ethics of writing about, and reading about, that violence. *Atonement* is metafiction all the way through, as it traces the sixty-four-year fictional history of the writing by its fictional protagonist of a realist fiction that turns out not simply to resemble but to *be* the novel published by McEwan as *Atonement*. At the same time, it is a metafictional mapping of the literary history of novelistic realism and its influence, from Samuel Richardson's *Clarissa* (1748) and Austen's *Northanger Abbey* (1818) to Virginia Woolf's interwar novel, *Mrs Dalloway* (1925) and Elizabeth Bowen's most famous novel of the Blitz, *The Heat of the Day* (1948).

By means of postmodern parody, *The Innocent* questions constructions of a heroic post-war pitting of western political ideals of social and political freedom against the threat of the expansion of Soviet communism. Except for the brief, ruminative final chapter in which the protagonist, Leonard Marnham, returns to the scene of the crime after some thirty years, the narrative unfolds over a few months from 1955. Leonard's innocence ends in the double space that is the edgy occupied city of Cold-War Berlin, and the underground world that is the CIA–MI6 surveillance project. The geographies and timelines of *Black Dogs* and *Atonement* are contrastingly expansive – the narratives move through some forty-five and sixty-four years, respectively, and between London and rural England and France, and in the case of *Black Dogs*, Berlin. Space and time allow for a more reflective, ethical critique than that allowed to Leonard. By means of memory, *Black Dogs* moves back and forth from the last years of the Second World War, through the Cold War to the fall of the Wall as its narrator, somewhat half-heartedly, researches a memoir of his mother-in-law, June Tremaine. Memory's fallibility, combined with narrative motivation on the part of the memoirist and his subject, conspire against the desire to pin down the truth of what 'really happened'. It is only when Jeremy indulges a 'divagation' (*BD*, p. 37) that the fictional memoir becomes a vehicle for a dialogic investigation of Jeremy's parents-in-law's irreconcilable ideological responses to social injustice. This investigation allows its readers to consider how they might, as individual subjects, lead an ethical life in the face of a seemingly irremediably violent world. That is the question at the heart of *Atonement*, too, though its play with the idea of metafiction does mean it extends to ethical questions about the content and style of the novel, and the orientation of the reader.

The only character who would qualify as a spy in *The Innocent* is George Blake, who, in real life as in McEwan's novel, was the double agent who betrayed Operation Gold to the Soviets long before work on the tunnel began.[19] Leonard Marnham is a twenty-five-year-old English Post Office communications technician who, until his transfer to Berlin, has lived in Tottenham and commuted to the Post Office Research Station at Dollis Hill. Apart from the war years spent in his grandmother's house in 'a Welsh village over which no enemy aircraft had ever flown' and a 'lonely three years at Birmingham University', he has lived at home with his parents (*I*, pp. 5, 61). Dollis Hill has close links to Bletchley Park, famous for its codebreaking activities during the Second World War. The Government Code and Cipher School moved its headquarters in 1946, and although the Central Training School remained until 1987, there is little evidence in Leonard's focalized narrative that he has training in espionage beyond an expertise in tapping telephone lines.[20] *The Innocent* is set for the most part in the realistically detailed city of Berlin ten years after the Armistice and ten years into the Cold War. The focus, however, is not the struggle for world dominance between the two emerging superpowers, but an ironic, at times darkly comic, reading of the Anglo-American Special Relationship as a political attempt to negotiate the reality of the last stages of the waning of Britain's international economic and political power and influence in the face of the rise of United States hegemony.

The shift of power is parodied by means of the stereotyping of British and American behaviours. On his arrival in Berlin, Leonard is briefed by his British contact, Lieutenant Lofting, before being passed on to his American supervisor, Bob Glass. Lofting is defensive and Bob Glass correspondingly confident that only the United States's contribution to Operation Gold counts. Driving the parody home, there is an echo of nostalgia for the lost global power of the British Empire in Lofting's scorn for the Americans as once-were colonial subjects: 'it's not the Germans or the Russians who are the problem here … it's the Americans. They don't know a thing. What's worse, they won't learn, they won't be told. It's just how they are' (*I*, p. 1). For Lofting, the bone of contention, laid out in detail over the ten minutes the briefing lasts, is not the espionage operation, but the shifting of an inter-sector swimming match to the American sector. The briefing itself is no more than the advice that, owing to a perceived British breach of protocol, 'the Yanks' have insisted Leonard be 'handed over' (*I*, pp. 2–3). Leonard is secretly delighted.

For all that Leonard frequently feels insulted by Glass, he admires his self-assurance, and comes to appreciate for its clarity 'the near rudeness of the American's speech … the absence of the modifiers and hesitancies that were supposed to mark out a reasonable Englishman' (*I*, p. 124). Glass, on the other hand, is exasperated by the reticent British being too 'busy being gentlemen [to] do their jobs' (*I*, p. 10). His view of who is the junior partner in Operation Gold shows power equates to wealth. The United States has paid for the project, while the British have 'supplied the light bulbs' and engineering expertise in the form of the vertical tunnelling necessary to lay Leonard's taps. Glass is quick to put the latter contribution into perspective: 'You think we couldn't lay those taps ourselves? … It's for politics that we're letting you in on this. We're supposed to have a special relationship with you guys, that's why' (*I*, p. 24). When the project is exposed, the Berlin press, interested only in US–USSR conflict, chooses not to give Britain any credit: 'The fluorescent lightbulbs bore the name of Osram, England, "clearly an attempt to mislead. But screwdrivers and adjustable wrenches give the game away: all are marked 'Made in USA'"' (*I*, p. 215).

Because the narrative is almost entirely focalized through Leonard, tensions around the Special Relationship exist as personal antagonisms and petty games but, as is so often the case with McEwan's realism, personal relationships map onto broader, and in this case, national issues. Crucial in this connection is Leonard's physical and metaphorical myopia and his blinkered, tunnel vision. He imagines dispensing with his glasses since the 'things he really wanted to see were up close. A circuit diagram. A valve filament. … A girl's face' (*I*, p. 4). Within weeks he will have fallen in love, and Maria Eckdorf's face, to say nothing of her body, will be added to the things Leonard can see without his glasses. However, much that matters will remain distant, out of focus. Leonard has been in Germany for almost nine months when he goes home for Christmas to realize he identifies as a Berliner, and that he is homesick for Maria, and the tunnel: 'he had come to love its earth, water and steel smell ... He missed the perfection of the construction ... the habits of secrecy and all the little rituals that went with it' (*I*, pp. 123–4). This description uncannily mirrors his pleasurably claustrophobic experience of Maria's flat, where the bitter cold means their lovemaking takes place 'burrowed down into the humid gloom' of her bed, beneath an ingenious precarious construction of 'blankets, coats, bath towels, an armchair cover and a nursery quilt' (*I*, p. 77).

He and Maria follow Cold War politics on the radio and in the newspapers (*I*, pp. 116–17) and on his visit home he is aware his family and neighbours are oblivious to the power struggle that is being played out in Europe. Tottenham is 'drowning in ordinariness ... there was no tension, no purpose'. West Germany has been accepted into NATO, but the men 'at his father's local' have not heard of the Soviet response in the form of the recently ratified Warsaw Pact. '[T]he great struggle to keep Europe free', which Leonard now thinks of as his own, 'is as remote [from Tottenham] as the canals of Mars' (*I*, p. 123). Prompted by a friend of his father he gives an account of Berlin that, apart from 'the bomb damage', bears little resemblance to Leonard's experience as he makes his way back and forth 'between his two secret worlds' (*I*, p. 77). 'The fabulous money made by smugglers, the kidnappings – men dragged shouting and kicking into saloon cars and driven off into the Russian sector, never to be seen again' (*I*, p. 123) recall the British and US films likely to have been among those Leonard has 'studied ... in depth at his local Odeon' (*I*, p. 1).[21] Perhaps his mole-like blindness to the deadly reality and the folly of the US–USSR relationship that is so clear in le Carré's novels goes some way towards explaining the cognitive dissonance that allows Leonard to betray the tunnel he had loved: 'the tunnel was not on his conscience. If it was right to spy on the Americans for MacNamee's [i.e. Britain's] interests, it was fine to sell the tunnel for his own' (*I*, p. 222). In the light of his flight home and his failure ever to contact Maria, the absence of any mention of her 'interests' perhaps further links her to the tunnel: loved, certainly, but in the face of Leonard's understandable fear of being tried for her ex-husband's murder, 'not on his conscience'.

It is ten years since Germany surrendered to the Allies, bringing to an end the War le Carré, looking back after fifty years, describes as a mere 'distraction' in a longer struggle for power. As soon as it was over, 'hard-liners of East and West ... could get on with the real war that had started with the

Bolshevik Revolution in 1917, and had been running under different flags and disguises ever since'.[22] McEwan's parody raises the ethical question signposted by its title and complicated by its parodic engagement with three recognized realist Cold-War masterworks: le Carré's *The Spy Who Came in from the Cold* (1963), its 1965 film adaptation by Martin Ritt and Carol Reed's *The Third Man* (1947).[23] *The Innocent* echoes the cynical awareness of all three narratives of the power games that drove the Cold War and the effect of those games on 'the innocent'. In le Carré's novel, Fiedler, a committed Stalinist, challenges British agent Leamas to decide whether 'the taking of human life' as collateral damage can be justified, confessing 'I myself would have put a bomb in a restaurant if it brought us further along the road. Afterwards I would draw the balance—so many women, so many children; and so far along the road'.[24] Leamas refuses to be drawn, but in the film adaptation he puts his case in response not to Fiedler's but to Nan Perry's defence of communism.[25] He relates a traumatic personal anecdote that speaks to McEwan's novel: 'Communists, capitalists. It's *the innocent* who get slaughtered' (emphasis added).[26] In the novel, the anecdote is a reflective interior monologue, but in Ritt's adaptation Leamas's sense of his complicity is spelt out. In le Carré's novel, he recalls driving too fast on an autobahn, 'weaving between [a] hurtling stream of giant lorries', because he is late for a meeting with an East German agent. He narrowly avoids colliding with a car containing four 'waving and laughing' children, and has 'a vision of the little car ... pounded and smashed, until there was nothing left ... and the bodies of the children, torn' like the bodies of refugees he had seen bombed as they streamed along a road outside Rotterdam.[27] Both the novel and its film adaptation conclude as Perry and Leamas attempt to cross back to the West by climbing the Wall. Nan, suspected by Smiley of knowing too much, is shot by his people. Leamas climbs back down to die with her. His awareness of his complicity in the betrayal and death of an innocent is made clear by the novel's last sentence: 'As he fell, Leamas saw a small car smashed between great lorries, and the children waving cheerfully though the window'.[28]

In Reed's *The Third Man*, 'the innocent' are also figured as children although they suffer at the hands of the historical post-war black market in Vienna whose driving force is greed rather than political ideology. When the American innocent, Holly Martins, confronts his old school friend Harry Lime about his peddling of diluted and contaminated penicillin that has caused the deaths and permanent disability of children, the two men are poised high on a Ferris wheel overlooking a Viennese fairground.[29] The people below are reduced to 'dots' from this God's-eye view and Lime commands Martins to 'Look down there. ... Would you really feel any pity

if one of those dots stopped moving forever? If I offered you twenty thousand pounds for every dot that stopped, would you really, old man, tell me
to keep my money, or would you calculate how many dots you could afford
to spare?'³⁰ There is a philosophical difference between le Carré's and Ritt's
response to violence against the innocent and Reed's response. The moral
politics of the retributive justice Martins dispenses to Lime in *The Third Man*
are complex, but Martins is allowed to act to destroy Lime as a figure for evil
in a way that is refused Leamas. The innocent American kills Lime; the
world-weary Leamas can only refuse to continue his role in the corrupt game
that is Cold War espionage.

The Innocent's establishing shots of the city are as meticulously, realistically detailed as those in Reed's film, from streetscapes to domestic interiors
to bars to night clubs to the interior of the tunnel. The 1950s clothes are
described in similar detail for what they tell us about their wearers. But the
novel's third-person narration of this space is focalized almost entirely
through Leonard, whose view is shaped by Hollywood and British thrillers
and film noir.³¹ This is signalled early when the third-person narrator gently
mocks Leonard's desire to fit into this American-occupied space and establish himself as central to the operation. He practices his phone manner
before making the first contact – 'Relaxed. Purposeful. *Leonard Marnham
here. I think you've been expecting me*') – only to collapse 'into the English
dither he had wanted to avoid' as soon as Glass picks up and barks his name
into the receiver (*I*, p. 4).³²

The Innocent's historical realism is underpinned by Operation Gold,
which burrows its way into the heart of the fiction, and this enables another
nod to *The Third Man*, in this case its labyrinthine criminal underworld for
which human excrement is a metaphor. The fugitive Lime haunts Vienna's
elaborate system of tunnels that dispose of the city's waste, and it is here he is
shot by Martins. *The Innocent*'s tunnel parodies the iconicity of Reed's
Viennese metaphor as the American tunnellers entertain their colleagues in
the staff canteen by recounting how they 'had had to shovel their way
through the run-off of their own cesspit'. An 'English voice' reinforces the
element of absurdity underscoring the dirty business that is espionage:
'Digging through your own shit, that just about sums this business up' (*I*,
p. 65). Blake's betrayal of the project before it begins further underscores the
politics of the absurd surrounding Cold-War espionage and the brutal
division of Berlin and of Germany, the separation of communities and
'innocent' individual families that is so memorably metaphorized in the
grand guignol anatomization of the body of Maria's ex-husband, Otto,
which 'makes a gruesome point about the carving up of the global
body politic'.³³ 'So much wasted effort', as Maria writes to Leonard of

Operation Gold in her last attempt to reach him after his three decades of silence (*I*, p. 241).

Black Dogs, published two years after *The Innocent*, reflects on 'deep roots' theories of violence as the communal expression of a behaviour so embedded not only in human history, but also in the evolutionary history of our species, as to seem immutable. The novel is structured as a philosophical dialogue and may be seen as a complicating development of *The Innocent*'s exploration of Cold War politics. For example, *Black Dogs*, in its conversation with Albert Camus's *The Plague*, asks the reader to recognize war, and the Second World War in particular, to be a recurrent symptom of a disease that is the embedded human propensity for violence that will return to haunt Europe so long as its nature and causality continue to remain repressed. The narrative teases out an ethical dilemma by means of juxtaposing two grand narratives, metaphysical belief and materialist rationality.[34] McEwan's narrative fits Morris's argument that realism is 'constructed in accordance with secular empirical rules' but, as Morris also argues, 'realist forms have given expression to some of the most powerful representations of spiritual conviction'.[35] Jeremy illustrates the juxtaposition by means of June's and Bernard's vivid but necessarily fallible memories of an incident that set them on 'separate journeys' in the first weeks of their marriage (*BD*, p. 140).

Just married and newly signed up as members of the Communist Party of Great Britain, June and Bernard embark on a walking tour across the south of the Cevennes (*BD*, p. 26). The day before, June's rational materialism had been shaken when she and Bernard, an entomologist by training, have their first argument, triggered by the ethics of destroying animals for research – specifically a ruddy darter dragonfly, not rare 'but ... unusually large, a beauty' (*BD*, p. 76). Years later and after June's death, Bernard relates to Jeremy his recollection of what happened as foreshadowing the opening of an unbridgeable gap between his materialism and the 'consoling magic' that is June's 'hocus-pocus' spirituality (*BD*, pp. 80, 81). Bernard's memory, as Shields might explain it, is narrativized because it explains the marriage's failure. The anecdote 'has been mythologized by repetition into [a] well-wrought [chapter] in the story of [his life]',[36] the means, as Jeremy puts it, of making 'retroactive sense of an overcrowded memory' (*BD*, p. 50). According to Bernard, as he remembers events forty-three years later, June had accused him of wanting to 'control' '"creation", as she called it, ... I wanted to ... choke the life out of it, label it, arrange it in rows. ... It wasn't injustice that bothered me so much as untidiness. ... What I wanted was a society ... justified by scientific theories' (*BD*, p. 77). Their 'row' and the joyful reconciliation that follows, lead to their missing their train and changing their route to one that sets the scene for June's retroactive sense-making, the 'famous anecdote' of the encounter with the black dogs that she has narrativized as the turning point in the marriage. She insists this should 'be the centrepiece of [the] memoir, just as it was in her own story of her life – the defining moment . . . by whose light' we might also see Jeremy's third-person version of events (BD, p. 50). The vividly realist centrepiece, which Jeremy reads as 'family lore, a story burnished with repetition, no longer remembered so much as incanted like a prayer got by heart', duly replaces the memoir he had hesitated to write (BD, p. 49). The accuracy of the recollection of the event no longer matters as it becomes the vehicle for Jeremy's broader metaphysical discussion about living an examined life.

Jeremy begins with June's experience of the deserted, dramatic landscape of the limestone plateaux of the Cevennes. Before they reach the route she already '[feels] a sourceless fear' (BD, p. 141) that is intensified once they reach the path that leads 'a thousand feet down' to the river where the air contains a fear-inducing 'darkness just beyond the reach of vision' (BD, p. 141). June walks on ahead (echoing his recounting of the dragonfly episode, Bernard has become fascinated by the apparently 'purposeful' but incomprehensible behaviour of 'a caravan of two dozen brown furry caterpillars' BD, p. 146), where her path is 'blocked' by the 'mythical' dogs, which present 'an allegory for her decipherment alone' (BD, pp. 143, 144). She and Bernard will learn the dogs were abandoned when the German Army retreated north in 1944, so they bear ghostly traces of the region's wartime occupation. They stalk and then attack her. June attributes her ability to fight them off to a 'Presence', 'an oval penumbra many feet high', of which we read: 'if this was God, it was also, incontestably, herself' (BD, p. 150). She spends the rest of her life exploring what is revealed to her in this epiphany, and Jeremy allows her ideology equal space with Bernard's empirical view, which 'finds its truths in the particular and specific'.[37]

Jeremy envies his subjects their ideological passions, but his narrative makes it clear resolution was never the point. What matters is the invitation to engage in a hospitable reading that is a conversation about the nature of human evil as it plays out in the private and the public spheres. Black Dogs imagines into existence the potential for social and political change not through either of the philosophical ideologies espoused by June and Bernard, but through action aware of its inherent risks. Like Leonard, Jeremy is confronted with evil in the form of persistent domestic violence perpetrated by a 'couple [who] worked in evident harmony' to bully their small son physically and psychologically (BD, p. 128). Unlike The Innocent's Leonard and Maria, who accidently kill her violent former husband in self-defence, Jeremy has a choice. He can act to defend the innocent victim of the crime or he can decide to respect the 'inviolable, private space' that surrounds the idea of the family (*BD*, p. 129). His first thought is 'someone, not me, had to intervene', but when the father hits his son 'with the unrestrained force of adult hatred' Jeremy challenges him to a fight (*BD*, p. 129). Recalling warfare or espionage, Jeremy fights dirty – it is a fight he must win if he is to save the innocent. He stuns the Frenchman by breaking his nose before he has time to 'square up' and uses the opportunity to land three more punches to the 'face, throat and gut, before he went down'. He is only prevented from kicking him 'to death' by another restaurant guest, who calmly says 'Ça suffit' – June's words to the black dogs. Jeremy is horrified to realize that with victory had come an 'elation ... that had nothing to do with revenge and justice'; he recognizes he is capable of taking pleasure in perpetrating violence when the need for it has passed (*BD*, p. 131). This chimes with *The Innocent*'s context: the victors of the Second World War continue the punishment of a defeated Germany, and particularly of its innocent civilian population, in the service of the US–USSR struggle. As late as 1955, long after the Marshall Plan had come into effect, Leonard's first experience of Germany is one of personal 'pride' over 'a defeated nation'. Despite having been fourteen years old on V-E day and having been evacuated from London for the entirety of the Blitz and 'despite ... the fact that it had been the Russians who had liberated the city', he walks through a residential district 'with a certain proprietorial swagger' (*I*, p. 5). In *The Innocent*, we see the several components of McEwan's post-realism coming together: a thoughtful response to formal literary conventions (in this case spy fiction), in a rendering governed by verisimilitude, and the convincing evocation of a significant historical moment.

Readers of *Black Dogs*, as we have seen, must attend to the same combination of elements, where the self-conscious narrative construction of Jeremy's memoir conditions our reading of the end of the Cold War, and its historical significance. As a final example of this post-realism, and a continuing demonstration of the hold the legacy of the Second World War has had on McEwan's imagination, I turn to *Atonement*, and specifically Part Two of the novel. McEwan's realism here – by turns both savage and poignant – turns on the combined effects on the innocent of war and class (and juridical) violence. Robbie Turner, twenty-three when the novel opens, is the innocent 'vanished' victim of thirteen-year-old Briony Tallis, whose perjury brings to the surface old class antagonisms that, in 1935, enable a wealthy, more-or-less liberal middle-class family to destroy an intelligent, ambitious young man from a working-class family (*At*, p. 187). Part Two is exemplary of the postmodern strategies that are brought to bear to create post-realism in that it tells the silenced stories of the marginalized. Its object is not the familiar heroic Dunkirk narrative: instead it records the survival, and the deaths, of helpless soldiers and French civilians strafed by the Luftwaffe as they flee. It is working-class Robbie's story, but it is also a story of more marginalized streetwise soldiers, with little formal education. Corporal Mace and Corporal Nettle are smart, funny, cynical, generous and kind, and they resist the stupidity of their superior officers and instinctively know Robbie, whose rank is inferior to theirs, will guide them to safety. The carelessness with which Robbie's life has been destroyed finds a symbol in the dismembered pyjamaed leg of a French boy he witnesses in the forked branches of a tree, victim of a bombing raid (*At*, pp. 190, 194). That night as he lies sleepless in a French barn, nursing the shrapnel injury that will cause his death from septicaemia before he can be evacuated to England, he thinks of 'the French boy asleep in his bed, and about the indifference with which men could lob shells into a landscape ... without knowing or caring who was there. ... They need never see the end result – a vanished boy'. This vanishing recalls to him 'another vanished boy, another life that was once his own' (*At*, p. 202), and 'the indifference' with which the Tallises caused him to vanish is implicit in the recollection.

Briony's novel, for all that it foregrounds its strategic metafictionality, fulfils Pam Morris's explanation of nineteenth-century realism. True to the mode as she defines it, *Atonement* begins in uncertainties about characters and contexts, internal and external realities, that the reader can expect to be 'resolved by fuller knowledge gained during the course of the narrative'. *Atonement* achieves what Morris terms an 'epistemological progress' as its readers 'acquire empirical knowledge of the actual social and physical worlds' we are being invited to enter as they trace both Briony's and Robbie's journeys 'towards self-awareness'.[38] Part Two is narrated in the third person, and focalized through Robbie. It is central to Briony's confession in that it is her attempt to atone, but it is also an elegy in praise of an intelligent, decent man who dreamt of rediscovering his vanished life. The story is both a closely researched historical-realist recounting of the 1940 Allied retreat to Dunkirk, set against the beauty and the vulnerability of a rural landscape under attack for the second time in a quarter of a century, and an elegy that imagines Robbie into existence, rendering him immortal in its recording for posterity not a true account, but an immortalizing 'truth' of his life and death. In its combination of historical rootedness, formal virtuosity and deep affect, it is the epitome of McEwan's post-realist achievement.

NOTES

1 Josh Toth, *The Passing of Postmodernism: A Spectroanalysis of the Contemporary* (Albany: State University of New York Press, 2010), p. 123. For more detailed discussion of this topic see Toth and also David Rudrum and Nicholas

Stavris, eds., *Supplanting the Postmodern: An Anthology of Writings on the Arts and Culture of the Early 21st Century* (London: Bloomsbury, 2015).

2 Pam Morris, *Realism* (Abingdon: Routledge, 2004), p. 4; Judith Seaboyer, 'Ian McEwan: Contemporary Realism and the Novel of Ideas', in *The Contemporary British Novel*, eds. James Acheson and Sarah C. E. Ross (Edinburgh: Edinburgh University Press, 2005), pp. 23–34 (pp. 23, 29).

3 John le Carré, 'Fifty Years Later', Afterword to the fiftieth anniversary edition of *The Spy Who Came in from the Cold* (London: Penguin, 2014), pp. 275–82 (p. 279).

4 Jed Esty, 'Realism Wars', *Novel*, 49 (2016), 2, pp. 316–42 (p. 316).

5 Stephen Arata, 'Realism', in *The Cambridge Companion to the Fin de Siècle* (Cambridge: Cambridge University Press, 2007), pp. 169–87 (p. 171).

6 Ian McEwan, 'When I Stop Believing in Fiction', *The New Republic*, 15 February 2013. Retrieved from: https://newrepublic.com/article/112374/ian-mcewan-my-uneasy-relationship-fiction (accessed 24 June 2018).

7 Gillian Beer, *Darwin's Plots: Evolutionary Narrative in Darwin, George Eliot and Nineteenth-Century Fiction*, third edition (Cambridge: Cambridge University Press, 2009).

8 Morris, *Realism*, pp. 3–4.

9 Jeanette Winterson, *Art Objects: Essays on Ecstasy and Effrontery* (Toronto: Knopf, 1996), p. 176.

10 Sean O'Hagan, 'Reality Hunger by David Shields', *The Observer*, 28 February 2010. Retrieved from: www.theguardian.com/books/2010/feb/28/reality-hunger-book-review (accessed 24 June 2018).

11 David Shields, *Reality Hunger: A Manifesto* (London: Hamish Hamilton, 2010).

12 Esty, 'Realism Wars', pp. 316, 319.

13 Morris, *Realism*, p. 9.

14 Linda Hutcheon, *The Politics of Postmodernism*, second edition (London: Routledge, 2002), p. 181.

15 Ibid., pp. 166, 178, 181.

16 Josh Toth and Neil Brooks, 'Introduction: A Wake and Renewed?' in *The Mourning After: Attending the Wake of Postmodernism*, eds. Toth and Brooks (Amsterdam: Rodopi, 2007), pp. 1–13 (p. 2).

17 Esty, 'Realism Wars', p. 316; Shields, *Reality Hunger*, pp. 65, 25.

18 Shields, *Reality Hunger*, p. 57.

19 See McEwan's 'Author's Note'. Blake was discovered and tried in 1961, but he escaped Wormwood Scrubs in 1966, to take up residence outside Moscow. See George Blake, *No Other Choice* (London: Simon & Schuster, 1990).

20 'After World War II, the Government Code and Cipher School changed its name officially [to Government Communications Headquarters] and moved its head-quarters to Eastcote, Middlesex in 1946. ... The Central Training School stayed at Bletchley Park until 1987'. Retrieved from: www.gchq.gov.uk/features/bletchley-park-post-war (updated 1 April 2016; accessed 14 July 2018).

21 See, for example, *The Man Between*, dir. Carol Reed, 1953, British Lion Films; *Night People*, dir. Nunnally Johnson, 1954, Fox.

22 le Carré, 'Afterword', p. 279.

23 *The Spy Who Came in from the Cold*, dir. Martin Ritt, 1965, Paramount; *The Third Man*, dir. Carol Reed, 1949, Lionsgate.

24 *The Spy Who Came in from the Cold*, p. 138.
25 Nan Perry is named Liz Gold in the novel. I have used the film name throughout to avoid confusion.
26 *The Spy Who Came in from the Cold*, dir. Martin Ritt.
27 Ibid., pp. 115–16, 17.
28 Ibid., p. 253.
29 Holly Martins prefigures McEwan's innocent Leonard Marnham in that he too reads the European city he arrives in in terms of fictions – in this case the Western genre fictions he writes, in which the clearly delineated good guys act to destroy the clearly delineated bad guys. Paul N. Newton and Brigitte Timmerman, Fake Penicillin, '*The Third Man* and Operation Clap-Trap', *British Medical Journal* 355 (2016), i6494, doi: 10.1136/bmj.i6494 (published 13 December 2016; accessed 1 July 2018).
30 Penicillin, '*The Third Man*'.'
31 In an interview in 2017, le Carré said of *The Spy Who Came in from the Cold*, that it is, 'in effect, a film noir'. Nick Miller, 'John le Carré: Why I Brought Back Guillam, Smiley and the Cold War', *Sydney Morning Herald*, 12 September 2017. Retrieved from: www.smh.com.au/entertainment/books/john-le-carre-why-i-brought-back-guillam-smiley-and-the-cold-war-20170912-gyfjb5.html (accessed 24 June 2018).
32 McEwan overlays this Berlin with noir-esque images of a similarly ravaged and divided city, Harry Lime's Vienna. Leonard's disorientation is reinforced by *The Innocent*'s American first edition's black-and-white Dutch-angle photograph of a spiral staircase and peeling walls that is clearly a visual echo of the publicity stills from Reed's film that display the spiral staircase that leads down to Vienna's labyrinthine underworld of sewers and where Lime is eventually cornered and shot by Holly Martins.
33 Dominic Head, *Ian McEwan* (Manchester: Manchester University Press, 2007), p. 91.
34 As David Malcolm puts it, *Black Dogs* weighs up two of the themes of western civilization: the claims of metaphysical, religious belief and materialist rationality. See *Understanding Ian McEwan* (Columbia: University of South Carolina Press, 2002), pp. 149–50.
35 Morris, *Realism*, p. 3.
36 Shields, *Reality Hunger*, p. 25.
37 Morris, *Realism*, p. 3.
38 Ibid., pp. 11–12.

11

THOM DANCER

Limited Modernism

Ian McEwan has a thorny relationship with modernism. The influence of major modernist writers and aesthetic styles on McEwan's work has been well established; yet the works of his that are most deeply and obviously indebted to modernist style (*Atonement* and *Saturday*) are also the novels that most clearly evince serious doubts about the modernist project. David James and Urmila Seshargiri see McEwan's work as part of a metamodernist trend in contemporary fiction in which, as they describe, writers 'place a conception of modernism as revolution at the heart of their fictions, styling their twenty-first-century literary innovations as explicit engagements with the innovations of early twentieth-century writing'.[1] In this definition, metamodernism designates a relation to modernism 'as an era, an aesthetic, and an archive that originated in the late nineteenth and early twentieth centuries', and, therefore, is distinct from 'the current academic understanding of modernism as a temporally and spatially complex global impulse'.[2] James and Seshargiri's metamodernism offers a way to think of contemporary authors as actively responding to and transforming their literary heritage instead of being caught up in an ever expanding influence of a generalized 'modernist' innovation.

To call McEwan a metamodernist is, then, to emphasize the ongoing conversation in his fiction about what modernism means for the contemporary novelist today. Instead of tracing the influence of particular modernist writers, this chapter examines how McEwan actively engages with modernism on three distinct but related topics that, to him, animate the project of modernism: the aesthetics of transgression and rupture, the view of human nature, and modernism's claims for the literary. Focusing on those novels that most explicitly take up modernism on these grounds, *Atonement*, *Saturday*, *Solar* and *The Children Act*, makes visible McEwan's efforts to retrofit modernism for new conditions of living, writing and thinking in the twenty-first century, conditions in which the politics of rupture that modernism valued appear no longer tenable. In doing so, McEwan's novels revitalize modernist impressionistic aesthetics by making them modest, that is, by shedding them of their transgressive politics and grandiose claims about the literary. The modest modernism that remains reveals a disinterested aesthetic whose political and ethical claims are severely downsized. McEwan takes from modernism perspectival techniques of narration that suspend judgment and puts them to work in his own project of acceptance realism, which holds that there is no position outside our situation from which we can either judge or, more seriously, hope to escape. This is not, I think, as pessimistic as it seems, for it does not mean surrender but a recalibration of goals: an incremental approach better suited to the difficulties of contemporary life.

McEwan's thinking about modernism cannot be considered apart from his larger questions about the limits of fiction. Writing of McEwan's oeuvre in 2007, Dominic Head describes the 'greatest paradox of McEwan's career' as the conflict between an aesthetic program that seems to 'extend the category of the literary' and a pragmatic vision that seems to 'hedge it in with many damaging reservations'.[3] The discussions of McEwan's metamodernism that follow aim not to undo this knot; indeed, I agree with Head that this paradox is constitutive of McEwan's novelistic imagination. Instead, by following its contours I hope to show that for McEwan accepting the limits of the human and the need for a vocabulary that moves beyond objectivity and critical mastery, opens up new possibilities for action on a more modest and incremental scale.

In attempting to chart McEwan's metamodernist engagement across these three lines of inquiry, the chapter forgoes a chronological sequence. Though these three issues – the aesthetics of rupture, human nature, and the limitations of the literary – are significantly interrelated for McEwan, this discussion treats them as provisionally distinct to tease out the logic of their development and their role in McEwan's larger aesthetic project.

Vexed Modernism in *Atonement*

Despite almost two decades of scholarship on this novel, the relationship of *Atonement* to modernism in general and Woolf in particular remains one of the central critical problems for readers and critics. The novel's preoccupation with the claims of the literary means that Briony's story of guilt becomes inseparable from matters of literary history. The difficulties lie in the conflict between the influences and evocations of modernist style, techniques and themes throughout the novel and its explicit discussion of the ethical and aesthetic values of modernist fiction. On the one hand, we have the novel's technical adaptation of modernist styles; its fairly unambiguous echoes and borrowings from works like *To the Lighthouse*; its historical setting and locale; its thematic preoccupation with war and time; and its allusive relationship to English novels. On the other hand, we have McEwan's explicit denunciation of the aesthetic and ethical failing of modernist fiction, articulated in the rejection letter from *Horizon* in Part Three. Finally, by adopting a different form than Woolfian modernism, Briony-the-writer's final draft seems to endorse this condemnation of modernism's lack of plot and moral courage.

Though it is tempting to read the literary history story as one of progress in which Briony grows up and out of her flirtation with Woolf and modernism, the novel's seeming return to Victorian characterization and postmodern self-reflexivity disrupt the ease of this reading. C. C.'s (Cyril Connolly, presumably) rejection letter in Part Three proves a key interpretative crux for the novel's take on literary history. Though scholarly discussions have been preoccupied with the extent to which the letter accurately represents an assessment of modern fiction, the letter presents an effort to refigure modernism within the novel as a narrative resource for 'rendering consciousness' adapted to a contemporary context whose political and aesthetic conditions are dramatically different. Not a symbol of the novel's progress beyond the solipsistic elitism of modernism, the letter becomes a part of the novel's literary historical investigation, allowing McEwan to assess retrospectively modernism's claims from his contemporary perspective.

Atonement's affinities with modernism and its rejection of certain parts of the modernist project must both be accounted for. Laura Marcus's and David James's treatments of the novel are exemplary in this case. Both critics refuse the temptation to see the novel as taking a position, as either reproducing or parodying the modernist text.[4] Instead, in James's words the novel works 'at the confluence of what seem like extremes: where Victorian realism's commitment to character and modernism's commitment to sensory experience intersect with the breed of postmodern reflexivity that McEwan ... has never been drawn to anyway'.[5] Both Marcus and James see *Atonement* as working out a literary historical legacy for the twenty-first-century novelist. Marcus concludes that McEwan 'acknowledges the debt [to modernism] even as he calls attention to the necessary and inevitable distance between his own time and that of the modernist novelist'.[6]

In the third part of the novel, we learn that Briony has dabbled in modernist style, especially the mode of Woolf's *The Waves*. For Briony, the techniques of modernism represent more than a different way of telling stories: they are explicitly linked with progress, with the largest possible currents of literary history. To do away with character and plot is explicitly figured as a break with narrative tradition. Characters, Briony explains, 'belonged to the nineteenth century' while plot is a 'rusted machinery' that no longer works. In contrast Woolf's impressionism carries with it the spirit of revolution. *The Waves*, Briony thinks, captures a 'transformation ... being worked in human nature' expressed only by a 'new kind of fiction' (*At*, pp. 281–2). McEwan frames Briony's attraction to Woolfian style in terms of its revolutionary potential. Hoping modernism's break with literary history will also break her from her guilty past, Briony's embrace and then rejection of modernism speaks to a disenchantment with its claims to radicalism rather than a rejection of its techniques and of 'plotless modernism'.[7]

As David James has made clear, however, this apparent rejection of modernism is not the end of the story. James argues that the 'surface reading' rejection of modernist radicalism is undercut by the use of 'impressionism's methods of rendering interiority' throughout.[8] James makes a crucial point that the self-reflexive use of 'internalist focalisation ... encourages us to share the cognitive space ... that later becomes the subject' of the novel.[9] My experiences of teaching *Atonement* seem to provide confirmation for this argument in the form of my students' frequent and spirited professions of their discomfort, anger and horror at being forced to occupy Briony's not quite fully formed mind as she acts out her dreadful mistake. It is not only Briony's consciousness that is self-reflexively rendered. Whether it be through the highly stylized depiction of Emily Tallis's 'send[ing] her tendrils' of thought throughout the house, or Briony's foregrounding of the problem of other minds in aesthetic terms, or Robbie's literary imagination of his future as a doctor, McEwan takes care to keep the reader aware of the minds that are doing the thinking, describing, or writing (*At*, p. 65). The end of the novel, in which we come to learn that the story of Briony's accusation, Robbie's time in war, and Briony's final confrontation with Cecilia and Robbie is not McEwan's but Briony's, written late in her life, further magnifies all of the stylistic and formal decisions *as rhetorical choices*. The fictionality of the novel reveals for us the disjunction between our own habitation of an internalist perspective, crafted for us as readers, and the experience of what it is actually like to be thinking. For McEwan, the ethical value of representing consciousness is destroyed the very moment we lose track of the tension between our mind and the mind we are occupying.[10] Therefore, when McEwan writes that he 'is interested in how to represent, obviously in a very stylized way, what it's like to be thinking' the issue of it being 'stylized' is vital.[11] Internalized perspective fails in all of the ways Briony, the *Horizon* editors, and McEwan himself point out when it claims some special access or knowledge to the real, to human nature, to represent what it is *really like* to think. At the heart of Briony's misapprehension, is less her 'modernist style' or her 'romantic imagination', though they play their part, than her belief that literature can convey meaning without deformation: 'a story was a form of telepathy ... Reading a sentence and understanding it were the same thing' (*At*, p. 37).

Atonement remains one of the greatest achievements in twenty-first-century fiction because it challenges us to open to our own minds a consciousness so 'radically different from [our] own to be almost offensive to reason'.[12] This is an extraordinary demand: to feel the world in the mistaken, half-clear way that Briony does but to be denied any means of judgment. To be without judgment is, of course, to be in the same position as the writer at the end of the novel. Briony-the-writer admits that there is no atonement for novelists because there are no criteria outside her own imagination. This admission differs from the evasion of responsibility that Briony identifies in her earlier drafts. Instead, the older Briony shifts the terms: there is no *moral* atonement in literature (only the young Briony would believe that anyway), but there is the possibility of atonement in the archaic sense of aesthetic harmony: 'to bring into artistic or logical harmony; to harmonize' (*OED*). Briony recognizes that as long as she thought her novel could atone in the moral sense, she clung to the magical view of language that led her astray all those years ago. A novel is not a meaning-producing machine – the order and closure it brings is aesthetic not ethical – this is its limit and its possibility. With the final revelation, Briony transmutes the question of moral good into an aesthetic one. The matter of atonement, of whether or not Briony-the-writer atones, becomes not a question of moral rebalancing, of the assignment of blame, or the confession to the 'true facts', or the taking of responsibility, but one of whether the story she tells is a good one. The question of whether she has written a 'good' story is one that allows for an answer since the reader is in a position to evaluate. Did she speak well (as she did not in 'Two Figures') by opening her mind up to readers capable of meeting that challenge of engaging with a mind that has acted so abominably?

Despite its doubts about the revolutionary impulse at the heart of modernism, *Atonement* makes visible a view that Woolf and McEwan share: 'that one of the great values of fiction was exactly this process of being able to enter other people's minds'.[13] I agree with Richard Robinson that 'the most conspicuous strain of modernism in *Atonement* is Woolfian', but not the Woolf of *To the Lighthouse* or *The Waves* as Robinson argues.[14] McEwan and Woolf reach their closest rapprochement in her essays on the experience and value of reading. This is the 'theorist of reading' Woolf that we find in 'The Common Reader', 'Robinson Crusoe' and 'How Should One Read a Book?' In Woolf's theory of reading, the difficulty, if not impossibility, of entering another's mind takes on central importance.

In 'Robinson Crusoe', Woolf explains that the first task for any reading is to attempt 'to master his [the author's] perspective'.[15] But, she insists, it is not as easy as it seems, 'for we have our own vision of the world; we have made it from our own experience and prejudices, and it is therefore bound up with our own vanities and loves'.[16] As a result, the reading experience is one that hurts: '[the author] inflicts his own perspective upon us so severely that as often as not we suffer agonies – our vanity is injured because our own order is being upset; we are afraid because the old supports are being wrenched from us ... yet from anger, fear, and boredom a rare and lasting delight is sometimes born'.[17] The experience of the failure of our sympathetic imagination is the engine that drives the literary experience, as she reminds us in 'How Should One Read a Book?': 'but we know we cannot sympathise wholly or immerse ourselves wholly'.[18] In talking about reading, Woolf offers a description of the function of interior perspective that seems to better fit its use by McEwan, where the disjunction between the mental processes being depicted and our own 'experiences and prejudices' is always centrally present. We come to know what it is really like to be thinking by way of a failure to do so. Indeed, it is this failure that seems so central to McEwan's aesthetics of perspective. Briony illustrates it not just in her own acts but also, self-reflexively in her representation of Robbie within her fiction, where she portrays him as being unable to imagine Briony's motives outside of his own tale of romance. In *The Children Act*, Fiona Maye comes to recognize her failure to 'sympathize wholly' as her crime against Adam Henry, a lapse caused in large part by her inability to see Adam outside the context of the courts. It is Woolf's understanding of the experience of reading, rather than her theories of fiction, that provide the richest resources for McEwan's metamodernist experimentation.

Literature and Human Nature

Though human nature is only briefly mentioned, *Atonement* demonstrates how deeply imbricated the 'concept of modernism as revolution' is with differences in how we view human nature. Recall that Briony phrases her attraction to Woolf in radical and transformational terms, figuring the revolution that *The Waves* heralds for literary history as reciprocal with a revolution in human nature. Both the aesthetic and political radicalism that McEwan attributes to modernist fiction cannot be divorced from its fundamental belief in a highly changeable human nature. He addresses the issue directly in a 2001 essay, 'Literature, Science, and Human Nature'. McEwan's thinking in this essay lays out his sense of the privileged place that modernism holds in courting a view of human nature as 'a frail entity subject to sudden lurches – exciting revolutionary improvements or deeply regrettable deterioration'.[19] It also allows us to see how the focus on medical and scientific matters in these novels participates in McEwan's larger project of scaling back the claims of the literary.

The essay expresses McEwan's well-known disdain for social constructivist views of human nature. Drawing on the work of Darwin and Paul Ekman, McEwan advocates a 'biological view' of human nature that emphasizes a baseline of continuity and similarity across the particularities of culture and society. In particular, McEwan seems deeply impressed by the 'universal expression of emotions' – the observation that the manner of expression of emotions seems commonly held across cultures even while the circumstances that provoke a particular emotion vary culturally. He argues that remarkable continuity in descriptive capacities of the literary further supports Darwin and Ekman's belief that 'behind the notion of a commonly held stock of emotion lies a universal human nature'. If we can understand Penelope's trepidation and Ulysses's anger across hundreds of generations, then, McEwan reasons, literature must contain the ability to tap into 'human universals that transcend culture'. The essay puts its emphasis on the difference between biological and social constructivist *views* of human nature, not on any definitive argument for what human nature *is*. McEwan is interested in the ways that different views of human nature have been historically mobilized to serve a range of agendas. For Darwin, McEwan reminds us, universalism in expression undermined the pseudoscientific basis for racism, but for Margaret Mead, the notion of a biological basis for expression appeared to support Western exceptionalism and racism. The point is that there is nothing automatically regressive or progressive about either view. Therefore, McEwan wonders why literature and criticism have been so drawn to 'the notion that human nature is a specific historical product, shaped by shared values'.[20] His answer has to do with modernism, which he understands as advancing an idea of a highly mutable human nature that is more suitable to its view of the human mind and its claims for the value of the literary. The essay goes on to paint a picture of modernism as committed to an aesthetics of rupture and transformation. He cites the typical examples: Virginia Woolf's famous claim that 'human nature changed' around December 1910; T. S. Eliot's belief that poetry could restore the dissociation of sensibility that took place in the seventeenth century; the radical power of Stravinsky's *Rite of Spring* and the subversive publication of Joyce's *Ulysses*. These are works that sought to scandalize, outrage, offend and shock; central to McEwan's modernism is its assumption that transgression itself is subversive. Though these examples are utterly predictable, they reveal that McEwan's understanding of modernism has much in common with Eric Hayot's claim that modernism is a 'mode of negation and refusal' or Susan Stanford Friedman's similarly 'relational' definition of modernism as a 'principle of radical rupture'.[21] Seeing human nature as susceptible to ruptures, paradigm shifts and radical transformations granted literature an important role in both describing and participating in them. The tabula rasa view of human nature endows literature with the ability to *intervene*, while the biological view limits it only to *description*. It is no surprise, McEwan concludes, that 'literary writers seem to prefer an explosive, decisive moment, the miracle of birth, to a dull continuum of infinitesimal change'.[22]

McEwan challenges this settlement between literature and the constructivist view on two grounds. The first comes out of his observation that there is nothing automatically politically progressive about a changeable human nature. In fact, he suggests that the radical utopian hope that social constructive views once held may have run out of steam. *Saturday*'s representation of the anti-war protests is a case in point: by showing the protestors only through their intersections with the city's infrastructure – litter, traffic disruption and media coverage – McEwan reminds us that such outrage and transgression has been completely subsumed by political economy. Similarly, the artists and writers that gather with Michael Beard in *Solar* to talk about climate change appear ridiculous in their faith in the interventional potential of art in the face of planetary-scale problems. This critique of the political claims of cultural (and so literary) intervention flows into an open question about the need to 'invent a literature' based in the deep time continuity of the biological view.[23] A literature that 'is no less interesting', McEwan asserts, is one in which 'one speaks not of a moment but of an immeasurable tract of irreversible time ... which demands all of our interpretative genius'.[24] In this new writing, the literary assumes the more humble and limited function of 'giving voice to' what 'binds us, our common nature'.[25]

With its focus on science and climate change, *Solar* provides an even clearer example of McEwan's efforts to detach the focalized internal perspectives from the modernist tabula rasa view of human nature. Where *Atonement* and *Saturday* wear their use of impressionism on their sleeves through their literary references to the perspectival and narrative experiments of Woolf, Joyce, Elizabeth Bowen and Ford Maddox Ford, *Solar*'s debts to modernism are less immediately obvious. However, in some ways, *Solar* is the culmination of McEwan's experiments with impressionistic perspective. It combines *Saturday*'s limiting of perspective to a single mind with *Atonement*'s interest in inviting us to occupy a loathsome perspective while withholding any narrative indictment. The novel tells the story of fictional Nobel Prize-winning scientist Michael Beard's attempt to develop artificial photosynthesis panels as an alternative energy source. Yet, as the critical reception of the novel demonstrates, it gets its focus all wrong. The novel talks too much about Beard and his world and not enough about the scientific and political 'facts' outside it. Greg Garrard sums up these disappointments by suggesting that McEwan has erred not so much in turning his attention to 'human nature', in the figure of Beard, but in not condemning the 'moral failings' he finds there.[26] Thus, once again the issue appears to be a narrative one, a consequence of limiting itself to Beard's consciousness. The novel does not provide a contrasting perspective or position that 'corrects' – so to speak – Beard's obviously sceptical, selfish views. For Garrard, the focus on Beard means the exclusion of external issues; thus, he says the novel shows 'little interest' in the 'actual' world.[27] In all of these cases, the critics condemn the novel for violating what now seems to be an implicit but immutable rule of climate change fiction: it must address the actual world and attempt to change us.

These criticisms take as a mistake, a failing, in McEwan what is in fact one of the central principles of his of literary project: to imagine continuity and incrementalism as politically and aesthetically valuable. The social constructivist view of human nature subtends the criticism of John Banville and Garrard, who take as axiomatic that literature's main role is interventional: to change us. In turn, they cast the biological view of human nature as regressive and conservative, supporting the status quo. Yet, as we see so often in McEwan, he is sceptical of this power. One of the key points that McEwan makes in both 'Literature, Science, and Human Nature' and *Solar* is that a theory of human nature has no innate politics or morality. *Solar* wants us to increase our attention on the politics that motivate particular conceptions of science, nature and humanity, as well as the ways that the nonhuman world undermines the politics superimposed upon it. *Solar*'s careful, detailed depictions of Beard and other scientists in action affirm the value of incrementalism and continuity to scientific practice. In fact, the rhetoric of rupture, revolution, 'paradigm shifts' and 'transformation' turns up only in Beard's lecture to the venture capitalists (*S*, p. 156). *Solar* gives us a world where capitalism has so fully assimilated the logics of transgression and rupture that they 'actually work to promote and advance capitalism, by providing it with its fuel'.[28] If the political logics have been turned around in this way, then perhaps, McEwan's vision implicitly suggests, the most politically efficacious thing to do is to find a fiction able to extend continuity and incrementalism, and scale the claims of the literary back. In place of the vain dreams of shaping a malleable human nature into perfection, we find instead the modest hope of caring for and protecting our frail and flawed mutual humanity as the basis for any chance of achieving the common good. This localization about where human dignity needs defence might also help to explain the romantic streak in many of McEwan's novels, especially those that seem to rush towards their neat conclusions on the backs of romantic love.

Fiction at the Limits of the Literary

Saturday signals a redirection of McEwan's metamodernist investigation towards the epistemological and political limits of novelistic form. Taking up the single day novel form made famous by *Mrs Dalloway* and *Ulysses*, but setting it in the lead up to the 2003 invasion of Iraq, McEwan expresses his doubts that the resolution of personal time and historical time by Clarissa Dalloway remains possible in the current moment. The formal engagement with the modernist novel and its complex ways of rendering time fits with its other central concern, the status of the literary itself, particularly the way that a 'rejection of the idea of the literary [itself] becomes a bald topic', as Head argues.[29] Indeed, McEwan's doubts about the modernist stream-of-consciousness and his 'exploration of the equivocal nature of the literary' intersect in Perowne's reflection on 'the growing complication of the human condition, the expanding circle of moral sympathy' (*S*, p. 127). How to react to this new condition is the central dilemma of the novel, one that occupies neurosurgeons as much as novelists.

Saturday's inveterate materialism militates against the historical strategies for dealing with the impossible demands of sympathy on a planetary scale. Our increasing knowledge about the natural world, for Perowne (as for McEwan), does not provide us with comforts of technical mastery, but instead discloses the increased interconnection of the human and nonhuman worlds. No longer do we have access to the consolations of ignorance or religion that enable us to operate as if we are surrounded by 'edible automata'. We must confront the uncomfortable fact that not only do other humans feel pain, but also foxes, laboratory mice, lobsters and even fish (*S*, p. 127). But we are also denied the consolations of social constructivism. Reflecting at the end of his day about what is to be done about Baxter, the profoundly disturbed young man who assaulted Perowne's family earlier in the evening, Perowne meditates on the problem of moral luck: the notion that one's fate depends on conditions not just outside our personal or social control, but right 'down to invisible folds and kinks of character, written in code, at the level of molecules'. Given genetic and environmental sources of suffering, Perowne doubts that any 'amount of social justice' can provide a 'cure' (*S*, p. 272). However, despite the diagnostic language, Perowne with all of his medical expertise knows equally well that no amount of medicine will cure them either. Faced with the enormity of the problem, Perowne takes up his son Theo's motto of 'think small': 'you need to recognize bad luck when you see it' and try to 'minimize' the 'miseries' of those affected (S, pp. 34, 272). As a solution to the planetary scale of war, suffering and injustice, triage may not inspire, but it is a solution that fits not only Perowne's modest pragmatism, but also the novel's efforts to imagine the contemporary condition as an encounter with limits.

Perowne's solution of selective mercy is only one of many of the examples of 'thinking small' throughout a novel that envelops the intersection of the political and the literary with a sense of humility about human limits. The novel's privileging of scaled down and epistemologically modest ways of knowing mediate the 'encyclopaedic' function of the stream-of-consciousness, single-day novel. For Woolf and Joyce, restricting the action of the novel to one day in one location seems to expand the representational capacities of the novel, which paradoxically come to contain more by doing less. For Woolf, the compression of narrative into a day does away with the demands of Edwardian verisimilitude and plot, allowing the modernist writer to 'convey this varying, this unknown and uncircumscribed spirit'.[30] Perowne's professional interest in consciousness suggests an adjustment: though Perowne professes to believe only in science, his discussions of the brain, consciousness and cognition constantly refers to its limits. Perowne refers again and again to what we do not know about the physiology of the brain: how it stores information, gives rise to experience, accesses memories. These physical limitations determine all of the instances in the novel where a character's (mostly Perowne's) subjectivity fails them. Perowne's humiliation of Baxter results from a failure of imagination, of sympathy, instigated by his overly diagnostic perspective. Perowne's felicity with the diagnostic mode in the operating theatre continually leads him astray in the world. His anxiety at the sight of the plane on fire in the opening scene is an assemblage of cognitive and perceptual mistakes. Later, his preference for medical understanding causes him to misunderstand an argument between two junkies that he oversees from his window. Here, as in *Atonement*, McEwan deploys the resources of modernist impressionism, but in a highly self-reflexive mode. The use of internalist perspective allows us to occupy this mind, in real time, as it struggles with and often fails to recognize other people as people instead of bundles of symptoms.

The novel's emphasis on the failures of consciousness also, I think, helps to explain Perowne's philistinism with respect to literature. Though it is tempting to throw out Perowne's views, as John Banville does, calling them 'literally unbelievable', there is surely some affinity here between Perowne and McEwan.[31] In fact, Perowne figures much the way Robbie Turner does in *Atonement*, where he gives voice to a scepticism about the outsized claim that literature is the 'core' of a 'civilized existence' (*At*, p. 91). Robbie settles on a more modest role for the literary, a practical role of making him a 'better doctor for having read literature' (*At*, p. 93). Perowne's philistinism may be more extreme (he is a much worse reader than Robbie), but he serves the same function of projecting a more circumscribed vision of the literary.[32] Perowne's 'respect' for 'the material world, its limits, and what it can sustain' is part of the novel's project of epistemological modesty for literature, even if we simultaneously recognize the deficiencies in Perowne's actual literary judgments. That is, the novel allows us to endorse Perowne's goal for literature 'to inspire uncomplicated wonder' without agreeing with him about the works capable of doing it. When it comes to actual moments of literary judgment, like listening to 'Dover Beach' or reading *My Saucy Bark*, McEwan makes it clear that Perowne is just not a very good reader.

Nevertheless, the vision of the literary given in the novel is one that also must heed the material world and its limits. If science and social justice provide no consolation to the vast injustice and suffering in the world, then literature does not either. Against the 'utopianists' (*S*, p. 276), and the pursuit of transformation, revolution and rupture, McEwan brings together science and literature under the banner of the 'dull continuum of infinitesimal change'.[33] In a famous passage at the end of *Saturday*, in which Perowne expresses his faith in science, it is important not to pass over the conditions for progress, 'over decades, as long as the scientists and institutions remains in place' (*S*, p. 255). Perowne's faith is in slow science, the accumulation of information over the long continuum of biological time. The grandeur of the Darwinian view, for McEwan, is continuity, life 'steadily improved over the centuries' (*S*, p. 77). The incrementalist view has its correspondence in Perowne's description of the great nineteenth-century novel as 'steady, workmanlike accumulation' of details, observations (*S*, p. 67).

Saturday has been roundly criticized by reviewers and academics for this scaled back, incrementalist vision, which seems to evade the responsibilities of the public world by withdrawing into the comforts of bourgeois life.[34] Banville's excoriating review takes McEwan to task for writing such a 'comforting' novel.[35] *Saturday*, he says, is too much like the nineteenth-century novels of Anthony Trollope, instead of the difficult uncomfortable novels of the modernists. Banville's literary historical inversion is interesting, and, I think right, but not for the reasons that he intends. *Saturday* denies us all consolation. The only way that I can think that it is *comforting* is that it does not instil the reader with a sense of urgency (if anything the reigning mood is gentle pessimism). Banville may be correct in suggesting that this mood has more to do with the 'incalculably diffusive' agency of 'unhistoric acts' of the kind found in *Middlemarch* than with the belief in the possibility of radically transforming human nature, implicitly expressed in the encyclopaedic totality of *Ulysses*.[36] Interestingly, Banville and McEwan express the same understanding of modernism and differ only in their sense of its political and ethical value. It is also the meaning Hayot captures when he describes modernism as a world-making 'mode of negation and refusal'. It is in this sense that modernism expresses a kind of raw opposition that the two writers share but which McEwan rejects. The metamodernism of McEwan might well be described as one that attempts to revive what is left of modernism once the mode of negation and refusal is strained off. As I have been trying to demonstrate, for McEwan modernism cannot be distinguished from its relation to an aesthetics of transgression against which his novels present a comprehensive rejection. In a world where our circle of moral responsibility has expanded to include the entire planet, a politics of rupture and transgression serves only 'utopianists, zealous men' all 'totalitarians in different form' (*S*, pp. 276–7). McEwan's novels may borrow from modernism, may look like them in locale and form, but this only serves to highlight the contrasts. For all of the internalist perspectives of Woolf, of the localization of Joyce, of the impressionism of Ford Maddox Ford, McEwan's novels seem so much more like Victorian novels in their limited and humble vision.

This imposition of limits, this reduction, becomes starkly visible again in the allusion to Joyce's 'The Dead' in *The Children Act*. We have come far from the deep technical and thematic imbrications of *Atonement* and *Saturday*. *The Children Act* owes little to the techniques of Joyce; instead 'The Dead' appears in *The Children Act* as a loose homage. Mirroring the events at the end of the novella, Jack and Fiona find themselves alone after a social event. Jack, like Gabriel, hopes to 'take her to bed, make things easy between them once more' but the romantic reconciliation is disrupted by a song and a memory (*CA*, p. 207). (The circumstances of the case are discussed in Chapter 6.) As with Gretta, Fiona describes how he 'walked through the rain to find me', a memory that both associate with a sense of guilt for the death (*CA*, p. 209). Both express responsibility and guilt for being unable to understand properly and reciprocate the love of their young men, and it reduces them to sobs. There is much that could be said about McEwan's taking up of 'The Dead' from the perspective of Fiona, especially in terms of addressing the sometimes-troubling gender politics of the novella. Most striking about McEwan's homage is the way that it treats the moment of epiphany at the end of 'The Dead'. Gabriel's confrontation with Michael Furey's love, and with his wife's profound grief, allows him to transcend his 'shameful' personal self-interest into a 'generous' sense of collective moral sympathy.[37] The end of 'The Dead' is characterized by a 'fading out' of 'identity' and a radical expansion of sympathy in line with the famous image of 'the snow falling faintly through the universe'.[38] *The Children Act* inverts this ending, with a contraction of interest. Instead of emulating Gabriel casting his soul out like the snow, which 'was general all over Ireland', McEwan's final paragraph sees a progressive contraction.[39] It begins with just the 'rain-cleansed city', which further contracts to 'their marriage', and finally to a celebration of the private love between Fiona and Jack as she tells her story (*CA*, p. 213). The progressive narrowing in *The Children Act* is a striking riposte to the epiphanic power accorded to the literary by Joyce. This is especially true given that Fiona, in these last moments, characterizes her (unintended) abdication of responsibility for Adam as one of failing to provide 'meaning' (*CA*, p. 213). Throughout *The Children Act*, the literary has a utilitarian function, helping to serve a barrister or judge attempting to tell stories that will induce sympathy, empathy and responsibility, to facilitate moral rather than simply legal justice. As in *Saturday*, it is music that is the purest, most transcendental art form. It provides the only escape for Fiona from the fact of innocent suffering and human cruelty she encounters every day in the Family Division. Music is important in 'The Dead' too, of course, but for Joyce the literary is its equal. For McEwan, it is not certain that the literary can occupy this place of purity. The literary, in *The Children Act*, occupies a more worldly, humble and limited function, offering not a transcendence of ourselves but a reminder of our all too human failings. *The Children Act* ends in the same mood as *Atonement*, *Solar* and *Saturday* with the effort to reaffirm the literary constrained by a clear comprehension of its limits.

NOTES

1 David James and Urmila Seshagiri, 'Metamodernism: Narratives of Continuity and Revolution', *PMLA*, 129 (2014), 1, pp. 87–100 (p. 87).
2 Ibid., p. 88.
3 Dominic Head, *Ian McEwan* (Manchester: Manchester University Press, 2007).
4 Laura Marcus, 'Ian McEwan's Modernist Time: *Atonement* and *Saturday*', in *Ian McEwan: Contemporary Critical Perspectives*, ed. Sebastian Groes, second edition (London: Bloomsbury, 2013), pp. 83–98 (p. 85).
5 David James, *Modernist Futures: Innovation and Inheritance in the Contemporary Novel* (New York: Cambridge University Press, 2012), p. 146.
6 Marcus, 'Ian McEwan's Modernist Time', p. 85.
7 Alistair Cormack, 'Postmodernism and the Ethics of Fiction in Atonement', in *Ian McEwan: Contemporary Critical Perspectives*, pp. 70–83 (p. 77). As Briony realizes 'the evasions of her little novel were exactly those of her life' (*At*, p. 320).
8 James, *Modernist Futures*, p. 146.

9 Ibid.

10 Dora Zhang's work on the 'qualia' and description in Woolf suggests a deeper affinity with McEwan's views of consciousness. Dora Zhang, 'Naming the Indescribable: Woolf, Russell, James, and the Limits of Description', *New Literary History*, 45 (2014), pp. 51–70.

11 Zadie Smith and Ian McEwan, 'Zadie Smith Talks with Ian McEwan', *The Believer*, 3 (2005), 6; reprinted in *Conversations with Ian McEwan*, ed. Ryan Roberts (Jackson: University Press of Mississippi, 2010), pp. 108–33 (p. 113).

12 Zadie Smith, 'Fail Better', in *The Writer's Reader: Vocation, Preparation, Creation*, eds. Robert Cohen and Jay Parini (New York: Bloomsbury Academic, 2017), pp. 349–62 (p. 361).

13 Smith and McEwan, 'Zadie Smith Talks with Ian McEwan', p. 112.

14 Richard Robinson, 'The Modernism of Ian McEwan's Atonement', *Modern Fiction Studies*, 56 (2010), 3, 473–95 (p. 477).

15 Virginia Woolf, *The Second Common Reader* (New York: Harvest Books, 1986), p. 52.

16 Ibid., p. 53.

17 Ibid., p. 54.

18 Ibid., p. 269.

19 Ian McEwan, 'Literature, Science, and Human Nature', in *The Literary Animal: Evolution and the Nature of Narrative*, eds. Jonathan Gottschall and David Sloan Wilson (Evanston, IL: Northwestern University Press, 2005), pp. 5–19 (p. 12).

20 Ibid., pp. 10, 11, 13, 14.

21 Eric Hayot, *On Literary Worlds* (New York: Oxford University Press, 2012), p. 127; Susan Stanford Friedman, 'Definitional Excursions: The Meanings of Modern/Modernity/Modernism', *Modernism/Modernity*, 8 (2001), 3, 493–513 (p. 505).

22 Though it would be a stretch to call McEwan a literary naturalist, his preference for the dramas of human nature over aesthetic revolution reveals more of his debts to the nineteenth-century novel. McEwan, 'Literature, Science, and Human Nature', p. 14.

23 Smith and McEwan, 'Zadie Smith Talks with Ian McEwan', p. 118.

24 McEwan, 'Literature, Science, and Human Nature', p. 14.

25 Ibid., p. 19.

26 Greg Garrard, '*Solar*: Apocalypse Not', in *Ian McEwan*, second edition, ed. Sebastian Groes (London: Bloomsbury, 2013), pp. 123–36 (p. 126).

27 Ibid., p. 127.

28 Steven Shaviro, *No Speed Limit: Three Essays on Accelerationism* (Minneapolis: University of Minnesota Press, 2015), p. 34.

29 Head, *Ian McEwan*, p. 178.

30 Virginia Woolf, *The Common Reader: First Series, Annotated Edition* (Mariner Books, 2002), p. 150. Rebecca L. Walkowitz also reads Woolf's restricted attention as part of a commitment 'to the multiple, transient self, as opposed to the constricted, marmoreal self required by proportion, conversion, and triumphalism'. See Rebecca L. Walkowitz, *Cosmopolitan Style: Modernism Beyond the Nation* (New York: Columbia University Press, 2006), p. 96.

31 John Banville, 'A Day in the Life', *New York Review of Books*, 26 May 2005. Retrieved from: www.nybooks.com/articles/2005/05/26/a-day-in-the-life/ (accessed 25 February 2018).

32 Richard Rorty notes how ambivalent the idea of the literary expressed in *Atonement* and *Saturday* is with regard to the political imperatives of literary criticism. Richard Rorty, 'A Queasy Agnosticism', *Dissent*, 52 (2005), 4, pp. 91–4.

33 McEwan, 'Literature, Science, and Human Nature', p. 14.

34 Elaine Hadley, 'On a Darkling Plain: Victorian Liberalism and the Fantasy of Agency', *Victorian Studies*, 48 (2005), pp. 92–102 (p. 95).

35 Banville, 'A Day in the Life'.

36 See, for example: George Eliot, *Middlemarch: An Authoritative Text, Backgrounds, Criticism* (Norton, 2000); Paul K. Saint-Amour, *Tense Future: Modernism, Total War, Encyclopedic Form* (Oxford: Oxford University Press, 2015).

37 James Joyce, *Dubliners: Authoritative Text, Contexts, Criticism*, ed. Margot Norris (New York: W. W. Norton, 2006), pp. 191, 194.

38 Ibid., p. 194.

39 Ibid.

12

DAVID JAMES

Narrative Artifice

'The artifice of fiction can be taken for granted', declared McEwan in 1978, the year of his debut novel. McEwan staked out a self-assured position on the form's future by sizing up the novel's many possible paths. His own preferences were clear: after the 'experimentation of the late sixties and early seventies', he predicted, 'there can surely be no more mileage to be had from demonstrating yet again through self-enclosed "fictions" that reality is words and words are lies. There is no need to be strangled by that particular loop'. The priority instead, as the young McEwan envisaged it, was 'the representation of states of mind and the society that forms them'. Metafiction had had its day, as far as he was concerned; the very purpose of 'experimentation' ought to dispense with the Mobius strip model of fiction that perpetually restages its own involuted fascination with manufacturing worlds from words. Instead, experimentalism 'in its broadest and most viable sense', advised McEwan, 'should have less to do with formal factors like busting up your syntax and scrambling your page order, and more to do with content'.[1]

As it turned out, McEwan would not necessarily abide by his own recommendations. In the years that followed, his joint effort to represent minds and examine society did not always appear seamlessly integrated or evenly balanced if we recall the psychosexual focus of *The Cement Garden* (1978) and *The Comfort of Strangers* (1981); neither would he exactly dispense with formal experimentalism as a precondition for prioritizing content. In 1987, however, *The Child in Time* made apparent that McEwan wanted to do something different, something more explicit with the novel as an emphatically social medium. Heralding a new direction in his writing, *The Child in Time* spoke directly to McEwan's sentiments ten years earlier about the state and purposes of fictional experimentation. With a moving account of familial loss situated against a dystopian political backdrop, the novel acts as a barometer of the damaging policies and systemic costs of Thatcherism. Social critique – whose delivery in fiction carries its own ample supply of 'artifice', of course – coexists with the searing pathos of a young family torn apart. As such, *The Child in Time* will be one of my lodestones in the pages to come, because it is also a vivid demonstration of how nimbly McEwan combines 'formal factors' with political commentary when he wants to; but, before we get there, it will be worth considering the significance of his rather testy relationship with narrative artifice as a way of tracking his evolving concerns as an innovator who has not always been comfortable with the very idea of literary innovation itself.

If McEwan has never really been pyrotechnic, he has always seemed rebellious. In opposition to what he terms the 'overstuffed, overfurnished English novel', he has maintained a career-long commitment to the novel of ideas, one that enables him to 'deal in broad strokes', as Michael LeMahieu observes, 'with very old questions and debates: faith versus reason, religion versus science, logic versus emotion'.[2] Even a cursory survey of his oeuvre's modes proves that McEwan has produced alternative designs for fiction by constantly reconfiguring his relationship to genre, pursuing what he calls a 'constant ... element of self-reinvention' even while also upholding a certain fidelity to nineteenth-century realism as a high watermark in the evolution of British fiction.[3] Never satisfied with one particular aesthetic, McEwan has moved across multiple subgenres: from psychological thrillers (*The Comfort of Strangers, Enduring Love*) and espionage (*The Innocent*), to geopolitical history (*Black Dogs*) and the period romance (*Atonement, On Chesil Beach*). Black comedy has always played its part (*Amsterdam, Solar, Nutshell*); and recently he has combined several of these models in one endeavour, *Sweet Tooth*, which also turns out – rather theatrically, on its final page – to be a meditation on the ethics of authorship and artistic licence.

However wary he seems, then, of being 'strangled' by the 'loop' of producing novels solely preoccupied with their own artifice, McEwan has never quite relinquished an interest in the very act of writing as a source of dramatic material and moral argument. As the sheer variety of genre-models in my foregoing list attests, if he has taken anything for granted it is not simply the 'artifice of fiction' so much as the promise of generic innovation as a wellspring of linguistic, characterological and thematic opportunities. This enduring sense of generic possibility coexists with his lasting love for the heritage of literary realism, an affection for the emotional ambition and social scale of Victorian narrative which, over time, implies that McEwan has become 'a more traditional writer', as he himself admits, aware 'of the traditions of the English novel'.[4]

Self-conscious traditionalism? It verges on the oxymoronic. Being so attracted to the novel's back-catalogue of formal paragons surely implies the sort of self-referentiality from which McEwan has sometimes distinguished himself when dissociating his work from the creative echo chambers of metafiction. Traditionalism, after all, is no less of an artifice than postmodernism, however dichotomous these terms have often seemed in theory. On closer inspection, however, McEwan's innovative traditionalism looks more like a product of artistic conciliation than contradiction. Novelists today, he observed in 2009, 'now have a narrative self-awareness that we can never escape'; but that's not something they axiomatically need 'to be crushed by'.[5] Reflexivity cannot simply be dismissed or shed like a worn-out convention. It needs to be acknowledged and reincorporated, he implies, without compromising the novel's solicitation and cultivation of the reader's immersion. In this way, McEwan's work has lived up to the promise of resolution that David Lodge famously envisaged for postwar writers caught 'at the crossroads' between the seemingly antagonistic impulses of realism and experimentation – the promise of 'a new synthesis of pre-existing narrative traditions, rather than a continuation of one of them or an entirely unprecedented phenomenon'.[6]

The Child in Time epitomizes this sense of synthesis, not only formally (with its combination of urban realism with modernist simulations of pain, boredom and longing), but also thematically as it locates a sharply poignant bereavement narrative within a malignant political landscape. As the novel's central focalizing consciousness, Stephen Lewis's perspective combines mourning and intellection, as his susceptibility to plangent daydreams provides a vehicle for ruminations not only about his missing daughter, Kate, but on social inequity, the brute effects of privatization, generational contrasts and the phenomenal experience of time. The novel is thereby known for attempting too much. Political critique, an anatomy of grief, the state of a nation, the metaphysics of temporality and a 'two cultures'-style debate between Thelma and Stephen in which physics and literature come head-to-head – these topical constellations vie for attention in a plot anchored to the irresolvable nature of traumatic loss. The audacious reach of McEwan's subject matter is matched by his stylistic ambitions, when sorrow-inflected sensations of passing time are simulated through flashback episodes and sequences of extended duration, which interrupt an increasingly futile quest narrative that loosely forms the novel's spine.

Trumping all these aspirations, McEwan at one stage breaches the confines of verisimilitude altogether by having Stephen enter a time warp in which he encounters his parents, young and unmarried, as his mother contemplates her early pregnancy. Spotting her alone through the window of an uncannily recognizable pub, 'The Bell', Stephen peers into a world without him where his expecting mother returns his gaze, before then withdrawing deliriously from the scene. Pulling back from this spectacle of pre-existence, Stephen is consumed in a vertiginous onrush of abandonment, and the novel's language responds in kind by rapidly unravelling through metaphorical ornamentation and syntactic elaboration. 'Perhaps he was crying', we're told, 'as he backed away', the uncertainty of that leading adverb rendering ambivalent the provenance of this narrative's perspective, which has hitherto been tightly focalized by Stephen's consciousness (CT, p. 60). If free indirect style dissipates, then it is by no means replaced with an authoritative narrator; instead, the narration sits somewhere between modernist interiority and realist omniscience. A discrepancy thus emerges between the vocabulary born out of Stephen's perspective and the way his outward behaviour is delineated, as the reader is informed that 'perhaps he was wailing like a baby waking in the night', and yet 'to an observer he may have appeared silent and resigned'. Thereafter, subjective impressions prevail; inward and nebulous, they convey how the 'air he moved through was dark and wet, he was light, made of nothing'. After he falls 'helplessly through a void', McEwan's syntax reproduces in its parataxis an agonizing, convoluted odyssey that returns Stephen 'dumbly through invisible curves' to the womb. Landscape and uterus merge in a catalogue of 'sinuous tunnels of undergrowth, dank, muscular sluices', where Stephen's 'eyes' appear 'large and round and lidless with desperate, protesting innocence', his fingers reduced to 'scaly flippers' that beat 'urgent, hopeless strokes through the salty ocean that engulfed the treetops and surged between their roots'. Self-reflection somehow survives this metamorphosis, yielding 'a single thought' reminiscent of what Joyce would call a negative epiphany. Indeed, something like a recognition crystallizes, attesting that 'he had nowhere to go, no moment which could embody him, he was not expected, no destination or time could be named'. Initially, this realization seems like a self-elegy; but it then 'unwrapped a sadness which was not his own', being 'centuries, millennia old', a testament for all existence that 'nothing was nothing's own' (CT, p. 60).

We have journeyed a long way from realism. With Stephen propelled back to a foetal state, McEwan offers through accretive grammar and proliferating description a series of linguistic correlatives to the amniotic fluid whose 'salty ocean' engulfs the countryside surrounding 'The Bell'. Even the uterine conceit of Nutshell (2016), a novel to which I will later turn, does not push McEwan to these heights of rhetorical and perspectival peculiarity. That he reached this peak at all was something he subsequently felt he had to lampoon. In Saturday (2005), the neurosurgeon Henry Perowne feels certain that he does not 'really want to be a spectator of other lives, of imaginary lives'. Instead of seeing 'the world invented', Perowne 'wants it explained'

(*S*, p. 66). His daughter, Daisy, tries to persuade him otherwise, by inviting him to read not only the great realists – *Anna Karenina* and *Madame Bovary*, books that for him 'were the products of steady, workmanlike accumulation' – but also 'the so-called magical realists', whose novels he regards as 'irksome confections'. Disparaging Daisy's celebration of magical realism's 'liminality', Perowne's list of the genre's most gratuitous tendencies culminates in an example that holds up the mirror to his creator: 'one visionary saw through a pub window his parents as they had been some weeks after his conception, discussing the possibility of aborting him' (*S*, p. 67). If this allusion to *The Child in Time* serves to mock Perowne's narrow-mindedness as much as it caricatures the exhibitionism of McEwan's most ambitious novel of the 1980s, then something of Perowne's adamant materialism – by his own admission 'a realist' who does not possess 'the lyric gift to see beyond' the actual (*S*, p. 168) – directly informs McEwan's own view of how fiction best evokes lived experience. Perowne muses that 'the actual, not the magical, should be the challenge' and, in light of Daisy's 'reading list' of fabulists, he is left convinced 'that the supernatural was the recourse of an insufficient imagination, a dereliction of duty, a childish evasion of the difficulties and wonders of the real, of the demanding re-enactment of the plausible' (*S*, pp. 67–8).

We would be forgiven for suspecting some ventriloquism is at work here. When interviewed by Zadie Smith as *Saturday* appeared, McEwan confessed to having 'a sneaking sympathy with the view that the real, the actual, is so demanding and rich, that magical realism is really a tedious evasion of some artistic responsibility'.[7] *Saturday*'s sideswipe at *The Child in Time* thus confirms McEwan's mild contempt for novels that take leave from actuality to build their own marvellous worlds, a position that has endured despite his diegetic adventures in recent works like *Nutshell*. For without the conceit of its foetal narrator, *Nutshell* would be a conventionally plotted crime novel, interspersed with politically up-to-the-minute ruminations on the global resurgence of a protectionist Right along with the deleterious consequences for higher education of curricular trigger warnings and institutional safe spaces. In this way, *Nutshell* is as committed to the real as any of McEwan's more overtly social novels, which makes complete sense in view of the allegiances he earmarked a decade before in that interview with Smith. While hammering home an artistic conviction about the primacy of realism, McEwan also, more implicitly, asserted an ethical conviction about fiction's accountability toward the material world: 'The real, the actual, they place heavy demands on a writer – how to invent it, how to confront it or pass it through the sieve of your own consciousness'. Having never been 'a great Márquez person', McEwan equates magical realism with 'the international style in furniture', a 'sort of lingua franca that really defies the central notion of the novel which is that the novel is local'. By this McEwan means that fiction's responsiveness to the 'demands' of actuality constitutes a 'regional' or 'bottom-up process', yielding an aesthetic particularism that remains antithetical to 'international styles' that, for him, 'are too similar to each other'.[8]

According to this view, the artifice of magical realism is paradoxically recognizable because of the uniformity of its extravagance, all the more monochrome despite the mode's reputation for technicolour ostentation. Realist fiction, by contrast, will always have its work cut out, in McEwan's model, because realism has to do justice to the particularities of time and space without the crutch of fabulation to help language 'confront' and evoke experience. And yet, answering to those 'heavy demands' requires its own level of artifice, not least if one has to 'invent' 'the real', as McEwan advises, in the process of refracting the material world via one's 'own consciousness'. What's more, even the most autochthonous form is also an artifice; the specificity of 'regional' naturalism is itself a calculated style of observation, specification and exactitude, as indeed the early stages of *The Child in Time* reveal. The novel's exposition is worth lingering over, precisely because it offers an instructive counterpoint to its momentary modulation into magical realism later on. Renowned for its suspenseful build-up to Kate's abduction, *The Child in Time*'s opening passages record that horrific day in retrospect, and the seemingly humdrum descriptions through which tension mounts exemplify McEwan's effort to synchronize linguistic artistry and social concretion, artifice and actuality.

For first-time readers, the sequence in question is no less unsettling for being centred on such a routine matter as a weekend trip to the supermarket. A second reading reveals how dexterously McEwan laces the painstaking taxonomy of an ordinary chore with something intangible yet appalling. The sequence typifies the way McEwan can produce the effect of psychological realism – the immediacy of action and sensation, the tangible and credible sense of the passage of felt time – while also leaving us with the impression 'that every sentence contains a ghostly commentary on its own processes'.[9] Descriptions of action and object-matter carry their own sense of verbal artifice, without impairing the scene's vraisemblance or its slow insinuation (in the reader) of apprehensiveness, thanks to McEwan's intermittent proleptic hints. As Stephen and Kate step 'outdoors as though into a storm', phrases that at first resemble unremarkable environmental illustrations are soon freighted with hints toward the post-traumatic state that will ensue in the months and years to come, as this 'bitter, anti-cyclonic day was to serve an obsessive memory well with a light of brilliant explicitness, a cynical eye for detail' (*CT*, p. 14). Initially banal as information goes, incidental rather than dramatic, the cold bright morning turns out to be not only portentous but to offer an apprenticeship in the forensic way of seeing that will possess Stephen in his obsessive, harrowing search for his abducted daughter.

This is how seemingly rudimentary descriptions in McEwan's writing take on a dramatic charge; local specifications (of objects, of weather, of by-the-way actions) secrete emotive implications for the plot at large. And in this instance, the tactic of reinflecting ordinary observations soon builds. That 'eye for detail' gets to work promptly in *The Child in Time*, though, tragically, it is as yet unscarred – as yet unobstructed by the 'cynical' lens through which Stephen will later view the world in sorrow. In turn, the proliferation of details slows the pace of what unfolds, with McEwan's extended duration producing his hallmark suspense. Declarative statements – 'It was a two-minute walk to the supermarket, over the four-lane road by a zebra crossing' (*CT*, pp. 14–15) – sound suspiciously punctilious. Ancillary components of the setting – 'Near where they waited to cross was a motor-bike salesroom, an international meeting place for bikers' (*CT*, p. 15) – feel, similarly, as though incidental elements might be distracting us from what's lurking ahead. Of course, the first-time reader will not know this for sure, and may even be taken in by the topographical artifice surrounding this walk to the shops, an artifice that switches to the level of demographic diagnosis when Stephen and Kate reach their destination, where 'people who used the supermarket divided into two groups, as distinct as tribes or nations', split along class lines. Stephen has his own list too – 'toothpaste, tissues, washing-up liquid, and best bacon, a leg of lamb, steak, green and red peppers, radice, potatoes, tin foil, a litre of Scotch' – but this time the inventory of groceries gives way to the macabre: 'and who was there when his hand reached for these items? Someone who followed him as he pushed Kate along the stacked aisles, who stood a few paces off when he stopped, who pretended to be interested in a label and then continued when he did?' (*CT*, p. 15). This figure, the potential abductor, remains obscure. And the fact of that obscurity yields tremendous poignancy. For despite the precision with which Stephen recalls all the items he bought, he struggles in vain to describe Kate's captor. Foodstuffs loom in memory with exaggerated clarity, their legibility set in pathetic opposition to 'that shrouded figure at the periphery of vision'. Linguistically, the concrete enumeration of his purchases contrasts that menacing yet ephemeral presence, to whose indistinctness Stephen 'had been back a thousand times' in a desperate effort 'to move his eyes, lift them against the weight of time' and see 'the one who was always to the side and slightly behind, who, filled with a strange desire, was calculating odds, or simply waiting'. Again proleptically, McEwan affords us a glance ahead toward a life of unrelieved bereavement, the experience of which is plagued by the compulsion to redress irreparable loss by revisiting what was not seen, what Stephen did not sufficiently notice and describe to himself. This desire to undo time, to suture its wound, clashes with the modest urgency of getting a weekend task done. A casual chore overtakes in its descriptive vividness the culprit of calamity, as though the 'time' of 'mundane errands' had narrowed Stephen's 'sight for ever', blocking out the figures 'all about him' and reducing them, in retrospect, to mere 'shapes without definition'. The whole sequence moves from the crystalline vividness of a raw sunlit morning to the horror of suspects 'lost to categories' (CT, p. 16).

Iconic for McEwan's readers, thanks to what arrestingly happens, the scene is also remarkable for the affective tension it conjures from its *un*eventful terrain, as description manipulates quotidian materials. Indeed, the episode epitomizes the way description itself – as a vital component of, rather than something distinct from, narration – is neither neutral nor simply functional for McEwan. Sometimes accused of deadening artificiality, description was seen by Georg Lukács as a 'mere filler in the novel', a 'schematic' device that 'transforms people into conditions, into components of still lives'.[10] But for *The Child in Time* description could not be more essential or vitalizing, emotionally electrifying even when its objects seem plain and innocuous. To draw an apposite formulation from Deborah Nelson's recent work on documentary photography, we are in the presence of 'a kind of realism ... that will not confuse the artifact with the thing it represents because it calls the distinction to the viewer's attention', producing in McEwan's case a modality of realist narration 'which includes the made-ness of the work of art as part of its reality'.[11] And that reality could not be more emotional in this early scene. Taxonomies elevate suspense, delaying the onset of alarm. Proleptic fragments of life ahead provoke pathos. And, finally, failures of categorization ignite ceaseless regret, perpetuating Stephen's longing to redescribe what 'was hardly an awareness at all', to decipher and give form to the 'weakest suspicion brought to life by a desperate memory' (CT, p. 16).

When that desperation is so elegantly delineated, when searing loss is offset for us by the thrill of suspense, *The Child in Time* shows how narrative artifice compels attention to the ethics of style. For if style captures violence so nimbly, what might its virtuosity occlude? Does McEwan's commitment to cultivating a form for capturing minute fluctuations of consciousness detract from his fiction's capacity for ethical commentary or social critique? Is linguistic athleticism, in other words, inimical to moral inquiry? These are time-honoured questions, of course, but they shadow McEwan's earliest convictions, as we have heard, about the responsibility fictional experimentation might have toward evoking 'states of mind and the society that informs them'. Two decades later, they endure in his most explicit and self-reflexive engagement with the ethics of fiction: *Atonement* (2001).

In this multi-generic work, McEwan operates within the coordinates of historical fiction while also producing a self-conscious meditation on the very history and moral efficacy of the modern novel as such. A parable of moral accountability and remorse; a trauma novel about the horrific personal costs of war; a reflection on how intertwined artistic ambitions and ethical actions can become, and how devastating it can be to regard them as distinct – *Atonement* is all of these things. It is also a pointed critique of modernism, calling to account what McEwan sees as the morally questionable artifice of subjectivism. As an exhibition of interiority, Part One belies how enchanted Briony Tallis is with producing her own version of the psychologically textured, densely particularized mode of represented thought we might associate with Henry James or Virginia Woolf. For the young Briony, reality comes to reciprocate her belief in conscious artistry, such that her 'wish for a harmonious, organized world denied her the reckless possibilities of wrongdoing' (*At*, p. 5). By giving herself over to 'all the pleasures of miniaturisation', her affectively intensive, scenically elaborate descriptions complement that 'love of order', however much they aspire to capture at the same time 'the vagaries and unpredictability of the private self' (*At*, p. 312). Part One is an exhibition, a pastiche even, of Woolfian impressionism, some way from the 'impartial psychological realism' (*At*, p. 41) that we are proleptically told will become Briony's chosen aesthetic as a mature writer some decades later. McEwan's aesthetic affinities are patent: whereas 'the nineteenth-century novel' displays '[b]road tolerance and the long view, an inconspicuously warm heart and cool judgment', a virtually therapeutic form 'alive to the monstrous patterns of fate' (*At*, p. 93), modernist writing is by contrast insulated from what really matters in life, obsessed instead (as a fictionalized Cyril Connolly later complains) with 'the quality of light and shade' (*At*, p. 313), evoking 'random impressions' in conspicuous disregard for a reader with the 'desire to be told a story, to be held in suspense, to know what happens' (*At*, p. 314). The novel is of course as much about the process by which Briony atones for the ethical atrocities these modernist obsessions can supposedly perpetuate as it is about the impossibility of ever rehabilitating the relationship between Robbie and Cecilia she blighted as a precocious and jealous child. *Atonement*, that is, directs its ethical scrutiny as intensely toward literary artifice as toward the fatal accusation that triggers the irremediable tragedy at its centre.

By drawing attention to how ethically disabled Briony becomes in her devotion to modernist aesthetics, *Atonement* ponders Theodor Adorno's hunch that the 'aesthetic stylistic principle' can 'make the unthinkable appear to have had some meaning', when historical catastrophe 'becomes transfigured' through its artful expression, leaving 'something of its horror removed'.[12] The artifice of impressionism that McEwan recreates for us in Part One seems to evidence in turn Fredric Jameson's warning that modernist fiction promised a 'transformation' of 'realities into style', deflecting modernity's violence into the compensations of verbal plenitude and thereby repackaging it 'for consumption on some purely aesthetic level'.[13] McEwan would probably agree. He has praised Victorian fiction for the way it 'brought the form to its point ... of perfection', arguing that where 'the creation of character' is concerned the 'great nineteenth-century novels' remain 'unsurpassed'.[14] Accordingly, he has blamed 'the dead hand of modernism' for triggering in twentieth-century fiction a 'dereliction of duty' with respect to 'the backbone' of 'plot'.[15] At the same time, however, the hallmark suspense and penetration of his writing arise from a degree of psychological realism that would not be possible without the innovations in perspectivism, episodic structure, depictive obliquity and extended duration that modernist fiction brought into being. McEwan himself acknowledges that he has tried to 'remain faithful to the sensuous, telepathic capabilities of language as it transfers thoughts and feelings from one person's mind to another's', a distinctly modernist artifice if ever there was one.[16] Hence, his allegiances cut both ways: admiring the moral architecture and epic sweep of Victorian realism while participating in the legacies of modernism's iconic concern with consciousness. Although McEwan attests that 'the nineteenth century' novel 'invented the notion of character', he concedes that '*Atonement* could not have been written without all the experiments in fiction and reflections on point of view' pioneered by early twentieth-century innovators like James, Woolf and Joyce.[17] As such, it joins a corpus of McEwan's career-long attempts to convey in a 'stylized way what it's like to be thinking', as he put it in that interview with Smith, while also exploiting the dramatic and ethical consequences of 'how much perception is distorted by will'.[18]

Atonement therefore stands at a crossroads, to borrow again Lodge's metaphor, poised between continuing certain facets of the realist project (notably in the way McEwan affirms fiction's role as a calibrator of moral error and its human costs), while at the same time folding into our reading experience an awareness of the artifice that is realism itself, whether bleak or gratifying, devastating or consoling.[19] By dramatizing through the figure of Briony the moral implications of artistic self-involvement yet without perpetuating the 'narcissism' of postmodern self-reflexivity,[20] and by initially assuming the guise of a Victorian 'big house' novel evoked in the manner of Virginia Woolf before then switching to the taut register of a war-torn psychological thriller, *Atonement* straddles periods and genres to stage what McEwan has called his conscious 'attempt' on behalf of postmillennial fiction 'to discuss where we stand'.[21] The precocious Briony enters that discussion in the final act to ramp up its ethical stakes. In a postscript, 'London, 1999', we find her making no apologies for the counterfactual narrative of Cecilia and Robbie's survival we have just read. If modernism once morally derailed her, Briony now attempts to make impossible amends in the form of alternative history, 'a final act of kindness, a stand against oblivion and despair' (*At*, p. 372). Such a romance is too poignant, too compelling, in her view, for the reader not to be granted the gratifications of seeing the 'lovers live' (*At*, p. 372). No one 'would want to believe' that they 'never fulfilled their love', she insists; to do without that uplifting artifice would be to 'do without hope or satisfaction'. Indeed, it would be to press the novel irrevocably into 'the service of the bleakest realism' (*At*, p. 371), a form that scuppers fiction's potential to recoup some quantum of consolation from the harm it plots. 'Bleak truths can be purging', reckons Julian Barnes, for 'describing things as they are rather than as we would like them to be can have a consoling effect'.[22] But Briony would not be convinced by this ascetic solace. Instead, she defends what we might call a strategic sentimentalism: gesturing to the salubrious benefits of finding fulfilment in fiction-*reading*, she regards fiction-*writing* in turn as salvage work, not only for her own sake as a novelist who has 'absolute power of deciding outcomes', but also for her audience who, she believes, ought to welcome her mission to substitute the sentimental yet salutary artifice of optimism for the realistic yet dour 'courage of … pessimism' (*At*, p. 371). If *Atonement* thus sits at the crossroads where modernism, metafiction and McEwan's own admiration for nineteenth-century realist characterization meet, then Briony is presented as notably less amenable to this colloquy of alternative practices, committed as she is to the idea that to '[b]ring down the fogs of the imagination' is precisely what novelists are for, as they 'set the limits and the terms' (*At*, pp. 370, 371).

Limits, both physical and philosophical, would subsequently become a pressing concern for one of McEwan's most extravagant narrator's yet. A foetus who already knows 'life's most limiting truth', the unborn boy of *Nutshell* ponders the constraints of being unable to divert his mother from conspiring to murder his father. All he can do is 'divert' himself: in place of frustrated action, 'I send my thoughts ahead to spy on them. Purely an exercise of the imagination. Nothing here is real' (*N*, p. 35).

Given these conditions, he never quite gives up the possibility of authoring his own reality, of becoming the novelist who hopes, to adapt Briony's terms, to 'set the limits' on a homicidal outcome that might yet be avoided. His apprenticeship as a fictioneer is fuelled by his mother's drinking habits, and after 'the last of the Sauvignon Blanc arrives' amid a London heatwave he wonders whether in fact his 'limiting truth was untrue', wondering in turn if '[o]ne could make a living devising such excursions' (N, p. 38). One of his emboldening tales envisions his twenty-eight-year-old self 'moving sleekly like a panther, temporarily immortal' (N, p. 35), ready to avenge his father's murder. Yet it is as though these projections provide hollow gratifications. The here and now contains threats too pressing for daydreams of retribution, too immediate for the escapism of hypothesized heroism. In an echo of McEwan's own misgivings about magical realism – that material reality is demanding enough as it is, without the high jinks of supernaturalism complicating the novel's task further – our narrator admits that 'the actual, the circumscribed real, is absorbing too' (N, p. 38).

Henceforth *Nutshell* schools us, through a sequence of mock-metaphysical vignettes, in 'the condition of the modern foetus' (N, p. 74). As an experiment in 'what it's like to be thinking', it is surely among McEwan's most peculiar, even though the language is for the most part stately, urbane, perfectly approachable if occasionally baroque. This unborn soliloquist, with 'nothing to do but be and grow', conveys without hesitation how enamoured he seems with his own eloquent meditations on 'the joy of pure existence' amid 'the tedium of undifferentiated days' (N, p. 74). Like a Romantic lyricist, he pictures himself 'owed the privilege and luxury of solitude', bemoaning the fact he was once 'in the realm of the sublime', 'until my mother wished my father dead' (N, p. 74–7). While diegetically outlandish, the novella's scenario could not be more recognizably allusive: an embryonic Prince of Denmark intimates 'the pain of unnamed, unreachable remorse, a sense of having left someone or something behind in a betrayal of duty or love' (N, p. 105). And, again despite its fantastic setting, *Nutshell* showcases what has become a familiar preoccupation of McEwan with the rhetorical artifice of mentation; or, more precisely, with the distance between the vicissitudes of thought and the language in which thinking is evoked, a distance that may remain insuperable for fiction but which writers since modernism have aspired to bridge. Philosophizing from the womb, we are told that in the beginning 'pain begat consciousness', since 'felt sensations are the beginning of the invention of the self'. Culture becomes a big beneficiary in this potted history: 'God said, Let there be pain. And there was poetry. Eventually' (N, p. 46).

The atheistic McEwan is evidently having some fun. Yet the style in which he posits consciousness at the epicentre of Creation exemplifies an interest that has remained central to his most serious fiction, namely, an interest in that 'matrix of shifting patterns, consolidating and compressing meaning in fractions of a second, and blending it inseparably with its distinctive emotional hue', which in *Saturday* is celebrated as the marvellous stuff of thought (*S*, p. 81). In this respect, *Nutshell*'s self-elegizing narrator echoes Perowne's awed fascination with 'mentalese', that 'pre-verbal language' of introspective sensation that 'even with a poet's gift of compression' could 'take hundreds of words and many minutes to describe' (*S*, p. 81). McEwan of course takes up the gauntlet. By exploiting the ironic inconsistency between Perowne's misgivings about literary fiction and his own dexterity as a choreographer of free indirect style, McEwan pursues a vocabulary for minute, incremental fluctuations in the translation of perception into thought, sensation into comprehension, that seem (to his neurologically expert protagonist) virtually ineffable. The artifice of this endeavour is revealed by how strenuously McEwan's language ventures to capture mental processes. In his initial confrontation with Baxter, for instance, a standoff in the wake of their collision is delineated moment by moment with a serenity that seems implausible given Perowne's apprehensiveness, his suspicion that 'there are reasons to be cautious'. The episode is given over to extended duration, as paragraphs expand to sync with a 'half-minute's pause' that 'has given the situation a game-like quality in which calculations have already been made' (*S*, p. 83). One is reminded of another driving incident, from *The Child in Time*, where 'duration shaped itself round the intensity of the event' as Stephen swerves to avoid a somersaulting lorry, experiencing as he does so a radical 'slowing of time' (*CT*, pp. 95, 94). Just as Stephen gauged in seconds his options for avoiding impact 'in a detached kind of way' (*CT*, p. 94), so Perowne too weighs up his options with a measured impartiality that seems affectively out of sync with his 'rising irritation' (*S*, p. 82). Instead of simulating the extent to which 'he's angry', the language records point by point what 'Perowne thinks as he goes round to the front of his car'. What McEwan offers is not so much a syntax that formally reciprocates the texture of unfolding sensations as a catalogue of intellectually processed reactions, not visceral perceptions but nicely rounded discussions, as Perowne acknowledges how caution should counterbalance his annoyance. Despite the possibility of imminent threat, he serenely documents how 'these contradictory notions aren't helpful, and he decides he'll be better off feeling his way into the confrontation, rather than troubling himself with ground rules' (*S*, p. 83). It is almost as though Perowne has a map of his own mental tendencies to hand that allows him to plot a course ahead, minute by minute – analysing in advance how he should behave in response to the impressions he forms of the world. It is artful. And it is very artificial.

In a novel about a man who is professionally and personally enchanted with the 'sinuous, snaking quality' of feelings – and who, 'in his usual manner', likes to 'break them down into their components, the quanta, and find all the distal and proximal causes' (S, p. 262) – style announces its own difference from mentation. This interval between the workings of the mind and the workings of language seems as important to McEwan as any effort to mimic in fictional discourse a definitive, 'irrefutable truth about consciousness' (S, p. 255). If a sense of dislocation thus emerges in *Saturday* between descriptive detail and felt experience, between the breadth and composure of granular observations and what a mind in Perowne's stressful situation might really be focusing on, then it is perhaps less an aesthetic shortfall or compromise on McEwan's part than a knowing recognition of what the novel strives against all odds to accomplish, a recognition that narrative artifice need not only be taken for granted but that it need not be concealed either. This is a style of concession, whereby McEwan's fiction builds into itself an admission of narrative deficit without capitulating to an outright acceptance of inexpressibility. As concessions go, it has played a paradoxically enabling role in his aesthetic, one perfectly suited to his inkling 'that every sentence contains a ghostly commentary on its own processes' – a commentary that may well pinpoint for us what it is in felt experience that fiction cannot comprehensively capture.[23]

Such is the extent, suggests McEwan, to which the artifice of composition is revealed, staged even, by the artifice of execution. Far from aspiring to what Susan Sontag once called the 'tenacious fantasies' of stylistic transparency that for her plagued postwar culture, his writing elucidates rather than screens its own procedures, yet without inhibiting the immediate, affective experience of reading his fiction by subjecting us to self-enclosed meta-stories about literature's counterfeit realities. Artifice, as we have seen, takes many forms in McEwan's prose, sometimes operating at several levels at once: it may apply to characterization and voice (*Nutshell*), to the (in)credibility of represented thought (*Saturday*), to realism's sudden swerves into phantasmagoria (*The Child in Time*), or to ethical evaluations of modernism's aesthetic distinction and elevated prestige (*Atonement*). But whatever its thematic or generic context, narrative artifice is something McEwan has little interest in evading. In this respect, he presents a retort to Sontag's suspicion that writers only 'pretend to believe that it is no more possible to get the artifice out of art than it is for a person to lose his personality'.[24] If anything, McEwan has continued to embrace the constructedness of his medium not as an escapade in the unfolding legacies of postmodernism but in ways that endeavour to 'do justice to the twin aspects of art', in Sontag's model: 'as artifice and as living form of consciousness, as the overcoming or supplementing of reality and as the making explicit of forms of encountering reality'.[25] Often it is precisely that tension between overcoming and confronting – between grasping the fragile promise of compensating loss or atoning for error and encountering the actuality of what cannot be put back – which supplies pathos in McEwan's fiction and provokes us to look closer at its affective mechanics. If his style seems to offer an occasional 'commentary on its own creation', then that's rarely inimical to the reader's emotional participation.[26] In fact, such moments of self-commentary invite us to reflect as much on our own critical inclinations as on McEwan's formal aims.

NOTES

1 Ian McEwan, 'The State of Fiction: A Symposium', *The New Review*, 5 (Summer 1978), 1, pp. 14–76 (p. 51).

2 Interview with Daniel Zalewski, 'The Background Hum: Ian McEwan's Art of Unease', *The New Yorker*, 23 February 2009; Michael LeMahieu, 'The Novel of Ideas', in *The Cambridge Companion to British Fiction since 1945*, ed. David James (New York: Cambridge University Press, 2015), pp. 177–91 (p. 182).

3 Jon Cook, Sebastian Groes and Victor Sage, 'Journeys without Maps: An Interview with Ian McEwan', in *Ian McEwan: Contemporary Critical Perspectives*, second edition, ed. Sebastian Groes (London: Continuum, 2013), pp. 144–55 (p. 145).

4 Ian McEwan, 'I Will Have to Make It Up', *The Guardian*, 'Saturday Review', 26 March 2011, 2.

5 Zalewski, 'The Background Hum'.

6 David Lodge, 'The Novelist at the Crossroads' (1969), in *The Novel Today: Contemporary Writers on Modern Fiction*, new edition, ed. Malcolm Bradbury (London: Fontana, 1990), pp. 87–114.

7 Zadie Smith and Ian McEwan, 'Zadie Smith Talks with Ian McEwan', *The Believer*, 3 (2005), 6; reprinted in *Conversations with Ian McEwan*, ed. Ryan Roberts (Jackson: University Press of Mississippi, 2010), pp. 108–33 (p. 115)

8 Ibid., p. 116.

9 Adam Begley, 'Ian McEwan: The Art of Fiction CLXXIII', *The Paris Review*, 162 (2002); reprinted in *Conversations with Ian McEwan*, ed. Ryan Roberts, pp. 89–107 (p. 107).

10 Georg Lukács, 'Narrate or Describe', in *Writer and Critic, and Other Essays*, ed. and trans. Arthur Kahn (London: Merlin, 1970), pp. 110, 139.

11 Deborah Nelson, *Tough Enough: Arbus, Arendt, Didion, McCarthy, Sontag, Weil* (Chicago: University of Chicago Press, 2017), p. 132.

12 Theodor W. Adorno, 'Commitment', in *Notes to Literature*, trans. Shierry Weber Nicholsen (New York: Columbia University Press, 1992), p. 88.

13 Fredric Jameson, *The Political Unconscious: Narrative as a Socially Symbolic Act* (1981; London: Routledge, 1996), p. 214.

14 Margaret Reynolds and Jonathan Noakes, 'Interview with Ian McEwan' (2001), in *Ian McEwan: The Essential Guide*, eds. Reynolds and Noakes (London: Vintage, 2002), p. 23.

15 Zalewski, 'The Background Hum: Ian McEwan's Art of Unease'; Ian McEwan, interview with Michael Silverblatt, *Bookworm* (Santa Monica, CA: KCRM, 11 July 2002).

16 Adam Begley, 'Ian McEwan: The Art of Fiction', in *Conversations with Ian McEwan*, ed. Ryan Roberts, p. 107.

17 David Lynn, 'A Conversation with Ian McEwan' (2006), in *Conversations with Ian McEwan*, ed. Ryan Roberts, pp. 143–55 (p. 154).

18 Zadie Smith and Ian McEwan, 'Zadie Smith Talks with Ian McEwan', in *Conversations with Ian McEwan*, ed. Ryan Roberts, p. 113.

19 Lodge notes that there are 'formidable discouragements to continuing serenely along the road of fictional realism. The novelist who has any kind of self-awareness must at least hesitate at the crossroads; and the solution many novelists have chosen in their dilemma is to *build that hesitation into the novel itself*'. See 'The Novelist at the Crossroads', in *The Novel Today: Contemporary Writers on Modern Fiction*, ed. Malcolm Bradbury, p. 105.

20 I am drawing this characterisation of postmodern narrative from Linda Hutcheon's *Narcissistic Narrative: The Metafictional Paradox* (London: Methuen, 1984).

21 Zalewski, 'The Background Hum: Ian McEwan's Art of Unease'.

22 Julian Barnes, 'Julian Barnes: The Final Interview', by Vanessa Guignery and Ryan Roberts (2007), in *Conversations with Julian Barnes*, eds. Guignery and Roberts (Jackson: University of Mississippi Press, 2009), pp. 161–88 (p. 169).

23 Adam Begley, 'Ian McEwan: The Art of Fiction' in *Conversations with Ian McEwan*, ed. Ryan Roberts, p. 107.

24 Susan Sontag, 'On Style' (1965), *Against Interpretation* (London: Vintage, 1994), p. 17.

25 Ibid., p. 31.

26 Zadie Smith and Ian McEwan, 'Zadie Smith Talks with Ian McEwan', in *Conversations with Ian McEwan*, ed. Ryan Roberts, p. 122.

FURTHER READING

Selected Essays by and Interviews with McEwan

Begley, Adam, 'Interview with Ian McEwan', *The Paris Review* (2002), 162, pp. 30–60.
Cook, Jon, Sebastian Groes and Victor Sage, 'Journeys without Maps: An Interview with Ian McEwan', in *Ian McEwan*, second edition, ed. Sebastian Groes (London: Bloomsbury, 2013), pp. 144–55.
Garner, Dwight, 'The Salon Interview – Ian McEwan', 31 March 1998. Retrieved from: www.salon.com/1998/03/31/cov_si_31int/ (accessed 6 June 2018).
Haffenden, John, *Novelists in Interview* (London: Methuen, 1985).
Louvel, Liliane, Gilles Ménégaldo and Anne-Laure Fortin, 'An Interview with Ian McEwan' (conducted November 1994), *Études Britanniques Contemporaines*, 8 (1995), pp. 1–12; reprinted in *Conversations with Ian McEwan*, ed. Ryan Roberts (Jackson: University Press of Mississippi, 2010), pp. 67–78.
McEwan, Ian, 'The State of Fiction: A Symposium', *The New Review*, 5, 1 (Summer 1978), pp. 14–76.
'Schoolboys', in *William Golding: The Man and His Books*, ed. John Carey (London: Faber, 1986), pp. 157–60.
'Move Over, Darwin', review of *Consilience* by Edward O. Wilson, *The Observer*, 'Review', 20 September 1998, 13.
'Wild Man of Literature (c1976): A Memoir', *The Observer*, 'Review', 7 June 1998, 16 (a memoir for inclusion in a festschrift for Ian Hamilton).
'Beyond Belief', *The Guardian*, 'G2', 12 September 2001, p. 2.
'Only Love and Then Oblivion. Love Was All They Had to Set Against Their Murderers', front-page article, *The Guardian*, 15 September 2001.
'Mother Tongue: A Memoir', in *On Modern British Fiction*, ed. Zachary Leader (Oxford: Oxford University Press, 2002), pp. 34–44. (The piece was first published in *The Guardian*, 13 October 2001.)
'Faith v Fact', (contribution), *The Guardian*, 7 January 2005, 'G2', p. 6.
'Literature, Science, and Human Nature', in *The Literary Animal: Evolution and the Nature of Narrative*, eds. Jonathan Gottschall and David Sloan Wilson (Evanston, IL: Northwestern University Press, 2005), pp. 5–19.
'Ian McEwan & Antony Gormley: A Conversation about Art and Nature', *The Kenyon Review* 28 (2006), 1, pp. 104–12. Reprinted in *Conversations with Ian McEwan*, ed. Ryan Roberts, pp. 134–42.

'A Parallel Tradition', *The Guardian*, 1 April 2006. Retrieved from: www.theguar dian.com/books/2006/apr/01/scienceandnature.richarddawkins (accessed 6 June 2018).

'The Originality of the Species', *The Guardian*, 23 March 2012. Retrieved from: www.theguardian.com/books/2012/mar/23/originality-of-species-ian-mcewan (accessed 6 June 2018).

'Some Notes on the Novella', *The New Yorker*, 29 October 2012. Retrieved from: www.newyorker.com/books/page-turner/notes-n-the-novella (accessed 1 January 2018).

'The God That Fails', *New Republic* 244, 2 (25 February 2013), pp. 7–8. Published online as 'When I Stop Believing in Fiction', 15 February 2013. Retrieved from: https://newrepublic.com/article/112374/ian-mcewan-my-uneasy-relationship-fic tion (accessed 6 June 2018).

'The Law versus Religious Belief', *The Guardian*, 5 September 2014, pp. 38, 57, 60–1, 62. Retrieved from: www.theguardian.com/books/2014/sep/05/ian-mce wan-law-versus-religious-belief (accessed 3 January 2018).

Ricks, Christopher, 'Adolescence and After – An Interview with Ian McEwan', *The Listener*, 12 April 1979, pp. 526–7.

Roberts, Ryan, ed., *Conversations with Ian McEwan* (Jackson: University Press of Mississippi, 2010).

Smith, Zadie and Ian McEwan, 'Zadie Smith Talks With Ian McEwan', *The Believer*, 3 (2005), 6; reprinted in *Conversations with Ian McEwan*, ed. Ryan Roberts (Jackson: University Press of Mississippi, 2010), pp. 108–33 (p. 113).

Works on McEwan

Banville, John, 'A Day in the Life', *New York Review of Books*, 26 May 2005. Retrieved from: www.nybooks.com/articles/2005/05/26/a-day-in-the-life (accessed 25 February 2018).

Baxter, Jeannette, 'Surrealist Encounters in McEwan's Early Work', in *Ian McEwan: Contemporary Critical Perspectives*, ed. Sebastian Groes (London: Continuum, 2009), pp. 13–25.

Berndt, Katrin, 'Science as Comedy and the Myth of Progress in Ian McEwan's *Solar*', *Mosaic*, 50 (2017), 4, pp. 85–101.

Brown, Richard, 'Postmodern Americas in the Fiction of Angela Carter, Martin Amis and Ian McEwan', in *Forked Tongues? Comparing Twentieth-Century British and American Literature*, eds. Anna Massa and Alistair Stead (London: Longman, 1994), pp. 92–110.

'A Wilderness of Mirrors: The Mediated Berlin Backgrounds for Ian McEwan's *The Innocent*' in *Anglistik: International Journal of English Studies* (Heidelberg) 21 (September 2010), 2.

Byrnes, Christina, *The Work of Ian McEwan: A Psychodynamic Approach* (Notting-ham: Paupers' Press, 2002).

Carbonell, Curtis D., 'A Consilient Science and Humanities in Ian McEwan's *Enduring Love*', *CLCWeb: Comparative Literature and Culture*, 12 (2010), 3. Retrieved from: https://doi.org/10.7771/148-4374.1425 (accessed 15 February 2018).

Childs, Peter, *Contemporary Novelists: British Fiction Since 1970* (Basingstoke: Palgrave, 2005).

The Fiction of Ian McEwan: A Reader's Guide to Essential Criticism (Basingstoke: Palgrave Macmillan, 2006).

'Ian McEwan's *Sweet Tooth*: "Put in Porphyry and Marble Do Appear"', in *Ian McEwan*, ed. Sebastian Groes, second edition (London: Bloomsbury, 2013), pp. 139–43.

Clark, Roger and Andy Gordon, *Ian McEwan's 'Enduring Love'* (London: Continuum, 2003).

Cormack, Alistair, 'Postmodernism and the Ethics of Fiction in *Atonement*', in *Ian McEwan: Contemporary Critical Perspectives*, pp. 70–83.

Dobrogoszcz, Tomasz, *Family and Relationships in Ian McEwan's Fiction: Between Fantasy and Desire* (Lanham, MD: Lexington Books, 2018).

Dodou, Katherina, *Childhood without Children: Ian McEwan and the Critical Study of the Child* (Uppsala, Sweden: Uppsala Universitet, 2009).

Edwards, Paul, 'Time, Romanticism, Modernism and Moderation in Ian McEwan's *The Child in Time*', *English*, 44 (Spring 1995), 178, pp. 41–55.

Evans, Walter, 'The English Short Story in the Seventies', *The English Short Story 1945–1980: A Critical History*, ed. Dennis Vannatta (Boston: Twayne Publishers, 1985), pp. 120–72.

Finney, Brian, 'Briony's Stand Against Oblivion: The Making of Fiction in Ian McEwan's *Atonement*', *Journal of Modern Literature*, 27 (2004), 3, pp. 68–82.

Garrard, Greg, 'Ian McEwan's Next Novel and the Future of Ecocriticism', *Contemporary Literature*, 50 (2009), 4, pp. 695–720.

'*Solar*: Apocalypse Not', in *Ian McEwan*, second edition, ed. Sebastian Groes, pp. 123–36.

Goodbody, Axel, '*Die Ringe des Saturn* und *Solar*: Sinnbilder und Schreibstrategien in Literarischen Stellungnahmen zur Ökologischen Krise von W. G. Sebald und Ian McEwan', in *Ökologische Transformationen und Literarische Repräsentationen*, eds. Maren Ermisch, Ulrike Kruse and Urte Stobbe (Göttingen: Universitätsverslag Göttingen, 2010), pp. 131–48.

Greenberg, Jonathan, 'Why Can't Biologists Read Poetry? Ian McEwan's *Enduring Love*', *Twentieth Century Literature*, 53 (2007), 2, pp. 93–124.

Groes, Sebastian, ed., *Ian McEwan*, second edition (London: Bloomsbury, 2013).

Hamilton, Ian, 'Points of Departure', *New Review*, 5 (1978), 2, pp. 9–21.

Hanson, Clare, *Short Stories and Short Fictions: 1880 – 1980* (Basingstoke: Macmillan, 1985).

Head, Dominic, *Ian McEwan* (Manchester: Manchester University Press, 2007).

Holland, Rachel, 'Reality Check: Ian McEwan's Rational Fictions', *Critique: Studies in Contemporary Fiction*, 58 (2017), 4, pp. 387–400.

Horton, Emily, *Contemporary Crisis Fictions: Affect and Ethics in the Modern British Novel* (London: Palgrave Macmillan, 2014).

Hubble, Nick, John McLeod and Philip Tew, eds., *The 1970s: A Decade of Contemporary British Fiction* (London: Bloomsbury, 2014).

James, David, '"A Boy Stepped Out": Migrancy, visuality, and the Mapping of Masculinities in the Later Fiction of Ian McEwan', *Textual Practice*, 17 (2003), 1, pp. 81–100.

Modernist Futures: Innovation and Inheritance in the Contemporary Novel (New York: Cambridge University Press, 2012).

ed., *The Cambridge Companion to British Fiction Since 1945* (New York: Cambridge University Press, 2015).

James, David and Urmila Seshagiri, 'Metamodernism: Narratives of Continuity and Revolution', *PMLA*, 129 (2014), 1, pp. 87–100.

Lee, Hermione, 'First Rites', Review of *The Cement Garden*, *New Statesman*, 29 (September 1978), p. 416.

Kimber, Gerri, 'The Novella: Between the Novel and the Story', in *The Cambridge History of the English Short Story*, ed. Dominic Head (Cambridge University Press, 2016), pp. 530–46.

Knights, Ben, *Writing Masculinities: Male Narratives in Twentieth-Century Fiction* (Basingstoke: Macmillan, 1999).

von der Lippe, George B., 'Death in Venice in Literature and Film: Six Twentieth-Century Versions', *Mosaic*, 32 (March 1999), 1, pp. 35–54.

McCrum, Robert, 'The Story of His Life' (author profile), *The Observer*, 'Review', 23 January 2005, p. 5.

Macfarlane, Robert, 'A Version of Events', review of *Atonement*, *TLS*, 5139 (28 September 2001), p. 23.

Malcolm, David, 'Narrational Strategy, Intertextuality and their Functions in Ian McEwan's Early Fiction', in *Approaches to Fiction*, ed. Leszek S. Kolek (Lublin, Poland: Folium, 1996), pp. 161–77.

'The Media-Genic and Victorian Mr McEwan?', *Anglistik*, 21 (2010), 2, pp. 13–22.

Understanding Ian McEwan (Columbia: University of South Carolina Press, 2002).

Marcus, Laura, 'Ian McEwan's Modernist Time: *Atonement* and *Saturday*', in *Ian McEwan: Contemporary Critical Perspectives*, ed. Sebastian Groes, second edition (London: Bloomsbury, 2013), pp. 83–98.

Mars-Jones, Adam, '*Venus Envy*', in *Blind Bitter Happiness* (London: Chatto and Windus, 1997), pp. 128–56.

Morrison, Jago, 'Narration and Unease in Ian McEwan's Later Fiction', *Critique: Studies in Contemporary Fiction*, 42 (2001), 3, pp. 253–68.

Morrison, Richard, 'Opera gets between the sheets with Ian McEwan's For You', *The Times*, 9 May 2008, p. 2.

Nicklas, Pascal, ed., *Ian McEwan: Art and Politics* (Heidelberg, Germany: Universitätsverlag Winter, 2009).

Reynolds, Margaret and Jonathan Noakes, eds., *Ian McEwan: The Essential Guide* (London: Vintage, 2002).

Robinson, Richard, 'The Modernism of Ian McEwan's Atonement', *Modern Fiction Studies*, 56 (2010), 3, pp. 473–95.

Ryan, Kiernan, *Ian McEwan* (Plymouth: Northcote House/British Council, 1994).

'Sex, Violence and Complicity: Martin Amis and Ian McEwan', in *An Introduction to Contemporary Fiction*, ed. Rod Mengham (Cambridge: Polity, 1999), pp. 203–18.

'After the Fall', in *Ian McEwan's Enduring Love*, Peter Childs (London and New York: Routledge, 2007), pp. 44–54.

Schemberg, Claudia, Achieving 'At-one-ment': Storytelling and the Concept of the Self in Ian McEwan's 'The Child in Time', 'Black Dogs', 'Enduring Love', and 'Atonement' (Frankfurt: Peter Lang, 2004).

Scurr, Ruth, 'Happiness on a Knife-edge' (review of Saturday), The Times, Saturday, 29 January 2005, 'Weekend Review', 13.

Seaboyer, Judith, 'Sadism Demands a Story: Ian McEwan's The Comfort of Strangers', Modern Fiction Studies, 45 (1999), 4, pp. 957–86.

'Ian McEwan: Contemporary Realism and the Novel of Ideas', The Contemporary British Novel Since 1980, eds. James Acheson and Sarah C. E. Ross (New York: Palgrave Macmillan, 2005), pp. 23–34.

Seligman, Craig, review of Amsterdam, Salon.com, 9 December 1998. Retrieved from: http://dir.salon.com/books/sneaks/1998/12/09sneaks.html (accessed 12 June 2005).

Slay, Jack, 'Vandalizing Time: Ian McEwan's The Child in Time', Critique: Studies in Contemporary Fiction, 35 (1994), 4, pp. 205–18.

Ian McEwan (New York: Twayne, 1996).

Stevenson, Randall, The Oxford English Literary History, Volume 12, 1960—2000: The Last of England? (Oxford: Oxford University Press, 2004).

Sutcliffe, William, review of Atonement, Independent on Sunday, 16 September 2001, 'LifeEtc.', p. 15.

Sutherland, John, 'What's It All About?', (review of Amsterdam), The Sunday Times, 'Books', 13 September 1998, 12.

Tait, Theo, 'A Rational Diagnosis', (review of Saturday), TLS, 5315, 11 February 2005, 21–2.

Tayler, Christopher, 'A Knife at the Throat', (review of Saturday), London Review of Books, 27 (3 March 2005), 5, pp. 31–3.

Taylor, D. J., A Vain Conceit: British Fiction in the 1980s (London: Bloomsbury, 1989). After the War: The Novel and England Since 1945 (1993; London: Flamingo, 1994).

Vannatta, Dennis, ed., The English Short Story 1945–1980: A Critical History (Boston: Twayne Publishers, 1985).

Wallace, Elizabeth Kowaleski, 'Postcolonial Melancholia in Ian McEwan's Saturday', Studies in the Novel 39 (2007), 4 (Winter), pp. 465–80 (p. 470).

Wally, Johannes, Secular Falls from Grace: Religion and (New) Atheism in the Implied Worldview of Ian McEwan's Fiction (Trier: Wissenschaftlicher Verlag, 2015).

Waugh, Patricia, 'Science and Fiction in the 1990s', in British Fiction of the 1990s, ed. Nick Bentley (London: Routledge, 2005), pp. 57–77.

Wells, Lynn, Ian McEwan (Basingstoke: Palgrave Macmillan, 2010).

Zalewski, Daniel, 'Ian McEwan's Art of Unease', The New Yorker (23 February 2009). Retrieved from: www.newyorker.com/magazine/2009/02/23/the-back ground-hum (accessed 15 February 2018).

Zemanek, Evi, 'A Dirty Hero's Fight for Clean Energy: Satire, Allegory, and Risk Narrative in Ian McEwan's Solar', Ecozon@, 3 (2012), 1 (2012), pp. 51–60 (p. 51). Retrieved from: http://ecozona.eu/article/view/450/472 (accessed 23 March 2018).

Other Works Cited

Abrams, M. H., *The Mirror and the Lamp* (Oxford: Oxford University Press, 1953).

Ackroyd, Peter, *Dressing Up: Transvestism and Drag – The History of an Obsession* (New York: Simon & Shuster, 1979) .

Adamson, Jane, 'Against Tidiness: Literature and/versus Moral Philosophy', in *Renegotiating Ethics in Literature, Philosophy, and Theory*, eds. Jane Adamson, Richard Freadman and David Parker (Cambridge: Cambridge University Press, 1998), pp. 84–110.

Andrew, Christopher, *The Defence of the Realm: The Authorized History of MI5* (Canada: Penguin, 2009).

Amis, Martin *Einstein's Monsters* (London: Jonathan Cape, 1987).

Barthes, Roland, 'The Death of the Author', in *Image, Music, Text* (London: Fontana, 1977), pp. 142–8.

A Lover's Discourse, trans. Richard Howard (London: Jonathan Cape, 1979).

Beckett, Andy, *When the Lights Went Out: Britain in the Seventies* (London: Faber and Faber, 2009).

Bellow, Saul, *Herzog* (1964; London: Penguin, 2001).

Bewes, Timothy, 'What Is "Philosophical Honesty" in Postmodern Literature?', *New Literary History*, 31 (2000), 3 (Summer), pp. 421–34.

Bohm, David, *Wholeness and the Implicate Order* (London: Routledge, 1980).

Bradbury, Malcolm, *The Modern British Novel* (London: Penguin, 1993).

Bradley, Arthur and Andrew Tate, *The New Atheist Novel: Fiction, Philosophy, and Polemic after 9/11* (London: Continuum, 2010).

Brightman, Carol, *Writing Dangerously: Mary McCarthy and Her World* (New York: Clarkson Potter, 1992).

Brockman, John, ed., *The Next Fifty Years: Science in the First Half of the Twenty-First Century* (New York: Touchstone, 1995).

Bronfen, Elisabeth, *Over Her Dead Body: Death, Femininity, and the Aesthetic* (Manchester: Manchester University Press, 1992).

Brooks, Peter, *Psychoanalysis and Storytelling* (Oxford: Blackwell, 1994).

Butler, Judith, *Gender Trouble: Feminism and the Subversion of Identity* (1990; rep. London: Routledge, 2006).

Cavell, Stanley, *Must We Mean What We Say?* (Cambridge: Cambridge University Press, 1969).

Chambers, Ross, *Room for Maneuver: Reading the Oppositional in Narrative* (Chicago: University of Chicago Press, 1991).

Clark, Timothy, 'Nature, Post Nature', in *The Cambridge Companion to Literature and the Environment*, ed. Louise Westling (Cambridge: Cambridge University Press, 2014), pp. 75–89.

Cohen, David, *Being a Man* (London: Routledge, 1990).

Damasio, Antonio, *Descartes' Error: Emotion, Reason, and the Human Brain* (1994; New York: Quill, 2000).

Eliot, T. S., 'In Memory of Henry James', *The Complete Prose of T. S. Eliot: The Critical Edition*, Vol. 1, eds. Jewel Spears Brooker and Ronald Schurchard (Baltimore: Johns Hopkins University Press, 2014).

Forster, E. M., *Aspects of the Novel and Related Writings* (1927; London: Edward Arnold, 1974).

Friedman, Susan Stanford, 'Definitional Excursions: The Meanings of Modern/ Modernity/Modernism', *Modernism/Modernity*, 8 (2001), 3, pp. 493–513.

Gardner, John, *On Moral Fiction* (New York: Basic Books, 1978).

Girard, René, *Deceit, Desire, and the Novel: Self and Other in Literary Structure* (Baltimore: Johns Hopkins University Press, 1972).

Gittins, Diana, 'The Historical Construction of Childhood', in *An Introduction to Childhood Studies*, second edition, ed. M. J. Kehily (Milton Keynes: Open University Press, 2009), pp. 35–49.

Guignery, Vanessa and Ryan Roberts, eds., *Conversations with Julian Barnes* (Jackson: University of Mississippi Press, 2009).

Hadley, Elaine, 'On a Darkling Plain: Victorian Liberalism and the Fantasy of Agency', *Victorian Studies*, 48 (2005), pp. 92–102.

Hayot, Eric, *On Literary Worlds* (New York: Oxford University Press, 2012).

Heise, Ursula, *Sense of Place and Sense of Planet* (Oxford and New York: Oxford University Press, 2008).

Hennessey, Thomas and Claire Thomas, *Spooks: The Unofficial History of MI5* (London: Amberley Publishing, 2010).

Hillis Miller, J., *Fiction and Repetition: Seven English Novels* (Cambridge, MA: Harvard University Press, 1982).

Hunt, R. N. Carew, *The Theory and Practice of Communism: An Introduction* (1951; London: Penguin Books, 1973).

Hutcheon, Linda, *Narcissistic Narrative: The Metafictional Paradox* (London: Methuen, 1984).

Huxley, Aldous, *Point Counter Point* (New York: Grosset & Dunlap, 1928).

Jackson, David, *Unmasking Masculinity: A Critical Autobiography* (London: Unwin Hyman, 1990).

James, David and Urmila Seshagiri, 'Metamodernism: Narratives of Continuity and Revolution', *PMLA*, 129 (2014), 1, pp. 87–100.

James, David, *Modernist Futures: Innovation and Inheritance in the Contemporary Novel* (New York: Cambridge University Press, 2012).

James, David, ed., *The Cambridge Companion to British Fiction Since 1945* (New York: Cambridge University Press, 2015).

James, Henry, *The Art of Fiction and Other Essays* (New York: Oxford University Press, 1948).

Johns-Putra, Adeline, 'Climate Change in Literature and Literary Studies: From Cli-Fi, Climate Change Theater and Ecopoetry to Ecocriticism and Climate Change Criticism', *WIREs Climate Change*, 7 (2006), pp. 266–82. Retrieved from: https://doi.org/10.1002/wcc.385 (accessed 23 March 2018).

Kehily, Mary Jane, ed., *An Introduction to Childhood Studies*, second edition (Milton Keynes: Open University Press, 2009).

Kerridge, Richard, 'The Single Source', *Ecozon@*, 1 (2010), 1, pp. 155–61 (pp. 159–60). Retrieved from: https://core.ac.uk/download/pdf/58910792.pdf (accessed 15 February 2018).

'Ecocritical Approaches to Literary Form and Genre', in *The Oxford Handbook of Ecocriticism*, ed. Greg Garrard (Oxford and New York: Oxford University Press, 2014), pp. 361–76.

Kimber, Gerri, 'The Novella: Between the Novel and the Story', in *The Cambridge History of the English Short Story*, ed. Dominic Head (Cambridge: Cambridge University Press, 2016), pp. 530–46.

Kynaston, David, *Austerity Britain: 1945–51* (London: Bloomsbury, 2007).

Lashmar, Paul and James Oliver, *Britain's Secret Propaganda War: 1948–1977* (London: Sutton Publishing, 1998).

Leibowitz, Judith, *Narrative Purpose in the Novella* (The Hague: Mouton, 1974).

Levine, Caroline, *Forms: Whole, Rhythm, Hierarchy, Network* (Princeton, NJ: Princeton University Press, 2015).

Lodge, David, 'The Novelist at the Crossroads', in *The Novel Today: Contemporary Writers on Modern Fiction*, new edition, ed. Malcolm Bradbury (London: Fontana, 1990), pp. 87–114.

Lukács, Georg, *Writer and Critic, and Other Essays*, ed. and trans. by Arthur Kahn (London: Merlin, 1970).

McCarthy, Mary, *Ideas and the Novel* (New York: Harcourt Brace Jovanovich, 1980).

McGowan, Todd, *The End of Dissatisfaction? Jacques Lacan and the Emerging Society of Enjoyment* (Albany: State University of New York Press, 2004).

McGurl, Mark, *The Novel Art: Elevations of American Fiction after Henry James* (Princeton, NJ: Princeton University Press, 2001).

Macintyre, Ben, *Operation Mincemeat* (London: Bloomsbury, 2010).

Martin, David C., *Wilderness of Mirrors* (1980; Guilford, CT: The Lyons Press, 2003).

Morton, Timothy, *Hyperobjects* (Minneapolis: University of Minnesota Press, 2013).

Nairn, Tom, *The Break-Up of Britain: Crisis and Neo-Nationalism* (London: NLB, 1977).

Nelson, Deborah, *Tough Enough: Arbus, Arendt, Didion, McCarthy, Sontag, Weil* (Chicago: University of Chicago Press, 2017).

Newton, Adam Zachary, *Narrative Ethics* (Cambridge, MA: Harvard University Press, 1995).

Nussbaum, Martha C., *Love's Knowledge: Essays on Philosophy and Literature* (Oxford: Oxford University Press, 1990).

Postman, Neil, *The Disappearance of Childhood*, second edition (New York: Vintage, 1994).

Rimington, Stella, *Open Secret: The Autobiography of the Former Director-General of MI5* (London: Hutchinson, 2001).

Robertson, Geoff, *Reluctant Judas: Life and Death of The Special Branch Informer Kenneth Lennon* (London: Maurice Temple Smith, 1976).

Rorty, Richard, 'A Queasy Agnosticism', *Dissent*, 52 (2005), 4, pp. 91–4.

Rutherford, Jonathan, *Men's Silences: Predicaments in Masculinity* (London: Routledge, 1992).

Saint-Amour, Paul K., *Tense Future: Modernism, Total War, Encyclopedic Form* (Oxford: Oxford University Press, 2015).

Sandbrook, Dominic, *State of Emergency: The Way We Were Britain 1970–1974* (London: Allen Lane, 2010).

Saunders, Frances Stonor, *Who Paid the Piper? The CIA and the Cultural Cold War* (London: Granta, 2009).

Schoene-Harwood, Berthold, *Writing Men: Literary Masculinities from 'Frankenstein' to the New Man* (Edinburgh: Edinburgh University Press, 2000).

Sedgwick, Eve Kosofsky, *Between Men: English Literature and Male Homosocial Desire* (New York: Columbia University Press, 1985).

Segal, Lynne, *Slow Motion: Changing Masculinities, Changing Men* (London: Virago, 1990).

Seidler, Victor J., ed., *The Achilles Heel Reader: Men, Sexual Politics, and Socialism* (London: Routledge, 1991).

Shaviro, Steven, *No Speed Limit: Three Essays on Accelerationism* (Minneapolis: University of Minnesota Press, 2015).

Smith, Zadie, 'Fail Better', in *The Writer's Reader: Vocation, Preparation, Creation*, eds. Robert Cohen and Jay Parini (New York: Bloomsbury Academic, 2017), pp. 349–62.

Sontag, Susan, *Against Interpretation* (London: Vintage, 1994).

Springer, Mary Doyle, *Forms of the Modern Novella* (Chicago: University of Chicago Press, 1975).

Toye, Richard, 'From "Consensus" to "Common Ground": The Rhetoric of the Postwar Settlement and Its Collapse', *Journal of Contemporary History*, 48 (2013), 1, pp. 3–23.

Trexler, Adam, *Anthropocene Fictions* (Charlottesville and London: University of Virginia Press, 2015).

Turner, Alwyn W., *Crisis? What Crisis? Britain in the 1970s* (London: Aurum Press, 2008).

Vannatta, Dennis, ed., *The English Short Story 1945–1980: A Critical History* (Boston: Twayne Publishers, 1985).

Vinen, Richard, *National Service: A Generation in Uniform 1945–63* (London: Penguin, 2014).

Walkowitz, Rebecca L., *Cosmpolitian Style: Modernism Beyond the Nation* (New York: Columbia University Press, 2006).

Walther, LuAnn, 'The Invention of Childhood in Victorian Autobiography', in *Approaches to Victorian Autobiography*, ed. G. Landow (Athens: Ohio University Press, 1979), pp. 64–83.

Whedon, Tony, 'Notes on the Novella', *Southwest Review*, 96 (2011), 4, pp. 565–71.

Wheen, Francis, *Strange Days Indeed: The Golden Age of Paranoia* (London: Harper Collins, 2008).

Wilford, Hugh, *The CIA, the British Left and the Cold War: Calling the Tune?* (London: Routledge, 2003).

Williams, Raymond, *Marxism and Literature* (Oxford: Oxford University Press, 1977).

Wilson, E. O., *Consilience: The Unity of Knowledge* (1998; London: Abacus, 2003).

Wittgenstein, Ludwig, *Zettel*, eds. G. E. M. Anscombe and G. H. von Wright, trans. G. E. M. Anscombe (Berkeley: University of California Press, 1967).

Tractatus Logico-Philosophicus, trans. D. F. Pears and B. F. McGuinness (1921; London: Routledge, 1961).

Woolf, Virginia, *The Common Reader: First Series, Annotated Edition* (Wilmington, MA: Mariner Books, 2002).

The Second Common Reader (New York: Harvest Books, 1986).

Wright, Peter, *Spycatcher: The Candid Autobiography of a Senior Intelligence Officer* (Australia: Heinemann, 1987).

Wyness, Michael, *Childhood and Society*, second edition (London: Palgrave, 2012).

Zhang, Dora, 'Naming the Indescribable: Woolf, Russell, James, and the Limits of Description', *New Literary History*, 45 (2014), pp. 51–70.

INDEX

Cambridge Companions To...

AUTHORS

TOPICS